Arlie Hochschild, a sociologist at the University of California, Berkeley, has co-edited one book and authored seven others, three of these *New York Times Review* Notable Books of the Year. She was won Guggenheim, Fulbright, Mellon, and Alfred P. Sloan awards, and her books have been translated into fourteen languages.

Newsweek describes *The Second Shift* as having the "detail and texture of a good novel"; *Publishers Weekly* noted that "the concept of the second shift . . . has entered the language"; and in the *New York Times Book Review*, Robert Kuttner described her "subtlety of . . . insights" and "graceful, seamless narrative," and called *The Second Shift* the "best discussion I have read of what must be the quintessential domestic bind of our time." The *Financial Times* said of the *Time Bind*, "there are wit, humour, and joy as well as portents of doom." In Christine Stansell's *Washington Post* review of *The Commercialization of Intimate Life*, she describes Hochschild's "curious, roving mind, her big ideas . . . No one," she writes, "has written about (family dilemmas) with Hochschild's intelligence, originality, and on-the-ground knowledge."

Hochschild has written for the *New York Times Book Review* and *Magazine*, the *Atlantic Monthly*, *O, The Oprah Magazine*, *Ms.*, the *American Prospect*, and *Mother Jones*, directed the U.C. Berkeley–based Alfred P. Sloan Center on Working Families, and lectures widely in Europe and elsewhere. She lives in San Francisco with her husband, the writer Adam Hochschild. They have two sons and share the second shift on the weekly overnight visits of their two small granddaughters.

Anne Machung currently works as director of accountability for the University of California. She received a Ph.D. in political science from the University of Wisconsin-Madison and has published articles on higher education and family in *Change* and *Feminist Studies*.

Other Books by Arlie Hochschild

The Outsourced Self

Global Woman: Nannies, Maids, and Sex Workers in the
New Economy *(co-edited with Barbara Ehrenreich)*

The Commercialization of Intimate Life:
Notes from Home and Work

The Time Bind: When Work Becomes Home
and Home Becomes Work

The Managed Heart: The Commercialization of Human Feeling

Coleen the Question Girl *(a children's story)*

The Unexpected Community

THE
SECOND
SHIFT

Working Families and the Revolution at Home

ARLIE HOCHSCHILD
WITH ANNE MACHUNG

PENGUIN BOOKS

PENGUIN BOOKS
Published by the Penguin Group
Penguin Group (USA) Inc., 375 Hudson Street, New York, New York 10014, U.S.A.
Penguin Group (Canada), 90 Eglinton Avenue East, Suite 700, Toronto, Ontario, Canada M4P 2Y3
(a division of Pearson Penguin Canada Inc.) • Penguin Books Ltd, 80 Strand, London WC2R 0RL,
England • Penguin Ireland, 25 St Stephen's Green, Dublin 2, Ireland (a division of Penguin Books Ltd) •
Penguin Group (Australia), 250 Camberwell Road, Camberwell, Victoria 3124, Australia (a division of
Pearson Australia Group Pty Ltd) • Penguin Books India Pvt Ltd, 11 Community Centre, Panchsheel
Park, New Delhi – 110 017, India • Penguin Group (NZ), 67 Apollo Drive, Rosedale, Auckland 0632,
New Zealand (a division of Pearson New Zealand Ltd) • Penguin Books (South Africa) (Pty) Ltd,
24 Sturdee Avenue, Rosebank, Johannesburg 2196, South Africa

Penguin Books Ltd, Registered Offices: 80 Strand, London WC2R 0RL, England

First published in the United States of America by Viking Penguin Inc. 1989
Edition with a new introduction published in Penguin Books 2003
This edition with a new preface published 2012

7 9 10 8 6

Copyright © Arlie Hochschild, 1989, 2003, 2012
All rights reserved

LIBRARY OF CONGRESS CATALOGING IN PUBLICATION DATA
Hochschild, Arlie Russell, 1940-
The second shift : working families and the revolution
at home / Arlie Hochschild, with Anne Machung.
p. cm.
Rev. ed. of: The second shift : working parents and the revolution at home. 1989.
Includes bibliographical references and index.
ISBN 978-0-14-312033-9
1. Dual-career families—United States.   2. Dual-career families—United States—
Case studies.   3. Sex role—United States.   4. Working mothers—United States.
I. Machung, Anne.   II. Title.
HQ536.H63 2012
306.872–dc23   2011043651

Printed in the United States of America
Set in Adobe Garamond Pro   Designed by Alice Sorensen

For Adam

Contents

Preface

When I was thirty-one, a moment occurred that crystallized the concern that drives this book. At the time, I was an assistant professor in the sociology department at the University of California, Berkeley, and the mother of a three-month-old child. I wanted to nurse the baby—and to continue to teach. Several arrangements were possible, but my solution was a pre-industrial one—to reintegrate the family into the workplace, which involved taking the baby, David, with me for office hours on the fourth floor of Barrows Hall. From two to eight months, he was nearly the perfect guest. I made him a little box with blankets where he napped (which he did most of the time) and I brought along an infant seat from which he kept a close eye on key chains, colored notebooks, earrings, and glasses. Sometimes waiting students took him out into the hall and passed him around. He became a conversation piece with shy students, and some returned to see him rather than me. I put up a fictitious name on the appointment list every four hours and fed him alone.

The baby's presence was like a Rorschach test for people entering my office. Older men, undergraduate women, and a few younger men seemed to like him and the idea of his being there. In the next office there was a seventy-four-year-old distinguished emeritus professor; it was our joke that he would stop by when he heard my son crying and say, shaking his head, "Beating the baby again, eh?" Textbook salesmen with briefcases and striped suits

were generally shocked at the unprofessional gurgles (and sometimes unprofessional odors) from the box. Many graduate student
women were put off, partly because babies were out of fashion in
the early 1970s, and partly because they were afraid that I was deprofessionalizing myself, women in general, and, symbolically,
them. I was afraid of that too. Before having David, I saw students
all the time, took every committee assignment, worked evenings
and nights writing articles, and had in this way accumulated a certain amount of departmental tolerance. I was calling on that tolerance now, with the infant box, the gurgles, the disturbance to
the dignity and sense of purpose of my department. My colleagues
never seemed to talk about children. They talked to each other
about research and about the department's ranking—still "number 1" or slipping to "number 2"? I was just coming up for tenure
and it wasn't so easy to get. And I wanted at the same time to be
as calm a mother for my son as my mother had been for me. In
some literal way I had brought together family and work, but in a
more basic way, doing so only made the contradictions between
the demands of baby and career all the more clear.

One day, a male graduate student came early for his appointment. The baby had slept longer than usual and hadn't been
hungry at my appointed Barrows Hall time. I invited the student
in. Since we had never met before, he introduced himself with
extreme deference. He seemed acquainted with my work and intellectual tastes in the field, and perhaps responding to his deference, I behaved more formally than usual. He began tentatively
to elaborate his interests in sociology and to broach the subject of
my serving on his Ph.D. orals committee. He had the task of explaining to me that he was a clever student, trustworthy and obe-
dient, but that academic fields were not organized as he wanted
to study them, and of asking me whether he could study the collected works of Karl Marx under the rubric of the sociology of
work.

In the course of this lengthy explanation, the baby began to cry.
I slipped him a pacifier, and continued to listen all the more in-

tently. The student went on. The baby spat out the pacifier and began to wail. Trying to be casual, I began to feed him. At this point, he let out the strongest, most rebellious wail I had ever heard from this small person.

The student uncrossed one leg, crossed the other and held a polite smile, coughing a bit as he waited for this little crisis to pass. I excused myself and got up to walk back and forth with the baby to calm him down. "I've never taken the baby here all day before," I remember saying, "it's just an experiment."

"I have two children of my own," he replied. "Only they live in Sweden. We're divorced and I miss them a lot." We exchanged a human glance of mutual support, talked of our families more, and soon the baby calmed down.

A month later, when the student signed up for a second appointment, he entered the office and sat down formally. "As we were discussing last time, Professor Hochschild . . ." Nothing further was said about what had, for me, been an utterly traumatic little episode. Astonishingly, I was still Professor Hochschild. He was still John. Something about power lived on regardless.

In retrospect I felt a little like that character in *Dr. Doolittle and the Pirates*, the pushmi-pullyu, a horse with two heads that see and say different things. The pushmi head felt relieved that motherhood had not reduced me as a professional. But the pullyu wondered why children in offices were not occasionally part of the "normal" scene. Where, after all, were the children of my male colleagues?

Part of me felt envious of the smooth choicelessness of those male colleagues who did not bring their children to Barrows Hall but who knew their children were in loving hands. I sometimes felt this keenly when I met one of these men jogging on the track (a popular academic sport because it takes little time) and then met his wife taking their child to the YMCA kinder-gym. I felt it too when I saw wives drive up to the building in the evening in their station wagons, elbow on the window, two children in the back, waiting for a man briskly walking down the steps, briefcase in hand. It seemed a particularly pleasant moment in their day. It reminded me of those summer Friday evenings, always a great treat, when my older brother and I would pack into the back of our old Hudson, and my mother with a picnic basket would drive up from Bethesda, Maryland, to Washington, D.C., at five o'clock to meet my father, walking briskly down the steps of the government office building where he worked, briefcase in hand. We picnicked at the Tidal Basin surrounding the Jefferson Memorial, my parents sharing their day, and in that end-of-the-week mood, we came home. When I see similar scenes, something inside rips in half. For I am neither and both the brisk stepping carrier of a briefcase and the mother with the packed picnic supper. The university is still designed for such men and their homes for such women. Both the woman in the station wagon and I with the infant box are trying to "solve" the work-family problem. As things stand now, in either case women pay a cost. The housewife pays a cost by remaining outside the mainstream of social life. The career woman pays a cost by entering a clockwork of careers that permits little time or emotional energy to raise a family. Her career permits so little of these because it was originally designed to suit a traditional man whose wife raised his children. In this arrangement between career and family, the family was the welfare agency for the university and women were its social workers. Now women are working in such institutions without benefit of the social worker. As I repeatedly heard career women in this study say, "What I really need is a wife." But maybe they don't need "wives"; maybe they need careers basically redesigned to suit workers who also care for families. This redesign would be nothing short of a revolution, first in the home, and then at places of work—universities, corporations, banks, and factories.

In increasing numbers women have gone into the workforce, but few have gone very high up in it. This is not because women cool themselves out by some "auto-discrimination." It is not because we lack "role models." Nor is it simply because corporations and other institutions discriminate against women. Rather, the career system inhibits women, not so much by malevolent disobedience to good rules as by making up rules to suit the male half of the population in the first place. One reason that half the lawyers, doctors, businesspeople are not women is because *men do not share the raising of their children and the caring of their homes*. Men think and feel within structures of work which presume they don't do these things. The long hours men devote to work and to recovering from work are often taken from the untold stories, unthrown balls, and uncuddled children left behind at home.

Women who do a first shift at work and all of a second shift at home can't compete on male terms. They find that their late twenties and mid-thirties, the prime childbearing years, are also a peak period of career demands. Seeing that the game is devised for family-free people, some women lose heart.

Thus to look at the system of work is to look at half the problem. The other half occurs at home. If there is to be no more mother with the picnic basket, who is to take her place? Will the new working woman cram it all in, baby and office? Will the office take precedence over the baby? Or will babies appear in the daily lives, if not the offices, of male colleagues too? What will men and women allow themselves to feel? How much ambition at work? How much empathy for children? How much dependence on a spouse?

Five years after David was born, we had our second child, Gabriel. My husband, Adam, didn't take either of our boys to his office, but overall, we have cared for them equally, and he cares for them as a mother would. Among our close friends, fathers do the same. But ours are highly unusual circumstances—middle-class jobs, flexible work schedules, a supportive community. These special circumstances make women like me and my friends "lucky." Some women colleagues have asked me, lids lowered, "I'll bet you really *struggled* to get that." But the truth is I didn't. I was "lucky."

Once the occupant of an infant box in my office, David is now a busy working father himself. Do working mothers have more help from partners than they did when David was a baby? Is the problem solved?

If I listen to what my students have told me, the answer is no. The women students I talk with don't feel optimistic that they will find a man who plans to share the work at home, and the women whose partners fully share still consider themselves "unusual," while the women whose partners don't share consider themselves "normal."

I began to think about this matter of feeling "lucky" again while driving home from my interviews in the evening. One woman, a bank clerk and mother of two young children, who did nearly everything at home, ended her interview as many women did, talking about how lucky she felt. She woke at 5:00 a.m., crammed in housework before she set off for the office, and after she got back, asked her husband for help here and there. She didn't seem lucky to me. Did she feel lucky because her husband was doing more than the "going rate" for men she knew? As I gradually discovered, husbands almost never talked of feeling "lucky" that their wives worked, or that they "did a lot" or "shared" the work of the home. They didn't talk about luck at all, while this bank clerk and I seemed to be part of a long invisible parade of women, one feeling a little "luckier" than the other because their man did a bit more at home. But if women who have an equal deal feel "lucky" because it is so rare and precious and unusual and precarious an arrangement to have—if all of us who have some small shard of help are feeling "lucky"—maybe something is fundamentally wrong with the usual male outlook on the home, and with the cultural world of work that helps create and reinforce it. But if sharing work at home, as I shall argue, is vitally linked to marital harmony, should something so important hinge on luck? Wouldn't it be far better if ordinary men and women lived in "lucky" structures of work and believed in ideas about men and women that brought that "luck" about?

Nearly all my women students want to have full-time jobs and rear children. How will this work out? Sometimes I ask women students, "Do you ever talk with your boyfriends about sharing child care and housework?" Often they reply with a vague "Not really." I don't believe these lively, inquiring eighteen- to twenty-two-year-old students haven't thought about the problem. I believe they are afraid of it. And since they think of it as a "private" problem, each also feels alone. At twenty-two, they feel they have time. But in a short ten years, many are likely to fall into a life like that of my harried bank clerk. I have explored the inner lives of two-job families in the faith that taking a very close look now can help these young women find solutions for the future that go far beyond an infant box and luck.

really," I don't believe these twelve inquiring eighteen- to twenty-two-year-old students haven't thought about the problem. I believe they are afraid of it. And since they drink of it as a "private" problem, each also feels alone. At twenty-two, they feel they have time. But in a short ten years, many are likely to fall into a life like that of my harried bank clerk. I have explored the inner lives of two-job families in the faith that taking a very close look now can help these young women find solutions for the future that go far beyond an infant box and brief.

Acknowledgments

I owe thanks in many directions. First of all, thanks to the National Institutes of Mental Health for generous funding of this research and to Elliot Liebow of the Center for the Study of Metropolitan Problems for administrative support. Many thanks to Troy Duster, chair of the Institute for the Study of Social Change, and longtime friend, for offering me an office, a file cabinet, and an atmosphere of warm support. My warm thanks to the research team that helped me conduct the research: Amanda Hamilton for help with preliminary interviews; Elaine Kaplan for interviewing and coding; Lynett Uttal for help with coding and statistical analysis; Basil Browne for help in distributing over 400 questionnaires to employees of a large Bay Area company; Brian Phillips for his excellent typing, and his encouragement even when the drafts seemed endless ("This one again? But I liked the last draft."); Virginia Malcolm and Joanna Wool and Pat Frost for their interest in the project as well as their careful transcriptions; and thanks for additional pages of perceptive commentary from Pat Frost. For help in library research, thanks to Wes Ford and Grace Benveniste. For historical references, thanks to Susan Thistle. To my research assistant and collaborator, Anne Machung, my enormous thanks and a hug. Anne conducted nearly half of the interviews, did all that it took to keep the interviews confidential, did the lion's share of some very complex coding, and put parts of our data on computer. She administered the project and helped a continual stream of out-of-town scholars, curious students, and volunteers that knocked on the door of our office at the Institute for the Study of Social Change. I have fond memories of those Thursday afternoon discussion sessions with Anne Machung, Elaine Kaplan, Lynett Uttal, Wes Ford, and Junko Kuninobi, a visiting scholar from Japan. Although I did all of the on-the-scene observations and writing, the initial research has all our hearts in it. Only when the project came to a close and I sat down to write and think alone did the comradely "we" become the "I" with which I write.

For helpful readings of early, off-the-mark drafts, and for loving me as deeply as they have, I am ever grateful to my parents, Ruth and Francis Russell. For their good advice, thanks to Todd Gitlin, Mike Rogin, Lillian Rubin, and Ann Swidler. For rescuing me in my hour of need, my loving thanks to Orville Schell and Tom Engelhardt. Thanks also to Gene Tanke, whose support and help at an earlier stage means a great deal. And to Nan Graham of Viking Penguin, whose faith in me, editorial guidance, and emotional beauty mean more than I can say. Thanks also to Beena Kamlani, who saw this book through production with grace and competence.

I would like to thank the graduate students who attended my seminar in the Sociology of Gender in the spring of 1986, on whom I first tried out the idea that there is a "his" and "hers" of industrialization.

I also want to thank the couples in this study. Although they were busy, they generously allowed me into their homes and into their lives in the faith that this research would help couples in similar situations to understand more about themselves. To protect their identities, I have transposed episodes and changed identifying characteristics. Some people may not see themselves exactly as I did, but I hope they find a mirror here that is faithful to important aspects of their experience as pioneers on a new family frontier.

Thanks to Ayi Kwei Armah, who had faith and combed out

the knots with loving patience. Thanks also to Eileen O'Neill for her warm, loving care of Gabriel and David.

Thanks to my husband, Adam, whose idea it was to write this book. One weekend afternoon over ten years ago, as we were hiking up a mountain and I had talked for half the climb about women's "double day," Adam suggested on our way down, "Why not write about it?" For that idea, for the good-humored encouragement, and for the love I have felt all along our way, my deepest gratitude.

Thanks to my son David, who sets aside his schoolwork and political and ecological concerns to pitch in with the second shift and regale me with hilarious imitations of figures on the American political scene. Thanks also to Gabriel, who took time away from his dog-walking business and poetry writing to bring me cups of Dr. Chang's herb tea. To inspire me, he even drafted some fictional case studies of Ted and Mary, Robin and Peter, Dick and Rosemary, Sally and Bill, and Asia and Frank, which are more gripping and action-packed than any the reader will find here. One day, he also left a note on my desk under the tea mug, with a small white bow attached, which said, "Congratulations for finishing, Mom." No mother could ask for more.

Introduction

In a society marked by individualism, we often think of problems at home as matters of clashing personality ("He's so selfish," "She's so anxious"). But when millions of couples are having similar conversations over who does what at home, it can help to understand just what's going on outside marriage that's affecting what goes on inside it. Without that understanding, we can simply continue to adjust to strains of a stalled revolution, take them as "normal," and wonder why it's so hard these days to make a marriage work.

After *The Second Shift* was published, I talked informally to many readers and in the 1990s conducted interviews with more working couples at a Fortune 500 company for *The Time Bind*, the following book. Based on these talks I began to conclude that for many couples the basic dilemma remains.

Among the variety of responses I encountered, one reader, Shawn Dickinson Finley, wrote a poem about one finding in this book, for the *Dallas Morning News*:

> *Weekends come. I'd like to relax.*
> *But he's tired of work and needs to crash.*
> *So take care of everything, would you dear?*
> *While he watches TV and drinks lots of beer.*
> *At last I'm through—I'm finally done.*
> *So good night. I have to run*

And hit the pillow and dream a dream,
Of the 18 percent who help to clean.

In New York, an imaginative bride and groom made up marriage vows designed to avoid Finley's dilemma. "I vow to cook dinners for Dhora," the groom said, before a stunned and delighted gathering of family and friends. And with a twinkle, the bride replied, "And I promise to eat what Oran cooks."

Other couples had become more seriously locked in an anguished struggle, not for time to relax but for time to work. One young Latino father of a two-year-old child explained, "My wife and I both work at low-paying jobs we love and believe in. [He worked for a human rights organization and she worked for an environmental group.] And we can't afford a maid. We love Julio but he's two and he's a handful. I do a lot with him, which I love. [Here his voice was soft, and slow.] But it's tough because my wife and I have no time for a marriage. It makes me think the unthinkable [Here his voice quavered.]: should we have *had* Julio?"

Some women found in these pages aid in an ongoing struggle. One working mother left xeroxed pages from the chapter on Nancy and Evan Holt on the refrigerator door. When her husband failed to notice, she placed the pages on his pillow in their bed. As she recounted, "He finally read about how Nancy Holt did all the housework and child care and expressed her resentment for doing so by excluding her husband from the love nest she made for herself and their child. The parallels began to hit him the way they had me."

I was sad to learn about what some people imagined as solutions to their struggles. One woman declared, with straightened shoulders and hands on hips, "The house is a mess. It's a pit. That's my solution." Another proudly responded to her husband's refusal to help at home by making meals for herself but not for him. Yet another woman described placing second-shift requirements into her prenuptial agreement. If women are that upset and that armed, I wonder if these apparent "solutions" haven't inadvertently become a problem all their own. What we really need to do is solve the original problem. And where in the design of our jobs, in the hierarchy of our values, in the policies of our government is the nurturing social stage on which to do that? That's the unanswered question behind this book.

THE
SECOND
SHIFT

The Family Speed-up

SHE is not the same woman in each magazine advertisement, but she is the same idea. She has that working-mother look as she strides forward, briefcase in one hand, smiling child in the other. Literally and figuratively, she is moving ahead. Her hair, if long, tosses behind her; if it is short, it sweeps back at the sides, suggesting mobility and progress. There is nothing shy or passive about her. She is confident, active, "liberated." She wears a dark tailored suit, but with a silk bow or colorful frill that says, "I'm really feminine underneath." She has made it in a man's world without sacrificing her femininity. And she has done this on her own. By some personal miracle, this image suggests, she has managed to combine what 150 years of industrialization have split wide apart—child and job, frill and suit, female culture and male.

When I showed a photograph of a supermom like this to the working mothers I talked to in the course of researching this book, many responded with an outright laugh. One day-care worker and mother of two, ages three and five, threw back her head: "Ha! They've got to be *kidding* about her. Look at me, hair a mess, nails jagged, twenty pounds overweight. Mornings, I'm getting my kids dressed, the dog fed, the lunches made, the shopping list done. That lady's got a maid." Even working mothers who did have maids couldn't imagine combining work and family in such a carefree way: "Do you know what a baby *does* to your life, the two o'clock feedings, the four o'clock feedings?" Another mother of two said: "They don't show it, but she's whistling"—she imitated a whistling woman, eyes to the sky—"so she can't hear the din." They envied the apparent ease of the woman with the flying hair, but she didn't remind them of anyone they knew.

The women I interviewed—lawyers, corporate executives, word processors, garment pattern cutters, day-care workers—and most of their husbands, too—felt differently about some issues: how right it is for a mother of young children to work a full-time job, or how much a husband should be responsible for the home. But they all agreed that it was hard to work two full-time jobs and raise young children.

How well do couples do it? The more women work outside the home, the more central this question. The number of women in paid work has risen steadily since before the turn of the century, but since 1950 the rise has been staggering. In 1950, 30 percent of American women were in the labor force; by 2011, that had risen to 59 percent. Over two-thirds of mothers, married or single, now work; in fact more mothers than non-mothers work for pay. Women now make up half of the labor force and two-job marriages now make up two-thirds of all marriages with children.

But the biggest rise by far has been among mothers of small children. In 1975, only 39 percent of women with children six and under were in the civilian labor force—doing or looking for paid work. By 2009, that had risen to 64 percent. In 1975, 34 percent of moms of children three and under were in the labor force; in 2009 that had risen to 61 percent. And it was the same story for moms of children one and younger: 31 percent in 1975 and 50 percent in 2009. Since more mothers of small children are now in the labor force, we might expect more to be working part time. But that's not what we find; in 1975, 72 percent of women worked full time and a bit more than that in 2009. Of all employed moms with babies under age one, 69 percent in 2009 worked full time.[1]

If more mothers of young children are stepping into full-time jobs outside the home, and if most couples can't afford household help, how much more are fathers doing at home? As I began exploring this question I found many studies on the hours working men and women devote to housework and child care. One national random sample of 1,243 working parents in forty-four American cities, conducted in 1965–66 by Alexander Szalai and his coworkers, for example, found that working women averaged three hours a day on housework while men averaged seventeen minutes; women spent fifty minutes a day of time exclusively with their children; men spent twelve minutes. On the other side of the coin, working fathers watched television an hour longer than their working wives, and slept a half hour longer each night. A comparison of this American sample with eleven other industrial countries in Eastern and Western Europe revealed the same difference between working women and men in those countries as well.[2] In a 1983 study of white middle-class families in greater Boston, Grace Baruch and R. C. Barnett found that working men married to working women spent only three-quarters of an hour longer each week with their kindergarten-aged children than did men married to housewives.[3]

Szalai's landmark study documented the now familiar but still alarming story of the working woman's "double day," but it left me wondering how men and women actually felt about all this. He and his coworkers studied how people used time, but not, say, how a father felt about his twelve minutes with his child, or how his wife felt about it. Szalai's study revealed the visible surface of what I discovered to be a set of deeply emotional issues: What should a man and woman contribute to the family? How appreciated does each feel? How does each respond to subtle changes in the balance of marital power? How does each develop an unconscious "gender strategy" for coping with the work at home, with marriage, and, indeed, with life itself? These were the underlying issues.

But I began with the measurable issue of time. Adding together the time it takes to do a paid job, housework, and child care, I averaged estimates from the major studies on time use done in the 1960s and 1970s, and discovered that women worked roughly fifteen hours longer each week than men. Over a year, they worked an *extra month of twenty-four-hour days*. Over a dozen years, it was an extra year of twenty-four-hour days. Most women without children spend much more time than men on housework; with children, they devote more time caring for both house and children. Just as there is a wage gap between men and women in the workplace, there is a "leisure gap" between them at home. Most women work one shift at the office or factory and a "second shift" at home.

Studies show that working mothers have higher self-esteem and get less depressed than housewives, but compared to their husbands, they're more tired and get sick more often. In Peggy Thoits's 1985 analysis of two large-scale surveys, each of about a thousand men and women, people were asked how often in the preceding week they'd experienced each of twenty-three symptoms of anxiety (such as dizziness or hallucinations). Thoits found working mothers more likely than any other group to be "anxious."

In light of these studies, the image of the woman with the flying hair seems like an upbeat cover for a grim reality, like those pictures of Soviet tractor drivers smiling radiantly into the distance as they think about the ten-year plan. The Szalai study was conducted in 1965–66. I wanted to know whether the leisure gap he found back then still existed or whether it has disappeared. Since most married couples work two jobs, since more will in the future, since most wives in these couples work the extra month a year, I wanted to understand what this "extra month" means for each person, and what it does to love and marriage in an age of high divorce.

MY RESEARCH

With my research associates Anne Machung and Elaine Kaplan, I interviewed fifty couples very intensively, and I observed in a dozen homes. We first began interviewing artisans, students, and professionals in Berkeley, California, in the late 1970s. This was at the height of the women's movement, and many of these couples were earnestly and self-consciously struggling to modernize the ground rules of their marriages. Enjoying flexible job schedules and intense cultural support to do so, many succeeded. Since their circumstances were unusual they became our "comparison group" as we sought other couples more typical of mainstream America. In 1980 we located more typical couples by sending a questionnaire on work and family life to every thirteenth name—from top to bottom—of the personnel roster of a large, urban manufacturing company. At the end of the questionnaire, we asked members of working couples raising children under age six and working full-time jobs if they would be willing to talk to us in greater depth. Interviewed from 1980 through 1988, these couples, their neighbors and friends, their children's teachers, day-care workers, and baby-sitters form the heart of this book.

When we called them, a number of baby-sitters replied as one woman did: "You're interviewing *us*? Good. We're human too." Or another, "I'm glad you consider what we do work. A lot of people don't." As it turned out, many day-care workers were themselves juggling two jobs and small children, and so we talked to them about that, too.

We also talked with other men and women who were not part of two-job couples, divorced parents who were war-weary veterans of two-job marriages, and traditional couples, to see how much of the strain we were seeing was unique to two-job couples.

I focused on heterosexual, married couples with children under age six, their child-care workers, and others in their world from the top to the bottom of the social class ladder. But the second shift is front and center for many other kinds of couples as well—the unmarried, gay, and lesbian couples, nonparents, and parents of older children. In particular, gay and lesbian partners are more likely than heterosexual ones, research suggests, to share the second shift— gay partners by specializing in tasks, lesbians by doing similar tasks.[4]

I also watched daily life in a dozen homes during a weekday evening, during the weekend, and during the months that followed, when I was invited on outings, to dinner, or just to talk. I found myself waiting on the front doorstep as weary parents and hungry children tumbled out of the family car. I shopped with them, visited friends, watched television, ate with them, walked through parks, and came along when they dropped their children at day-care, often staying on at the baby-sitter's house after parents waved good-bye. In their homes, I sat on the living-room floor and drew pictures and played house with children. I watched as parents gave them baths, read bedtime stories, and said good night. Most couples tried to bring me into the family scene, inviting me to eat with them and talk. I responded if they spoke to me, from time to time asked questions, but I rarely initiated conversation. I tried to become as unobtrusive as a family dog. Often I would base myself in the living room, quietly taking notes. Sometimes I would follow a wife upstairs or down, accompany a child on her way out to "help Dad" fix the car, or watch television with the other watchers. Sometimes I would break out of my peculiar role to join in the jokes they often made about acting like the "model" two-job couple. Or perhaps the joking was a subtle part of my role, to put them at ease so they could act more naturally. For a period of two to five years, I phoned or visited these couples to keep in touch even as I moved on to study the daily lives of other working couples—black, Chicano, white—from every social class and walk of life.

I asked who did how much of a wide variety of household tasks. I asked who cooks. Vacuums? Makes the beds? Sews? Cares for plants? Sends Christmas or Hanukkah cards? I also asked: Who washes the car? Repairs household appliances? Does the taxes? Tends the yard? I asked who did most household planning, who noticed such things as when a child's fingernails need clipping, cared more how the house looked or about the change in a child's mood.

INSIDE THE EXTRA MONTH A YEAR

The women I interviewed seemed to be far more deeply torn between the demands of work and family than were their husbands. They talked with more animation and at greater length than their husbands about the abiding conflict between them. Busy as they were, women more often brightened at the idea of yet another interviewing session. They felt the second shift was *their* issue and most of their husbands agreed. When I telephoned one husband to arrange an interview with him, explaining that I wanted to ask him about how he managed work and family life, he replied genially, "Oh, this will *really* interest my *wife.*"

It was a woman who first proposed to me the metaphor, borrowed from industrial life, of the "second shift." She strongly resisted the *idea* that homemaking was a "shift." Her family was her life and she didn't want it reduced to a job. But as she put it, "You're on duty at work. You come home, and you're on duty. Then you go back to work and you're on duty." After eight hours of adjusting insurance claims, she came home to put on the rice for dinner, care for her children, and do laundry. Despite her resistance, her home life *felt* like a second shift. That was the real story and that was the real problem.

Men who shared the load at home seemed just as pressed for time as their wives, and as torn between the demands of career and small children, as the stories of Michael Sherman and Art Winfield will show. But the majority of men did not share the load at home. Some refused outright. Others refused more passively, often offering a loving shoulder to lean on, an understanding ear as their working wife faced the conflict they both saw as hers. At first it seemed to me that the problem of the second shift was hers. But I came to realize that those husbands who helped very little at home were often indirectly just as deeply affected as their wives through the resentment their wives feel toward them, and through their need to steel themselves against that resentment. Evan Holt, a warehouse furniture salesman described in Chapter 4, did very little housework and played with his four-year-old son, Joey, at his convenience. Juggling the demands of work with family at first seemed a problem for his wife. But Evan himself suffered enormously from the side effects of "her" problem. His wife did the second shift, but she keenly resented it, and half-consciously expressed her frustration and rage by losing interest in sex and becoming overly absorbed with Joey. One way or another, most men I talked with do suffer the severe repercussions of what I think is a transitional phase in American family life.

One reason women took a deeper interest than men in the problems of juggling work with family life is that even when husbands happily shared the hours of work, their wives felt more *responsible* for the home. More women kept track of doctors' appointments, arranged play dates, and kept up with relatives. More mothers than fathers worried about the tail on a child's Halloween costume or a birthday present for a school friend. While at work they were more likely to check in by phone with the baby-sitter.

Partly because of this, more women felt torn between one sense of urgency and another, between the need to soothe a child's fear of being left at day care, and the need to show the boss she's "serious" at work. More women than men questioned how good they were as parents, or if they did not, they questioned why they weren't questioning it. More often than men, women alternated between living in their ambition and standing apart from it.

As masses of women have moved into the economy, families have been hit by a "speed-up" in work and family life. There is no more time in the day than there was when wives stayed home, but there is twice as much to do. It is mainly women who absorb this "speed-up." Twenty percent of the men in my study shared housework equally. Seventy percent of men did a substantial amount (less than half but more than a third), and 10 percent did less than a third. Even when couples share more equitably in the work at home, women do two-thirds of the *daily* jobs at home, like cooking and cleaning—jobs that fix them into a rigid routine. Most women cook dinner and most men change the oil in the family car. But, as one mother pointed out, dinner needs to be prepared every evening around six o'clock, whereas the car oil needs changing every six months, any day around that time, anytime that day. Women do more child care than men, and men repair more household appliances. A child needs to be tended daily while household repair can often wait "until I have time." Men had more control over *when* they make their contributions than women do. They may be very busy with family chores but, like the executive who tells his secretary to "hold my calls," the man has more control over his time. The job of the working mother, like that of the secretary, is usually to "take the calls."

Another reason women may feel more strained than men is that women more often do two things at once—for example, write checks and return phone calls, vacuum and keep an eye on a three-year-old, fold laundry and think out the shopping list. Men more often cook dinner *or* take a child to the park. Indeed, women more often juggle three spheres—job, children, and housework—while most men juggle two—job and children. For women, two activities compete with their time with children, not just one.

Beyond doing more at home, women also devote *proportionately more* of their time at home to housework and proportionately less of it to child care. Of all the time men spend working at home, more of it goes to child care. That is, working wives spend relatively more time "mothering the house"; husbands spend more time "mothering" the children. Since most parents prefer to be with their children to cleaning house, men do more of what they'd rather do. More men than women take their children on "fun" outings to the park, the zoo, the movies. Women spend more time on maintenance, such as feeding and bathing children, enjoyable activities to be sure, but often less leisurely or special than going to the zoo. Men also do fewer of the "undesirable" household chores: fewer wash toilets and scrub the bathroom.

As a result, women tend to talk more intently about being over-tired, sick, and "emotionally drained." Many women I could not tear away from the topic of sleep. They talked about how much they could "get by on" . . . six and a half, seven, seven and a half, less, more. They talked about who they knew who needed more or less. Some apologized for how much sleep they needed—"I'm afraid I need eight hours of sleep"—as if eight was too much. They talked about the effect of a change in baby-sitter, the birth of a second child, or a business trip on their child's pattern of sleep. They talked about how to avoid fully waking up when a child called them at night, and how to get back to sleep. These women talked about sleep the way a hungry person talks about food.

All in all, if in this period of American history, the two-job family is suffering from a speed-up of work and family life, working mothers are its primary victims. It is ironic, then, that often it falls to women to be the "time and motion expert" of family life. Watching inside homes, I noticed it was often the mother who rushed children, saying, "Hurry up! It's time to go," "Finish your cereal now," "You can do that later," "Let's go!" When a bath was crammed into a slot between 7:45 and 8:00 it was often the mother who called out, "Let's see who can take their bath the quickest!" Often a younger child will rush out, scurrying to be first in bed, while the older and wiser one stalls, resistant, sometimes resentful: "Mother is always rushing us." Sadly enough, women are more often the lightning rods for family aggressions aroused by the speed-up of work and family life. They are the "villains" in a process of which they are also the primary victims. More than the longer hours, the sleeplessness, and feeling torn, this is the saddest cost to women of the extra month a year.

Marriage in a Stalled Revolution

❋

EACH marriage bears the footprints of economic and cultural trends which originate far outside marriage. The offshoring of industrial jobs and decline of unions which erode the earning power of men, an expanding service sector which opens up jobs for women, new cultural images—like the woman with the flying hair—that make the working mother seem exciting, all these changes do not simply go on *around* marriage. They occur *inside* marriage, and transform it. Problems between husbands and wives, problems which seem "individual" and "marital," are often individual experiences of powerful economic and cultural shock waves that are not caused by one person or two. Quarrels that erupt, as we'll see, between Nancy and Evan Holt, Jessica and Seth Stein, and Anita and Ray Judson result mainly from a friction between faster-changing women and slower-changing men, rates of change which themselves result from the different rates at which the industrial economy has drawn men and women into itself.

There is a "his" and "hers" to the economic development of the United States. In the latter part of the nineteenth century, it was mainly men who were drawn off the farm into paid, industrial work and who changed their way of life and identity. At that point in history, men became more different from their fathers than women became from their mothers. Today the economic arrow points at women; it is women who are being drawn into wage work, and women who are undergoing changes in their way of life and identity. Women are departing more from their mothers' and grandmothers' way of life, men are doing so less.*

Both the earlier entrance of men into the industrial economy and the later entrance of women have influenced the relations *between* men and women, especially their relations within marriage. The earlier increase in the number of men in industrial work tended to increase the power of men, and the present growth in the number of women in such work has somewhat increased the power of women. On the whole, the entrance of men into industrial work did not destabilize the family whereas *in the absence of other changes*, the rise in female employment has accompanied a rise in divorce.

The influx of women into the economy has not been accompanied by a cultural understanding of marriage and work that would make this transition smooth. Women have changed. But most workplaces have remained inflexible in the face of the family demands of their workers, and at home, most men have yet to really adapt to the changes in women. This strain between the change in women and the absence of change in much else leads me to speak of a stalled revolution.

A society which did not suffer from this stall would be a society *humanely* adapted to the fact that most women work outside the home. The workplace would allow parents to work part time, to share jobs, to work flexible hours, to take parental leaves to give birth, tend sick children, and care for well ones. As Dolores Hayden has envisioned in *Redesigning the American Dream*, it would include affordable housing closer to places of work, and perhaps community-based meal and laundry services. It would include men whose notion of manhood encouraged them to be active parents and householders. In contrast, a stalled revolution lacks social

---

* This is more true of white and middle-class women than it is of black or poor women, whose mothers often worked outside the home. But the trend I am talking about—an increase from 20 percent of American women in paid jobs in 1900 to 55 percent in 1986—has affected a large number of women.

arrangements that ease life for working parents, and lacks men who share the second shift.

If women begin to do less at home because they have less time, if men do little more, if the work of raising children and tending a home requires roughly the same effort, then the questions of who does what at home and of what "needs doing" become key. Indeed, they may become a source of deep tension in marriage, tensions I explore here one by one.

The tensions caused by the stall in this social revolution have led many men and women to avoid becoming part of a two-job couple. Some have married but clung to the tradition of the man as provider, the woman as homemaker. Others have resisted marriage itself. In *The Hearts of Men*, Barbara Ehrenreich describes a "male revolt" against the financial and emotional burden of supporting a family. In *Women and Love*, Shere Hite describes a "female revolt" against unsatisfying and unequal relationships with men. But the couples I focused on are not in traditional marriages and are not giving up on marriage. They are struggling to reconcile the demands of two jobs with a happy family life. Given this larger economic story and the present stalled revolution, I wanted to know how the two-job family was doing.

As I drove from my classes at Berkeley to the outreaching suburbs, small towns, and inner cities of the San Francisco Bay to observe and ask questions in the homes of two-job couples, and back to my own two-job marriage, my first question about who does what gave way to a series of deeper questions: What leads some working mothers to do all the work at home themselves—to pursue what I call a supermom strategy—and what leads others to press their husbands to share the load at home? Why do some men genuinely want to share housework and child care, others fatalistically acquiesce, and still others resist?

What do each husband's ideas about manhood lead him to think he "should feel" about what he's doing at home and at work? What does he really feel? Do his real feelings conflict with what he thinks he should feel? How does he resolve this conflict? The same questions apply to wives. What influence does each person's strategy for handling the second shift have on his or her children, job, and marriage? Through this line of questioning, I was led to the complex web of ties between a family's needs, the sometime quest for equality, and happiness in modern marriage.

We can describe a couple as rich or poor and that will tell us a great deal about their marriage. We can describe them as Catholic, Protestant, Jewish, black, Chicano, Asian, or white and that will tell us something more. We can describe their marriage as a combination of two personalities, one "obsessive compulsive," say, and the other "narcissistic," and again that will tell us something. But knowledge about class, ethnicity, and personality takes us only so far in understanding who does and doesn't share the second shift, and whether or not sharing makes marriage happier.

When I sat down to compare one couple that shared the second shift with another three that didn't, many of the answers that would seem obvious—a man's greater income, his longer hours of work, the fact that his mother was a housewife or his father did little at home, his ideas about men and women—all these factors didn't really explain why some women work the extra month a year and others don't. They didn't explain why some women seemed content to work the extra month, while this made others deeply unhappy. When I compared a couple who was sharing and happy with another couple who was sharing but miserable, it was clear that purely economic or psychological answers were not enough. Gradually, I felt the need to explore how *deep* within each man and woman gender ideology goes. For some, men and women seemed to be egalitarian "on top" but traditional "underneath," or the other way around. I tried to sensitize myself to the difference between shallow ideologies (ideologies which were contradicted by deeper feelings) and deep ideologies (which were reinforced by such feelings). I explored how each person reconciled ideology with the rest of life. I felt the need to explore what I call gender strategies.

THE TOP AND BOTTOM OF GENDER IDEOLOGY

A gender strategy is a plan of action through which a person tries to solve problems at hand, given the cultural notions of gender at play. To pursue a gender strategy, a man draws on beliefs about manhood and womanhood, beliefs that are forged in early childhood and usually anchored to deep emotion. He makes a connection between how he thinks about his manhood, what he feels about it, and what he does. It works in the same way for a woman. Each person's gender ideology defines what sphere a person *wants* to identify with (home or work) and how much power in the marriage one wants to have (less, more, or the same amount).

I found three types of ideology of marital roles: traditional, transitional, and egalitarian. Even though she works, the "pure" traditional woman wants to identify with her activities at home (as a wife, a mother, a neighborhood mom), wants her husband to base his identity on work, and wants less power than he has. The traditional man wants the same. The "pure" egalitarian wants to identify with the same spheres her husband does, and to have an equal amount of power in the marriage. Some want the couple to be jointly oriented to the home, others to their careers, or both of them to jointly hold some balance between the two. Between the traditional and the egalitarian is the transitional, any one of a variety of types of blending of the two. But, in contrast to the traditional, a transitional woman wants to identify with her role at work as well as at home, but she believes her husband should base his identity more on work than she does. A typical transitional wants to identify *both* with the care of the home and with helping her husband earn money, but wants her husband to focus on earning a living. A typical transitional man is all for his wife working, but expects her to do the lion's share at home too. Most people I talked with were transitional in their beliefs.

In actuality, I discovered contradictions between what people said they believed about their marital roles and how they seemed to *feel* about those roles. Some men seemed to me egalitarian on top but traditional underneath. Others seemed traditional on top and egalitarian underneath.[1] Often a person's deeper feelings were a response to the cautionary tales of childhood as well as to life as an adult. Sometimes these feelings *reinforced* the surface of a person's gender ideology. For example, the fear Nancy Holt was to feel of becoming a submissive "doormat," as she felt her mother had been, infused emotional steam into her belief that her husband, Evan, should share the second shift.

On the other hand, the dissociation Ann Myerson was to feel from her successful career undermined her ostensible commitment both to her career and to a shared second shift. She *wanted* to feel as engaged with her career as her husband was with his. She thought she *should* love her work. She *should* think it mattered. In fact, as she confessed in a troubled tone, she didn't love her work and didn't think it mattered. She felt a conflict between what she thought she ought to feel and did feel. Among other things, her gender strategy was a way of trying to resolve that conflict.

The men and women I am about to describe seem to have developed their gender ideology by unconsciously synthesizing certain cultural ideas with feelings about their past. But they also developed their ideology by taking opportunity into account. Sometime in adolescence they matched their personal assets against the opportunities available to men or women of their type; they saw which gender ideology best fit their circumstances, and—often regardless of their upbringing—they identified with a certain version of manhood or womanhood. It "made sense" to them. It felt like "who they were." For example, a woman sizes up her education, intelligence, age, charm, sexual attractiveness, type of sexuality, her dependency needs, her aspirations, and she matches these against her perception of how women like her are doing in the job and marriage market. What jobs could she get? What men? If she wishes to marry, what are her chances for an equal marriage, a traditional marriage, a happy marriage, any marriage? Her courtship pool has very traditional men? She takes these into account. She looks at job prospects with the same eye. *Then* a certain gender ideology, let's say a traditional one, "makes sense." She will embrace the ideology that suits her perception of her chances. She holds to a certain version of womanhood (the "wilting violet," say). She identifies with its customs (men opening doors), and symbols (lacy dress, long hair, soft handshakes, and lowered eyes). She tries to develop its "ideal personality" (deferential, dependent), not because this is what her parents taught her, not because this corresponds to how she naturally "is," but because these particular customs *make sense* of her resources and of her overall situation in a stalled revolution. The same principle applies to men. However wholehearted or ambivalent, a person's gender ideology tends to fit their situation.

GENDER STRATEGIES

When a man tries to apply his ideas about gender to the life unfolding before him, unconsciously or not he pursues a gender strategy.[2] He outlines a course of action. He might become a "superdad"— working long hours and keeping his child up late at night to spend time with him or her. Or he might cut back his hours at work. Or he might scale back housework and spend less time with his children. Or he might actively try to share the second shift.

The term "strategy" refers both to his plan of action and to his emotional preparation for pursuing it. For example, he may require himself to suppress his career ambitions to devote himself more to his children, or suppress his responsiveness to his children's adoring appeals in the course of steeling himself for struggles at work. He might harden himself to his wife's appeals, or he might be the one in the family who "lets" himself see when a child is calling out for help.

I have tried to attune myself to fractures in gender ideology, conflicts between thought and feeling and to the emotional work it takes to fit a gender ideal when inner needs or outer conditions make it hard.

As this social revolution proceeds, the problems of the two-job family will not diminish. If anything, as more and more women do paid work, these problems may well increase. If we can't return to traditional marriage, and if we are not to despair of marriage altogether, it becomes vitally important to understand marriage as a magnet for the strains of the stalled revolution, and to understand gender strategies as the basic dynamic of marriage.

THE ECONOMY OF GRATITUDE

The interplay between a man's gender ideology and a woman's implies a deeper interplay between his gratitude toward her, and hers toward him. For how a person wants to identify himself or herself influences what, in the back and forth of a marriage, will seem like a gift and what will not. If a man doesn't think it fits his male ideal to have his wife earn more than he, it may become his gift to her to "bear it" anyway. But a man may also feel like the husband I interviewed, who said, "When my wife began earning more than me I thought I'd struck gold!" In this case his wife's salary is the gift, not his capacity to accept it "anyway." When couples struggle, it is seldom simply over who does what. Far more often, it is over the giving and receiving of gratitude.

FAMILY MYTHS

As I watched couples in their own homes, I began to realize that they often improvise family myths—versions of reality that obscure a core truth in order to manage a family tension.[3] Evan and Nancy Holt managed an irresolvable conflict over the distribution of work at home through the myth that they now "shared it equally." Another couple unable to admit to the conflict came to believe "we aren't competing over who will take responsibility at home; we're just dreadfully busy with our careers." Yet another couple jointly believed that the husband was bound hand and foot to his career "because the job demanded it," while in fact his careerism covered the fact that they were avoiding each other. Not all couples need or have family myths. But when they do arise, I believe they often manage key tensions which are linked, by degrees, to the long hand of the stalled revolution.

After interviewing couples for a while, I got into the practice of offering families who wanted it my interpretation of how they fit into the broader picture I was seeing and what I perceived were their strategies for coping with the second shift. Couples were often relieved to discover they were not alone, and were encouraged to open up a dialogue about the origins of their troubles.

Many couples in this book worked long hours at their jobs and their children were very young: in this way their lot was unusually hard. But in one crucial way they had it far easier than most couples in America: most were middle class. Many also worked for a company that embraced progressive policies toward personnel, generous benefits and salaries. If *these* middle-class couples find it hard to juggle work and family, many other families across the nation—who earn less, work at less flexible, steady, or lucrative jobs, and rely on poorer day care—are likely to find it harder still.

Anne Machung and I began interviewing in 1976, and accomplished most of our interviews in the early 1980s. I finished in 1988. About half of my later interviews were follow-up contacts with couples we'd talked to earlier; the other half were new.

How much had changed from 1976 to 1988? In practice, little. But something was different, too. More couples *wanted* to share and imagined that they did. Dorothy Sims, a personnel director, summed up this new blend of idea and reality. She eagerly explained to me that she and her husband, Dan, "shared all the housework," and that they were "equally involved" in raising their nine-month-old son, Timothy. Her husband, a refrigerator salesman, applauded her career and was more pleased than threatened by her high salary; he urged her to develop such skills as reading ocean maps and calculating interest rates (which she'd so far resisted learning) because these days "a woman should." But one evening at dinner, a telling episode occurred. Dorothy had handed Timothy to her husband while she served us a chicken dinner. Gradually, the baby began to doze on his father's lap. "When do you want me to put Timmy to bed?" Dan asked. A long silence followed during which it occurred to Dorothy—then, I think, to her husband—that this seemingly insignificant question hinted to me that it was *she*, not he or "they," who usually decided such matters. Dorothy slipped me a glance, put her elbows on the table, and said to her husband in a slow, deliberate voice, "So, what do *we* think?"

When Dorothy and Dan described their "typical days," their picture of sharing grew even less convincing. Dorothy worked the same nine-hour day at the office as her husband. But she came home to fix dinner and to tend Timmy while Dan fit in a squash game three nights a week from six to seven (a good time for his squash partner). Dan read the newspaper more often and slept longer.

Compared to the early interviews, women in the later interviews seemed to speak more often in passing of relationships or marriages that had ended for some other reason but in which it "was also true" that he "didn't lift a finger at home." Or the extra month alone did it. One divorcee who typed part of this manuscript echoed this theme when she explained, "I was a potter and lived with a sculptor for eight years. I cooked, shopped, and cleaned because his art took him longer. He said it was fair because he worked harder. But we both worked at home, and I could see that if anyone worked longer hours, I did, because I earned less with my pots than he earned with his sculpture. That was *hard* to live with, and that's really why we ended."

Some women moved on to slightly more equitable arrangements in the early 1980s, doing a bit less of the second shift than the working mothers I talked to in the late 1970s. Comparing two national surveys of working couples, F. T. Juster found the male slice of the second shift rose from 20 percent in 1965 to 30 percent in 1981, and my study may be a local reflection of this slow national trend.[4] But women like Dorothy Sims, who simply add to their extra month a year a new illusion that they aren't doing it, represent a sad alternative to the woman with the flying hair—the woman who doesn't think that's who she is.

The Cultural Cover-up

❋

I~N~ the apartment across from the little study where I work there is a large bay window that never fails to catch my eye. Peering out from inside, wide-eyed and still, is a life-sized female mannequin in an apron. Her arms are folded and have been for years. She's there guarding the place, waiting. She reminds me and other passersby that no one is home. Maybe she's a spoof on the nostalgia for the 1950s "mom," waiting with milk and cookies for the kids to come home in the era before the two-job family.

Perhaps the mannequin mom is the occupant's joke about the darker reality obscured by the image of the woman with the flying hair—briefcase in one hand and child in the other. "There's really no one home," it seems to say, "only a false mother." She invites us to look again at the more common image of the working mother, at what that image hides. The front cover of the *New York Times Magazine* for September 9, 1984, features a working mother walking home with her daughter. The woman is young. She is good-looking. She is smiling. The daughter is smiling as she lugs her mother's briefcase. The role model is taking, the child is a mini-supermom already. If images could talk, this image would say, "*Women* can combine career and children." It would say nothing about the "extra month a year," nothing about men, nothing about flexible work hours. That would be covered up.

There is no trace of stress, no suggestion that the mother needs help from others. She isn't harassed. She's busy, and it's glamorous to be busy. Indeed, the image of the on-the-go working mother is very like the glamorous image of the busy top executive. The scarcity of the working mother's time seems like the scarcity of the top executive's time. Yet their situations are totally different. The busy top executive is in a hurry at work because his or her time is worth so much. He is in a hurry at home because he works long hours at the office. In contrast, the working mother is in a hurry because her time at work is worth so little, and because she has no help at home. The analogy suggested between the two obscures the wage gap between them at work and helps the gap between them at home.

The *Times* article gives the impression that the working mother is doing so well because she is *personally* competent, not because she has a sound *social* arrangement. Indeed the image of her *private* characteristics obscures all that is missing in *public* support for the working parent. In this respect, the image of the working mother today shares something with that of the black single mother of the 1960s. In celebrating such an image of personal strength, our culture creates an ironic heroism. It extends to middle-class white women a version of womanhood a bit like that offered to poor women of color.

In speaking of the black single mother, commentators and scholars have sometimes used the term "matriarch," a derogatory term in American culture, and a term brought to popular attention by Daniel Patrick Moynihan's controversial government report *The Negro Family: The Case for National Action*. In a section of the report entitled "Tangle of Pathology," Moynihan cited figures showing that black girls scored higher on school tests than black boys. He also showed that 25 percent of black wives in two-job families earned more than their husbands, while only 18 percent of white wives did. Moynihan quotes social scientist Duncan MacIntyre: ". . . the underemployment among Negro men and compensating higher labor force propensity among Negro women . . .

both operate to enlarge the mother's role, undercutting the status of the male and making many Negro families essentially matriarchal."[1] The implication was that black women should aspire to the standards of white women: perform more poorly on educational tests and earn less than their mates. Reading this, black social scientists such as Elaine Kaplan pointed out that black women were "damned if they worked to support their families and damned if they didn't." Black women were cautioned against being so "matriarchal." But as working mothers in low-paid jobs without much male support, they also legitimately felt themselves the victims of male underemployment. While at the bottom of the social totem pole, they were described as if they were at the top. These women pointed out that they "took charge" of their families not because they wanted to dominate, but because if they didn't pay the rent, buy the food, cook it, and look after the children, no one else would. Black women would have been delighted to share the work and the decision making with a man. But in Moynihan's report, the black woman's dominance came to seem like the problem itself rather than the result of the problem.

Similarly, the common portrayal of the supermom suggests that she is energetic and competent because these are her *personal* characteristics, not because she has been forced to adapt to an overly demanding schedule. What is hidden in both cases is the extra burden on women. The difference between Moynihan's portrayal of the black working mother as matriarch and the modern portrayal of the white supermom is an unconscious racism. The supermom has come to seem heroic and good, whereas the matriarch seems unheroic and bad.

This same extra burden on women was also disguised in the Soviet Union, a large industrial nation that had long employed over 80 percent of its women, and who, according to the Alexander Szalai study (described in Chapter 1), work the extra month a year. In a now legendary short story entitled "A Week Like Any Other" by Natalya Baranskaya, Olga, twenty-six, is a technician in a plastics testing laboratory in Moscow and a wife and mother of two. Olga's supervisor praises her for being a *real* Soviet Woman—a supermom. But when Olga is asked to fill out a questionnaire listing her hobbies, she answers, "Personally my hobby is running, running here, running there. . . ." Like the black matriarch, and the multiracial supermom, the image of the real Soviet woman confines a *social* problem to the realm of *personal* character.

Missing from the image of the supermom is the day-care worker, the baby-sitter, the maid—a woman usually in a blue collar position to whom some white collar couples pass much, although not all, of the work of the second shift. In the image, the supermom is almost always white and at least middle class. In reality, of course, day-care workers, baby-sitters, au pairs, nannies, maids, and housekeepers are often part of two-job couples as well. This growing army of women is taking over the parts of a mother's role that employed women relinquish. Most maids and baby-sitters also stay in their occupations for life. But who can afford a house cleaner? In 2010, the median household income was about $50,000. There were 1,470,000 maids and house cleaners and 312,000,000 Americans. So for the average American, outsourcing is not a primary solution.

In the world of advertising images, the maid is often replaced by a machine. In television ads, for example, we see an elegant woman lightly touching her new refrigerator or microwave oven. Her husband may not be helping her at home, but her *machine* is. She and *it* are a team.[2] In the real world, however, machines don't always save time. As the sociologist Joan Vanek pointed out in her study of homemakers in the 1920s and 1960s, even with more labor-saving appliances, the later homemakers spent as much time on housework as the earlier ones. The 1960s homemakers spent less time cleaning and washing the house; machines helped with that. But they spent more time shopping, getting appliances repaired, washing clothes (as standards of cleanliness rose), and doing bookkeeping. Eighty-five percent of the working couples I interviewed did not employ regular household help; it was up to them and their "mechanical helpmates." Since these took time they didn't have, many dropped their standards of housekeeping.

The image of the woman with the flying hair is missing someone else too: her husband. In the absence of a maid, and with household appliances that still take time, a husband's hand becomes important. Yet in the popular culture the image of the working father is largely missing, and with it the very issue of *sharing*. With the disappearance of this issue, ideas of struggle and marital tension over the lack of sharing are also smuggled out of view. One advertising image shows us a woman just home from work fixing a quick meal with Uncle Ben's rice; the person shown eating it with great relish is a man. In a 1978 study of television advertising, Olive Courtney and Thomas Whipple found that men are shown *demonstrating* products that help with domestic chores, but usually not *using* them. Women are often shown serving men and boys, but men and boys are seldom shown serving women and girls.

In the world of print as well, the male of the two-job couple is often invisible. There are dozens of advice books for working mothers, telling them how to "get organized," "make lists," "prioritize," but I found no such books for working fathers. In her book *Having It All*, Helen Gurley Brown, inventor of the "Cosmo Girl" and the author of *Sex and the Single Girl*, tells readers in a chatty, girl-to-girl voice how to rise from clerical work to stardom, and how to combine this career success with being feminine and married. She offers women flamboyant advice on how to combine being sexy with career success, but goes light and thin on how to be a good mother. Women can have fame and fortune, office affairs, silicone injections, and dazzling designer clothes, in Brown's world. But the one thing they can't have, apparently, is a man who shares the work at home. Referring to her own husband, Brown writes: "Whether a man will help in the kitchen depends on his mother, says Carol (a friend). Mine *doesn't*. You also can't send him to market . . . he comes back with tiny ears of corn vinaigrette, olives and pâté—but it's no good banging your head against the stove because he hasn't got a cassoulet simmering on top of it. Usually they do something to make up for household imbecility . . . like love you and pay a lot of bills."[3]

In another advice book to women, *The Superwoman Syndrome*, Marjorie Hansen Shaevitz more candidly admits to losing a struggle to get her husband to share housework: "I spent a lot of time smoldering internally over his apparent recalcitrance. I took it one step further by judging that if he really loved me, he would see how hard I was working, how tired I was and would come to my rescue with cheerful resourcefulness. Need I tell you this never happened?"[4]

Shaevitz became overworked, overwhelmed, and out of control. The answer? She should make lists, prioritize, or hire a maid. Shaevitz suggests having few children, having them late and close together because "this leaves more time in which the parents may pursue careers or other activities." She remarks that "some relief is available if you have a child-oriented spouse" but cautions "many women don't have that luxury. . . ." What changes does Shaevitz recommend? Ask more favors of friends and do fewer for them. Indeed, for the working woman the very principle of reciprocity is a "problem." As she explains, "The Superwoman not only has some anxiety about asking people for help, but the internal 'catch 22' is that she probably feels she's going to have to repay that help in some multiple way. *And that is also losing control of your life.*"[5] So she should not do such things as "agree to pick up your friend's child for a school play . . ." or "listen to a friend's laundry list of problems with her husband and kids."

Shaevitz doesn't feel sharing is wrong, only that women can't get it. In a four-page epilogue to *The Superwoman Syndrome*, the dread issue of sharing resurfaces in a strangely sour exchange between Shaevitz and her husband, Mort:

MARJORIE: . . . Right now I think we're in for some rough times between men and women, unless men begin participating a little more (you notice I say a *little* more) in the household and with their children. I don't think bright, competent, educated women are going to put up with men who are unwilling to participate in a sharing kind of relationship. You notice I say "sharing," not "equal sharing." Many women tell me they want to have a man in their life, but they are no longer willing to be the only person giving in the relationship. They don't want to be with a man who needs to be taken care of. In that case, it's easier and more pleasant to be without a man.

MORT: Marjorie, that's really infuriating to most men. It's quite clear that men are doing more and that this trend is likely to increase. What men find difficult to accept is that they get little credit for what they do, and an incredible list of complaints about what they don't do. Men and women may give in different ways. Women continue to set ground rules for what they expect, what they want, and how they want it delivered. I can tell you that most highly competent, successful men—the kind of men most women look for—simply will not respond to a behavioral checklist.

MARJORIE: . . . The consequence of letting your wife do it all is that she is likely to get angry, resentful, and maybe even sick.

MORT: Couples need to take a look at what this situation is behind the wife's pointing a finger at the husband. You know that doesn't work either. I think many men will probably be happy to "let her go"—they'll find someone else to take care of them.[6]

Marjorie talks about "many women" and Mort talks about "most men," but the dialogue seems obliquely infused with their own struggle. In the end, Mort Shaevitz refers obscurely to the idea of a woman "getting help from *everyone*—her husband, her children, and society," a faceless crowd through which the Superwoman once again strides alone. *Having It All* and *The Superwoman Syndrome* advise women on how to do without a change in men, how to be a woman who is different from her mother, married to a man not much different from her father. By adding "super" before "woman" and subtracting meaning from the word "all," these authors tell women how to gracefully accommodate to the stalled revolution.

There have been two responses that counter the supermom: one is to poke fun at her and one is to propose an alternative to her—"the new man." The humorous response is to be found in the joke books, memo pads, key chains, ashtrays, cocktail napkins, and coffee mugs sold in novelty and gift shops especially around Mother's Day. It critiques the supermom by making her look ridiculous. One joke book by Barbara and Jim Dale, entitled the *Working Woman Book*, advises, "The first step in a good relationship with your children is memorizing their names." In a section called "What You Can Do" in a chapter on raising children, *The Superwoman Syndrome* seriously advises: "A. Talk with your child, B. Play a game, C. Go to a sports event. . . ." and under "Demonstrate Your Affection By" it helpfully notes, "A. Hugging, B. Kissing. . . ."[7]

Or again: "The famous Flying Wallendas were renowned for their feat of balancing seven Wallendas on a thin shaft of wood supported only by four Wallendas beneath whom was but one, strong, reliable, determined Wallenda . . . undoubtedly *Mrs.* Wallenda."

One mug portrays a working mother with the familiar briefcase in one hand and baby in the other. But there is no striding, no smile, no backswept hair. The woman's mouth is a wiggly line. Her hair is unkempt. One shoe is red, one blue. In one hand she holds a wailing baby, in the other a briefcase, papers cascading out. Beneath her it says, "I am a working mother. I am nuts." There is nothing glamorous about being time-poor; the mug seems to say, "I'm not happy. I'm not fine." Implicitly the cup critiques the frazzled supermom herself, not her inflexible work schedule, not the crisis in day-care, not the glacial pace of change in our idea of "a real man." Her options were fine; what was crazy—and funny—was her *decision* to work. That's what makes the extra month a year a joke. In this way the commercial vision of the working mother incorporates a watered-down criticism of itself, has a good laugh, and continues on.

A serious critique of the supermom parallels the humorous one, and in popular journalism, this serious approach seemed to be crowding out many other journalistic approaches to the woman question. In *Woman on a Seesaw: The Ups and Downs of Making It*, for example, Hilary Cosell bitterly rues her single-minded focus on career, which barely made time for a husband and precluded having children. For example:

> There I was, coming home from ten or twelve or sometimes more hours at work, pretty much shot after the day, and I'd do this simply marvelous imitation of all the successful fathers I remembered from childhood. All the men I swore I'd never grow up and marry, let alone be like . . . the men who would come home from the office, grab a drink or two, collapse on the couch, shovel in a meal and be utterly useless for anything beyond the most mundane and desultory conversation. And there I'd be, swilling a vodka on the rocks or two, shoving a Stouffer's into my mouth and staggering off to take a bath, watch "Hill Street Blues" and fade away with Ted Koppel. To get up and do it all again.[8]

Like the frazzled coffee-mug mom, Cosell admits her stress. Like the coffee-mug mom, she deplores her "wrong decision" to enter the rat race, but does not much question the unwritten rules of that race. Both the humorous and the serious critiques of the supermom tell us things are not fine, but like the image of the working mother they criticize, they convey a fatalism. "That's just how it is," they say.

A second cultural trend tacitly critiques the supermom image by proposing an alternative—the new man. Increasingly, books, articles, films, and comics celebrate the man who feels that time with his child and work around the house are compatible with being a real man. Above a series of articles in his syndicated newspaper column about his first year as a father, a series which later became a popular book entitled *Good Morning, Merry Sunshine*, Bob Greene is pictured holding his baby daughter, Amanda. Greene is not in transit between home and work. He is sitting down, apparently at home, where he works as a writer. He is in a short-sleeved shirt instead of a coat and tie—no need to address the professional world outside. He is smiling and in his arms, his daughter is laughing. He is successful—he is writing this column, this book. He writes on "male" topics like the Chicago mayoral election. He's an involved father. But he's not a house husband, like the man in the movie *Mr. Mom*, who for a disastrous, funny period—role reversal is an ancient, always humorous theme in literature—exchanges roles with his wife. Greene's wife, Susan, is *also* home with Amanda; he joins, but doesn't replace, his wife at home. As he writes in his journal:

> Started early this morning. I worked hard on a column about the upcoming Chicago mayoral election. I had to go to the far north side of town to interview a man; then once I got back downtown I had several hours of phone checking to do. There were some changes to be made after I had finished writing. It was well after dark before I was finished. I was still buzzing from the nonstop reporting and writing when I got home, all of the elements of the story were still knocking around my head. Susan said, "Amanda learned how to drink from a cup today." I went into the kitchen and watched her. I watched Amanda drink from the cup, and nothing else mattered.[9]

The new man "has it all" in the same way the supermom has it all. He is a male version of the woman with the flying hair. Bob Greene is an involved father and also successful in a competitive field. In writing only about his own highly atypical experience, though, Greene unintentionally conveys the idea that men face no conflict between doing a job and raising a child.

In fact, most working fathers who fully share the emotional responsibility and physical care of children and do half the housework also face great difficulty. As long as the "woman's work" that some men do is socially devalued, as long as it is defined as woman's work, as long as it's tacked onto a regular work day, men who share it are likely to develop the same jagged mouth and frazzled hair as the coffee-mug mom. The image of the new man is like the image of the supermom: it obscures the strain.

The image of the supermom and, to a lesser extent, the image of the new man enter a curious cultural circle. First, more men and women become working couples. Spotting these men and women as a market, advertisers surround them with images—on computer Web sites, on magazine covers, in television commercials— mainly of the do-it-all woman. Then journalists write articles about her. Advice books follow, and finally, more ponderously, scientific word gets out. As a result of this chain of interpretations, the two-job couple see themselves down a long hall of mirrors.

What working mothers find in the cultured mirror has much to do with what the dilemmas in their lives make them look for. When the working mothers I talked with considered the image of the supermom, they imagined a woman who was unusually efficient, organized, energetic, bright, and confident. To be a supermom seemed like a good thing. To be called one was a compliment. She wasn't real, but she was ideal. Nancy Holt, a social worker and the mother of a son named Joey, found the idea of a supermom curiously *useful*. She faced a terrible choice between having a stable marriage and an equal one, and she chose the stable marriage. She struggled hard to suppress her conflict with her husband and to perform an emotional cover-up. The supermom image appealed to her because it offered her a cultural cover-up to go with her emotional one. It clothed her compromise with an aura of inevitability. It obscured the crisis she and her husband faced over the second shift, her conflict with her husband over it, and her attempts to suppress the conflict to preserve their marriage—leaving in their place the illusive, light, almost-winking image of that woman with the flying hair.

Joey's Problem:
Nancy and Evan Holt

✳

Nancy Holt arrives home from work, her son, Joey, in one hand and a bag of groceries in the other. As she puts down the groceries and opens the front door, she sees a spill of mail on the hall floor, Joey's half-eaten piece of cinnamon toast on the hall table, and the phone machine's winking red light: a still-life reminder of the morning's frantic rush to distribute the family to the world outside. Nancy, for seven years a social worker, is a short, lithe blond woman of thirty who talks and moves rapidly. She scoops the mail onto the hall table and heads for the kitchen, unbuttoning her coat as she goes. Joey sticks close behind her, intently explaining to her how dump trucks dump things. Joey is a fat-cheeked, lively four-year-old who chuckles easily at things that please him.

Having parked their red station wagon, Evan, her husband, comes in and hangs up his coat. He has picked her up at work and they've arrived home together. Apparently unready to face the kitchen commotion but not quite entitled to relax with the newspaper in the living room, he slowly studies the mail. Also thirty, Evan, a warehouse furniture salesman, has thinning pale blond hair, a stocky build, and a tendency to lean on one foot. In his manner there is something both affable and hesitant.

From the beginning, Nancy describes herself as an "ardent feminist"; she wants a similar balance of spheres and equal power. She began her marriage hoping that she and Evan would base their identities in both parenthood and career, but clearly tilted toward parenthood. Evan felt it was fine for Nancy to have a career, if she could handle the family too.

As I observe in their home on this evening, I notice a small ripple on the surface of family waters. From the commotion of the kitchen, Nancy calls, "Eva-an, will you *please* set the table?" The word "please" is thick with irritation. Scurrying between refrigerator, sink, and oven, with Joey at her feet, Nancy wants Evan to help; she has asked him, but reluctantly. She seems to resent having to ask. (Later she tells me, "I *hate* to ask; why should I ask? It's begging.") Evan looks up from the mail and flashes an irritated glance toward the kitchen, stung, perhaps, to be asked in a way so barren of respect. He begins setting out knives and forks, asks if she will need spoons, then answers the doorbell. A neighbor's child. No, Joey can't play right now. The moment of irritation has passed.

Later as I interview Nancy and Evan separately, they describe their family life as very happy—except for Joey's "problem." Joey has great difficulty getting to sleep. They start trying to put him to bed at 8:00. Evan tries but Joey rebuffs him; Nancy has better luck. By 8:30 they have him *on* the bed where he crawls and bounds playfully. After 9:00 he still calls out for water or toys, and sneaks out of bed to switch on the light. This continues past 9:30, then 10:00 and 10:30. At about 11:00 Joey complains that his bed is "scary," that he can only go to sleep in his parents' bedroom. Worn down, Nancy accepts this proposition. And it is part of their current arrangement that putting Joey to bed is "Nancy's job." Nancy and Evan can't get into bed until midnight or later, when Evan is tired and Nancy exhausted. She used to enjoy their lovemaking, Nancy tells me, but now sex seems like "more work." The Holts consider their fatigue and impoverished sex life as results of Joey's Problem.

The official history of Joey's Problem—the story Nancy and Evan give me—begins with Joey's fierce attachment to Nancy, and Nancy's strong attachment to him. On an afternoon walk through

Golden Gate Park, Nancy devotes herself to Joey's every move. Now Joey sees a squirrel; Nancy tells me she must remember to bring nuts next time. Now Joey is going up the slide; she notices that his pants are too short—she must take them down tonight. The two enjoy each other. Off the official record, neighbors and Joey's baby-sitter say that Nancy is a wonderful mother, but privately they add how much "like a single mother."

For his part, Evan sees little of Joey. He has his evening routine, working with his tools in the basement, and Joey always seems happy to be with Nancy. In fact, Joey shows little interest in Evan, and Evan hesitates to see that as a problem. "Little kids need their moms more than they need their dads," he explains philosophically; "All boys go through an oedipal phase."

Perfectly normal things happen. After a long day, mother, father, and son sit down to dinner. Evan and Nancy get the first chance all day to talk to each other, but both turn anxiously to Joey, expecting his mood to deteriorate. Nancy asks him if he wants celery with peanut butter on it. Joey says yes. "Are you sure that's how you want it?" "Yes." Then the fidgeting begins. "I don't like the strings on my celery." "Celery is made up of strings." "The celery is too big." Nancy grimly slices the celery. A certain tension mounts. Every time one parent begins a conversation with the other, Joey interrupts. "I don't have anything to drink." Nancy gets him juice. And finally, "Feed me." By the end of the meal, no one has obstructed Joey's victory. He has his mother's reluctant attention and his father is reaching for a beer. But talking about it later, they say, "This is normal when you have kids."

Sometimes when Evan knocks on the baby-sitter's door to pick up Joey, the boy looks past his father, searching for a face behind him: "Where's Mommy?" Sometimes he outright refuses to go home with his father. Eventually Joey even swats at his father, once quite hard, on the face, for "no reason at all." This makes it hard to keep imagining Joey's relationship to Evan as "perfectly normal." Evan and Nancy begin to talk seriously about a "swatting problem."

Evan decides to seek ways to compensate for his emotional distance from Joey. He brings Joey a surprise every week or so—a Tonka truck, a Tootsie Roll. He turns weekends into father-and-son times. One Saturday, Evan proposes the zoo, and hesitantly, Joey agrees. Father and son have their coats on and are nearing the front door. Suddenly Nancy joins them, and as she walks down the steps with Joey in her arms, she explains to Evan, "to help things out."

Evan gets few signs of love from Joey and feels helpless to do much about it. "I just don't feel good about me and Joey," he tells me one evening, "that's all I can say." Evan loves Joey. He feels proud of him, this bright, good-looking, happy child. But Evan also seems to feel that being a father is vaguely hurtful and hard to talk about.

The official history of Joey's Problem was that Joey felt the normal oedipal attachment of a male child to his mother. But Evan and Nancy add the point that Joey's problems are exacerbated by Evan's difficulties being an active father, which stem, they feel, from the way Evan's own father, remote and inexpressive self-made businessman, had treated him. Evan tells me, "When Joey gets older, we're going to play baseball together and go fishing."

As I recorded this official version of Joey's Problem through interviews and observation, I began to feel doubts about it. For one thing, clues to another interpretation appeared in the simple pattern of footsteps on a typical evening. There was the steady pacing of Nancy, preparing dinner in the kitchen, moving in zigzags from counter to refrigerator to counter to stove. There were the lighter, faster steps of Joey, running in large figure eights through the house, dashing from his Tonka truck to his motorcycle man, reclaiming his sense of belonging in this house, among his things. After dinner, Nancy and Evan mingled footsteps in the kitchen as they cleaned up. Then Nancy's steps began again: click, click, click, down to the basement for laundry, then thuck, thuck, thuck up the carpeted stairs to the first floor. Then to the bathroom where she runs Joey's bath, then into Joey's room, then back to the bath with Joey. Evan moved less—from the living room chair to Nancy in the kitchen, then back to the living room. He moved to the dining room to eat dinner and to the kitchen to help clean up. After dinner he went down to his hobby shop in the basement to sort out his tools; later he came up for a beer, then went back down. The footsteps suggest what is going on: Nancy is working second shift.

BEHIND THE FOOTSTEPS

Between 8:05 a.m. and 6:05 p.m., both Nancy and Evan are away from home, working a "first shift" at full-time jobs. The rest of the time they deal with the varied tasks of the second shift: shopping, cooking, paying bills; taking care of the car, the garden, and the yard; keeping harmony with Evan's mother, who drops over quite a bit, concerned about Joey, with neighbors, their voluble baby-sitter, and each other. And Nancy's talk reflects a series of second-shift thoughts: "We're out of barbecue sauce. . . . Joey needs a Halloween costume. . . . Joey needs a haircut. . . ." and so on. She reflects a certain second-shift sensibility, a continual attunement to the task of striking and restriking the right emotional balance between child, spouse, home, and outside job.

When I first met the Holts, Nancy was absorbing far more of the second shift than Evan. She said she was doing 80 percent of the housework and 90 percent of the child care. Evan said she did 60 percent of the housework, 70 percent of the child care. Joey said, "I vacuum the rug, and fold the dinner napkins," finally concluding, "Mom and I do it all." A neighbor agreed with Joey. Clearly, between Nancy and Evan, there was a leisure gap: Evan had more than Nancy. I asked both of them, in separate interviews, to explain to me how they had dealt with housework and child care since their marriage began.

One evening in the fifth year of their marriage, Nancy told me that when Joey was two months old (and almost four years before I met the Holts), she first seriously raised the issue with Evan. "I told him: 'Look, Evan, it's not working. I do the housework, I take the major care of Joey *and* I work a full-time job. I get pissed. This is *your* house too. Joey is *your* child too. It's not all *my* job to care for them.' When I cooled down I put to him, 'Look, how about this: I'll cook Mondays, Wednesdays, and Fridays. You cook Tuesdays, Thursdays, and Saturdays. And we'll share or go out Sundays.'"

According to Nancy, Evan said he didn't like "rigid schedules." He said he didn't necessarily agree with her standards of house-keeping, and didn't like that standard imposed on him, especially if she was "sluffing off" tasks on him, which from time to time he felt she was. But he went along with the idea in principle. Nancy said the first week of the new plan went as follows. On Monday, she cooked. For Tuesday, Evan planned a meal that required shopping for a few ingredients, but on his way home he forgot to shop for them. He came home, saw nothing he could use in the refrigerator or in the cupboard, and suggested to Nancy that they go out for Chinese food. On Wednesday, Nancy cooked. On Thursday morning, Nancy reminded Evan, "Tonight it's your turn." That night Evan fixed hamburgers and french fries and Nancy was quick to praise him. On Friday, Nancy cooked. On Saturday, Evan forgot again.

As this pattern continued, Nancy's reminders became sharper. The sharper they became, the more actively Evan forgot—perhaps anticipating even sharper reprimands if he resisted more directly. This cycle of passive refusal followed by disappointment and anger gradually tightened, and before long the struggle had spread to the task of doing the laundry. Nancy said it was only fair that Evan share the laundry. He agreed in principle, but, anxious that Evan would not share, Nancy wanted a clear, explicit agree-ment. "You ought to wash and fold every other load," she had told him. Evan experienced this plan as a yoke around his neck. On many weekdays, at this point, a huge pile of laundry sat like a disheveled guest on the living-room couch.

In her frustration, Nancy began to make subtle jabs at Evan. "I don't know *what's* for dinner," she would say with a sigh. Or "I can't cook now, I've got to deal with this pile of laundry." She tensed at the slightest criticism about household disorder; if Evan wouldn't do the housework, he had absolutely *no* right to criticize how she did it. She would burst out angrily: "After work *my* feet are just as tired as *your* feet. I'm just as wound up as you are. I come home. I cook dinner. I wash and I clean. Here we are, planning a second child, and I can't cope with the one we have."

About two years after I first began visiting the Holts, I started to see their problem in a certain light: as a conflict between their two views of gender, each with its load of personal symbols. Nancy wanted to be the sort of woman who was needed and appreciated both at home and at work. She wanted Evan to appreciate her for being a caring social worker, a committed wife, and a wonderful mother. But she cared just as much that she be able to appreciate *Evan* for what *he* contributed at home, not just for how he supported the family. She would feel proud to explain to women friends that she was married to such a man.

A gender ideology is often rooted in early experience and fueled by motives traced to some cautionary tale in early life. So it was for Nancy:

> My mom was wonderful, a real aristocrat, but she was also terribly depressed being a housewife. My dad treated her like a doormat. She didn't have any self-confidence. And growing up, I can remember her being really depressed. I grew up bound and determined not to be like her and not to marry a man like my father. As long as Evan doesn't do the housework, I feel it means he's going to be like my father—coming home, putting his feet up, and hollering at my mom to serve him. That's my biggest fear. I've had *bad* dreams about that.

Nancy thought that women friends her age in traditional marriages had come to similarly bad ends. She described a high school friend: "Martha barely made it through City College. She had no interest in learning anything. She spent nine years trailing behind her husband [a salesman]. It's a miserable marriage. She hand washes all his shirts. The high point of her life was when she was eighteen and the two of us were running around Miami Beach in a Mustang convertible. She's gained seventy pounds and hates her life." To Nancy, Martha was a younger version of her mother, depressed, lacking in self-esteem, a cautionary tale whose moral was "If you want to be happy, develop a career and get your husband to share at home." Asking Evan to help again and again felt like hard work but it was an effort to escape Martha's fate and her mother's.

For his own reasons, Evan imagined things very differently. He loved Nancy and if Nancy loved being a social worker, he was happy and proud to support her in it. He knew that because she took her caseload so seriously, it was draining work. But at the same time, he did not see why, just because she chose this demanding career, *he* had to change *his own* life. Why should her personal decision to work outside the home require him to do more inside it? Nancy earned about two-thirds as much as Evan, and her salary was a big help, but as Nancy confided, "If push came to shove, we could do without it." Nancy was a social worker because she loved it. Doing daily chores at home was thankless work, and certainly not something Evan needed her to appreciate about him. Equality in the second shift meant a loss in his standard of living, and despite all the high-flown talk, he felt he hadn't *really* bargained for it. He was happy to help Nancy at home if she needed help; that was fine. That was only decent. But it was too sticky a matter committing himself to some formal even-steven type plan.

Two other beliefs probably fueled his resistance as well. The first was his suspicion that if he shared the second shift with Nancy, she would dominate him. Nancy would ask him to do this, ask him to do that. It felt to Evan as if Nancy had won so many small victories that he had to draw the line somewhere. Nancy had a declarative personality; and as she confided, "Evan's mother sat me down and told me once that I was too forceful, that Evan needed to take more authority." Both Nancy and Evan agreed that Evan's sense of career and self was in fact shakier than hers. He had been unemployed. She never had. He had had some bouts of drinking in the past. Drinking was foreign to her. Evan thought that sharing housework would upset a certain balance of power that felt culturally right. He held the purse strings and made the major decisions about large purchases (like their house) because he "knew more about finances" and because he'd chipped in more inheritance than she when they married. His job difficulties had lowered his self-respect, and now as a couple they had achieved some ineffable balance—tilted in his favor, she thought—which, if corrected to equalize the burden of chores, would result in his giving in "too much." A certain driving anxiety behind Nancy's strategy of actively renegotiating roles had made Evan see agreement as "giving in." When he wasn't feeling good about work, he dreaded the idea of being under his wife's thumb at home.

Underneath these feelings, Evan perhaps also feared that Nancy was avoiding taking care of *him*. His own mother, a mild-mannered alcoholic, had by imperceptible steps phased herself out of a mother's role, leaving him very much on his own. Perhaps a personal motive to prevent that happening in his marriage—a guess on my part, and unarticulated on his—underlay his strategy of passive resistance. And he wasn't altogether wrong to fear this. Meanwhile, he felt he was offering Nancy the chance to stay home or cut back her hours, and that she was refusing his gift, while Nancy felt that, given her feelings, this offer was hardly a gift.

In the sixth year of their marriage, when Nancy again intensified her pressure on Evan to commit himself to equal sharing, Evan recalled saying, "Nancy, why don't you cut back to half time, that way you can fit everything in." At first Nancy was baffled:

"We've been married all this time, and you *still* don't get it. Work is important to me. I worked *hard* to get my MSW. Why *should* I give it up?" Nancy also explained to Evan and later to me, "I think my degree and my job has been my way of reassuring myself that I won't end up like my mother." Yet she'd received little emotional support in getting her degree from either her parents or her in-laws. (Her mother had avoided asking about her thesis, and her in-laws, though invited, did not attend her graduation, later claiming they'd never been invited.)

In addition, Nancy was more excited about seeing her elderly clients in tenderloin hotels than Evan was about selling couches to furniture salesmen with greased-back hair. Why shouldn't Evan make as many compromises with his career and his leisure as she'd made with hers? She couldn't see it Evan's way, and Evan couldn't see it hers.

In years of alternating struggle and compromise, Nancy had seen only fleeting mirages of cooperation, visions that appeared when she got sick or withdrew, and disappeared when she got better or came forward.

After seven years of loving marriage, Nancy and Evan had finally come to a terrible impasse. They began to snap at each other, to criticize, to carp. Each felt taken advantage of: Evan, because his offer of a good arrangement was deemed unacceptable, and Nancy, because Evan wouldn't do what she deeply felt was fair.

This struggle made its way into their sexual life—first through Nancy directly, and then through Joey. Nancy had always disdained any form of feminine wiliness or manipulation. She felt above the underhanded ways traditional women used to get around men. Her family saw her as a flaming feminist and that was how she saw herself. "When I was a teenager," she mused, "I vowed I would *never* use sex to get my way with a man. It is not self-respecting; it's demeaning. But when Evan refused to carry his load at home, I did, I used sex. I said, 'Look, Evan, I would not be this exhausted and asexual every night if I didn't have so much to face every morning.'" She felt reduced to an old strategy, and her modern ideas made her ashamed of it. At the same time, she'd run out of other modern ways.

The idea of a separation arose, and they became frightened. Nancy looked at the deteriorating marriages and fresh divorces of couples with young children around them. One unhappy husband they knew had become so uninvolved in family life (they didn't know whether his unhappiness made him uninvolved, or whether his lack of involvement made his wife unhappy) that his wife left him. In another case, Nancy felt the wife had nagged her husband so much that he abandoned her for another woman. In both cases, the couple was less happy after the divorce than before. Both wives took the children, fought with their exes about them, and struggled desperately for money and time. Nancy took stock. She asked herself, "Why wreck a marriage over a dirty frying pan?" Is it really worth it?

Upstairs-Downstairs:
A Family Myth as "Solution"

Not long after this crisis in the Holts' marriage, there was a dramatic lessening of tension over the second shift. It was as if the issue was closed. Evan had won. Nancy would do it. Evan expressed vague guilt but beyond that he had nothing to say. Nancy had wearied of continually raising the topic, wearied of the lack of resolution. Now in the exhaustion of defeat, she wanted the struggle to be over too. Evan was "so good" in *other* ways, why debilitate their marriage by continual quarreling? Besides, she told me, "Women always adjust more, don't they?"

One day, when I asked Nancy to tell me who did which tasks from a long list of household chores, she interrupted me with a broad wave of her hand and said, "I do the upstairs, Evan does the downstairs." What does that mean? I asked. Matter-of-factly, she explained that the upstairs included the living room, the dining room, the kitchen, two bedrooms, and two baths. The downstairs meant the garage, a place for storage and hobbies—Evan's hobbies. She explained this as a "sharing" arrangement, without humor or irony—just as Evan did later. Both said they had agreed it was the best solution to their dispute. Evan would take care of the car, the garage, and Max, the family dog. As Nancy explained, "The dog is all Evan's problem. I don't have to deal with the dog." Nancy took care of the rest.

For purposes of accommodating the second shift, then, the Holts' garage was elevated to the full moral and practical equivalent of the rest of the house. For Nancy and Evan, "upstairs and downstairs," "inside and outside," was vaguely described like "half and half," a fair division of labor based on a natural division of their house.

The Holts presented their upstairs-downstairs agreement as a perfectly equitable solution to a problem they "once had." This belief is what we might call a family myth, even a modest delusional system. Why did they believe it? I think they believed it because they needed to believe it, because it solved a terrible problem. It allowed Nancy to continue thinking of herself as the sort of woman whose husband didn't abuse her—a self-conception that mattered a great deal to her. And it avoided the hard truth that, in his stolid, passive way, Evan had refused to share. It avoided the truth, too, that in their showdown, Nancy was more afraid of divorce than Evan was. This outer cover to their family life was jointly devised. It was an attempt to agree that there was no conflict over the second shift, no tension between their versions of manhood and womanhood, and that the powerful crisis that had arisen was temporary and minor.

The wish to avoid such a conflict is natural enough. But their avoidance was tacitly supported by the surrounding culture, especially the image of the woman with the flying hair. After all, this admirable woman also proudly does the "upstairs" each day without a husband's help and without conflict.

After Nancy and Evan reached their upstairs-downstairs

agreement, their confrontations ended. They were nearly forgotten. Yet, as she described their daily life months after the agreement, Nancy's resentment seemed alive and well. For example, she said:

> Evan and I eventually divided the labor so that I do the upstairs and Evan does the downstairs and the dog. So the dog is my husband's problem. But when I was getting the dog outside and getting Joey ready for child care, and cleaning up the mess of feeding the cat, and getting the lunches together, and having my son wipe his nose on my outfit so I would have to change—then I was pissed! I felt that I was doing *everything*. All Evan was doing was getting up, having coffee, reading the paper, and saying, "Well, I have to go now," and often forgetting the lunch I'd bothered to make.

She also mentioned that she had fallen into the habit of putting Joey to bed in a certain way: he asked to be swung around by the arms, dropped onto the bed, nuzzled and hugged, whispered to in his ear. Joey waited for her attention. He didn't go to sleep without it. But, increasingly, when Nancy tried it at eight or nine, the ritual didn't put Joey to sleep. On the contrary, it woke him up. It was then that Joey began to say he could only go to sleep in his parents' bed, that he began to sleep in their bed and to encroach on their sexual life.

Near the end of my visits, it struck me that Nancy was putting Joey to bed in an exciting way, later and later at night, in order to tell Evan something important: "You win. I'll go on doing all the work at home, but I'm angry about it and I'll make you pay." Evan had won the battle but lost the war. According to the family myth, all was well: the struggle had been resolved by the upstairs-downstairs agreement. But suppressed in one area of their marriage, this struggle lived on in another—as Joey's Problem, and as theirs.

Nancy's "Program" to Sustain the Myth

There was a moment, I believe, when Nancy seemed to *decide* to give up on this one. She decided to try not to resent Evan. Whether or not other women face a moment just like this, at the very least they face the need to deal with all the feelings that naturally arise from a clash between a treasured ideal and an incompatible reality. In the age of a stalled revolution, it is a problem a great many women face.

Emotionally, Nancy's compromise from time to time slipped; she would forget and grow resentful again. Her new resolve needed maintenance. Only half aware that she was doing so, Nancy went to extraordinary lengths to maintain it. She could tell me now, a year or so after her decision, in a matter-of-fact and noncritical way: "Evan likes to come home to a hot meal. He doesn't like to clear the table. He doesn't like to do the dishes. He likes to go watch TV. He likes to play with Joey when he feels like it and not feel like he should be with him more." She seemed resigned.

Everything was "fine." But it had taken an extraordinary amount of complex emotion work—the work of *trying* to feel the right feeling, the feeling she wanted to feel—to make and keep everything fine. Across the nation at this particular time in history, this emotion work is often all that stands between the stalled revolution on the one hand, and broken marriages on the other.

It would have been easier for Nancy Holt to do what some other women did: indignantly cling to her goal of sharing the second shift. Or she could have cynically renounced all forms of feminism as misguided, could have cleared away any ideological supports to her indignation, so as to smooth her troubled bond with Evan. Or, like her mother, she could have sunk into quiet depression, disguised perhaps by overbusyness, drinking, overeating.

She did none of these things. Instead, she did something more complicated. She became *benignly* accommodating.

How did Nancy manage to accommodate graciously? How did she really live with it? In the most general terms, she had to bring herself to *believe* the myth that the upstairs-downstairs division of housework was fair, and that it had resolved her struggle with Evan. She had to decide to accept an arrangement which in her heart of hearts felt unfair. At the same time, she did not relinquish her deep beliefs about fairness.

Instead, she did something more complicated. Intuitively, Nancy *avoided* all the mental associations linked to this sore point: the connections between Evan's care of the dog and her care of their child and house, between her share of family work and equality in their marriage, and between equality and love. In short, Nancy refused to consciously recognize the entire chain of associations that made her feel that something was wrong. The maintenance program she designed to avoid thinking about these things and to avoid the connections between them was, in one way, a matter of denial, and in another way, it was a matter of intuitive genius.

First, it involved dissociating the inequity in the second shift from the inequity in their marriage, and in marriages in general. Nancy continued to care about sharing the work at home, about having an "equal marriage" and about other people having them too. For reasons that went back to her "doormat" mother, and to her own determination to forge an independent identity as an educated, working woman for whom career opportunities had opened up, Nancy cared about these things. Feminism made sense of her biography, her circumstances, and the way she had forged the two. How could she *not* care? But to ensure that her concern for equality did not make her resentful in her marriage to a man remarkably resistant to change, she "rezoned" this anger-inducing territory. She made that territory smaller: only if Evan did not take care of the dog would she be indignant. Now she wouldn't need to be upset about the double day *in general*. She could still believe in fifty-fifty with housework, and still believe that working toward equality was an expression of respect and respect the basis of love. But this chain of ideas was now anchored more safely to a more minor matter: how lovingly Evan groomed, fed, and walked the dog.

For Evan, also, the dog came to symbolize the entire second shift: it became a fetish. Other men, I found, had second-shift fetishes too. When I asked one man what he did to share the work of the home, he answered, "I make all the pies we eat." He didn't have to share much responsibility for the home; "pies" did it for him. Another man grilled fish. Another baked bread. In their pies, their fish, and their bread, such men converted a single act into a substitute for a multitude of chores in the second shift, a token. Evan took care of the dog.

Another way in which Nancy encapsulated her anger was to think about her work in a different way. Feeling unable to cope at home, she had with some difficulty finally arranged a half-time schedule with her boss at work. This eased her load, but it did not resolve the more elusive moral problem: within their marriage, her work and her time "mattered less" than Evan's. What Evan did with his time corresponded to what he wanted her to depend on him for, to appreciate him for; what she did with her time did not.

To deal with this, she devised the idea of dividing all of her own work into "shifts." As she explained: "I've been resentful, yes. I was feeling mistreated, and I became a bitch to live with. Now that I've gone part-time, I figure that when I'm at the office from eight to one, and when I come home and take care of Joey and make dinner at five—all that time from eight to six is my shift. So I don't mind making dinner every night *since it's on my shift.* Before, I had to make dinner on time I considered to be *after* my shift and I resented always having to do it."

Another plank in Nancy's maintenance program was to suppress any comparison between her hours of leisure and Evan's. In this effort she had Evan's cooperation, for they both clung hard to the notion that they enjoyed an equal marriage. What they did was to deny any connection between this equal marriage and equal access to leisure. They agreed it couldn't be meaningfully claimed that Evan had more leisure than Nancy or that his fatigue mattered more, or that he enjoyed more discretion over his time, or that he lived his life more as he preferred. Such comparisons could suggest that they were both treating Evan as if he were *worth more* than Nancy, and for Nancy, from that point on, it would be a quick fall down a slippery slope to the idea that Evan did not love and honor her as much as she honored and loved him.

For Nancy, the leisure gap between Evan and herself had never seemed to her a simple, practical matter of her greater fatigue. Had it been just that, she would have felt tired but not indignant. Had it been only that, working part time for a while would have been a wonderful solution, as many other women have said, "the best of both worlds." What troubled Nancy was the matter of her worth. As she told me one day: "It's not that I mind taking care of Joey. I love doing that. I don't even mind cooking or doing laundry. It's that I feel sometimes that Evan thinks his work, his time, is worth more than mine. He'll wait for me to get the phone. It's like his time is more sacred."

As Nancy explained: "Evan and I look for different signs of love. Evan feels loved when we make love. Sexual expression is very important to him. I feel loved when he makes dinner for me or cleans up. He knows I like that, and he does it sometimes." For Nancy, feeling loved was connected to feeling Evan was being considerate of her needs, and honoring her ideal of sharing. To Evan, "fairness" and respect seemed impersonal moral concepts, abstractions rudely imposed on love. He thought he expressed his respect for Nancy by listening carefully to her opinions on the elderly, on welfare, on all sorts of topics, and by consulting her on major purchases. But who did the dishes had to do with a person's role in the family, not with fairness or love. In my interviews, a surprising number of women spoke of their fathers helping their mothers "out of love" or consideration. As one woman said, "My dad helped around a lot.

He really loved my mom." But in describing their fathers, not one man made this link between help at home and love.

SUPPRESSING THE POLITICS OF COMPARISON

In the past, Nancy had compared her responsibilities at home, her identity, and her life to Evan's, and had compared Evan to other men they knew. Now, to avoid resentment, she seemed to compare herself more to *other working mothers*—how organized, energetic, and successful she was compared to them. By this standard, she was doing great: Joey was blooming, her marriage was fine, her job was all she could expect.

Nancy also compared herself to single women who had moved further ahead in their careers, but who fit another mental category. There were two kinds of women, she thought—married and single. "A single woman could move ahead in her career but a married woman has to do a wife's work and mother's work as well." She did not make this distinction for men.

When Nancy decided to stop comparing Evan to men who helped more around the house, she had to suppress an important issue that she had often discussed with Evan: How *unusually* helpful was Evan? How unusually lucky was she? Did he do more or less than men in general? Than middle-class, educated men? What was the going rate?

Before she made her decision, Nancy had claimed that Bill Beaumont, who lived two doors down the street, did half the housework without being reminded. Evan gave her Bill Beaumont, but said Bill was an exception. Compared to *most men*, Evan said, he did more. This was true if most men meant Evan's old friends. Nancy felt upwardly mobile compared to the wives of those men, and she believed that they looked upon Evan as a model for their own husbands, just as she used to look up to women whose husbands did more than Evan. She also noted how much the dangerous unionizer she had appeared to a male friend of theirs:

> One of our friends is a traditional Irish cop whose wife doesn't work. But the way they wrote that marriage, even when she had the kid and worked full time, she did everything. He couldn't understand our arrangement where my husband would help out and cook part time and do the dishes once in a while and help out with the laundry. We were *banned* from his house for a while because he told Evan, "Every time your wife comes over and talks to my wife, I get in trouble." I was considered a flaming liberal.

When the wife of Dennis Collins, a neighbor on the other side, complained that Dennis didn't take equal responsibility, Dennis in turn would look down the invisible chain of sharing, half-sharing, and nonsharing males to someone low on his wife's list of helpful husbands and say, "At least I do a hell of a lot more than *he* does." In reply, Dennis's wife would name a husband she knew who took fully half the responsibility of caring for child and home. Dennis would answer that this man was either imaginary or independently wealthy, and then cite the example of another male friend who, though a great humorist and fisherman, did far less at home.

I began to imagine the same evening argument extending down the street of this middle-class Irish neighborhood, across the city to other cities, states, regions, wives pointing to husbands who did more, husbands pointing to men who did less. I imagined it extending to Chinese, Mexican, Indian, Iranian families, to unmarried, and in a different but equally important way to lesbian and gay families. Comparisons like these—between Evan and other men, between Nancy and other women—reflect a semiconscious sense of *the going rates for a desirable attitude or behavior in an available member of the same and opposite sex.* If most of the men in their middle-class circle of friends had been given to drinking heavily, beating their wives, and having affairs, Nancy would have considered herself "lucky" to have Evan, because he didn't do those things. But most of the men they knew weren't like that either, so Nancy didn't consider Evan above the going rate in this way. Most of those men only halfheartedly encouraged their wives to advance at work, so Nancy felt lucky to have Evan's enthusiastic encouragement.

This idea of a going rate indicated the market value, so to speak, of a man's behavior or attitudes. If a man was really rare, his wife intuitively felt grateful, or at least both of them felt she ought to. How far the whole culture, and their particular corner of it had gotten through the feminist agenda—criminalizing wife battery, disapproving of a woman's need for her husband's permission to work, and so on—became the cultural foundation of the judgment about how rare and desirable a man was.

The going rate was a tool in the marital struggle, useful in this case mainly on the male side. If Evan could convince Nancy that he did as much or more than most men, she couldn't as seriously expect him to do more. Like most other men who didn't share, Evan felt the male norm was evidence on his side: men "out there" did less. Nancy was lucky he did as much as he did.

Nancy thought men out there did more at home but were embarrassed to say so. Given her view of men out there, "Nancy felt less lucky than seemed right to Evan, given his picture of things. Besides that, Nancy felt that sheer rarity was not the only or best measure. She felt that Evan's share of the work at home should be assessed not by comparing it to the real inequalities in other people's lives but to the ideal of sharing itself.

The closer to the ideal, the more credit. And the harder it was to live up to the ideal, the more pride-swallowing it took, or the more effort shown, the more credit. Since Evan and Nancy didn't see this going rate the same way, since they differed in their ideals, and since Evan hadn't actually shown much effort in changing, Nancy had not been as grateful to Evan as he felt she should have been. Not only had she not been grateful, she'd resented him.

But now, under the new maintenance program to support the necessary myth of equality in her marriage, Nancy set aside the tangles in the give and take of credit. She thought now in a more segregated way. She compared women to women, and men to men, and based her sense of gratitude on that way of thinking. Since the going rate was unfavorable to women, Nancy felt she should feel more grateful for what Evan gave her (because it was so rare in the world) than Evan should feel for what she gave him (which was more common). Nancy did not have to feel grateful because Evan had compromised his own views on manhood; actually he had made few concessions. But she did feel she owed him gratitude for supporting her work so wholeheartedly. That was unusual.

For his part, Evan didn't talk much about feeling grateful to Nancy. He avoided an Evan-Nancy comparison. He erased the distinction between Nancy and himself: his "I" disappeared into "we," leaving no "me" to compare to "you." For example, when I asked him if he felt that he did enough around the house, he laughed, surprised to be asked point-blank and replied mildly: "No, I don't think so. No. I would have to admit that we probably could do more." Then using "we" in an apparently different way, he went on: "But I also have to say that I think we could do more in terms of the household chores than we really do. See, we let a lot more slide than we should."

Nancy made no more comparisons to Bill Beaumont, no more unfavorable comparisons to the going rate. Without these frames of reference, the deal with Evan seemed fair. This did not mean that Nancy ceased to care about equality between the sexes. On the contrary, she cut out magazine articles about how males rose faster in social welfare than females, and she complained about the condescending way male psychiatrists treat female social workers. She pushed her feminism "out" into the world of work, a safe distance away from the upstairs-downstairs arrangement at home.

Nancy now blamed her fatigue on "everything she had to do."

When she occasionally spoke of conflict, it was conflict between her job and Joey, or between Joey and housework. Evan slid out of the equation. As Nancy spoke of him now, he had no part in the conflict.

Since Nancy and Evan no longer conceived of themselves as comparable, Nancy let it pass when Evan spoke of housework in a "male" way, as something he "would do" or "would not do," or something he did when he got around to it. Like most women, when Nancy spoke of housework, she spoke simply of what had to be done. The difference in the way she and Evan talked seemed to emphasize that their viewpoints were naturally different and again helped push the problem out of mind.

Many couples traded off tasks as the need arose; whoever came home first started dinner. In the past, Evan had used flexibility in the second shift to camouflage his retreat from it; he hadn't liked "rigid schedules." He had once explained to me: "We don't really keep count of who does what. Whoever gets home first is likely to start dinner. Whoever has the time deals with Joey or cleans up." He had disparaged a female neighbor who kept strict track of tasks as "uptight" and "compulsive." A couple, he had felt, ought to be "open to the flow." Dinner, he had said, could be anytime. The very notion of a leisure gap disappeared into Evan's celebration of happy, spontaneous anarchy. But now that the struggle was over, Evan didn't talk of dinner at "anytime." Dinner was at six.

Nancy's program to keep up her gracious resignation included another tactic: she would focus on the advantages of losing the struggle. She wasn't *stuck* with the upstairs. Now, as she talked she seemed to preside over it as her dominion. She would do the housework, but the house would feel like hers. The new living-room couch, the kitchen cabinet, she referred to as "mine." She took up supermom-speak and began referring to *my* kitchen, *my* living-room curtains, and, even in Evan's presence, to *my* son. She talked of machines that helped *her,* and of the work-family conflict itself as *hers.* Why shouldn't she? She felt she'd earned that right. The living room reflected Nancy's preference for beige. The upbringing of Joey reflected Nancy's ideas about fostering creativity by giving a child controlled choice. What remained of the house was Evan's domain. As she remarked: "I never touch the garage. Evan sweeps it and straightens it and arranges it and plays with tools and figures out where the equipment goes—in fact, that's one of his hobbies. In the evening, after Joey has settled down, he goes down there and putzes around; he has a TV down there, and he figures out his fishing equipment. The washer and dryer are down there, but that's the only part of the garage that's my domain."

Nancy could see herself as the winner—the one who got her way, the one whose kitchen, living room, house, and child these really were. She could see her arrangement with Evan as *more* than fair—from a certain point of view.

As a couple, Nancy and Evan together explained their division of the second shift in ways that disguised their struggle. Now they rationalized that it was a result of their two *personalities*. For Evan, especially, there was no problem of a leisure gap; there was only the continual, fascinating interaction of two personalities. "I'm lazy," he explained. "I like to do what I want to do in my own time. Nancy isn't as lazy as I am. She's compulsive and very well organized." The comparisons of his work to hers, his fatigue to hers, his leisure time to hers—comparisons that used to hurt— were melted into freestanding personal characteristics, his laziness, her compulsiveness.

Nancy now agreed with Evan's assessment of her, and described herself as "an energetic person" who was amazingly "well organized." When I asked her whether she felt any conflict between work and family life, she demurred: "I work real well overnight. I pulled overnighters all through undergraduate and graduate school, so I'm not too terribly uncomfortable playing with my family all evening, then putting them to bed, making coffee, and staying up all night [to write up reports on her welfare cases] and then working the next day—though I only go into overdrive when I'm down to the wire. I don't feel any conflict between my job and Joey that way at all."

Evan was well organized and energetic on his job. But as Nancy talked of Evan's life at home, he neither had these virtues nor lacked them; they were irrelevant. This double standard of virtue reinforced the idea that men and women cannot be compared, being "naturally" so different.

Evan's orientation to domestic tasks, as both described it now, had been engraved in childhood, and how could one change a whole childhood? As Nancy often reminded me, "I was brought up to do the housework. Evan wasn't." Many other men, who had also done little housework when they were boys, did not talk so fatalistically about "upbringing," because they were doing a lot of it now. But the idea of a fate sealed so very early was oddly useful in Nancy's program of benign resignation. She needed it, because if the die had been cast in the dawn of life, it was inevitable that she should work the extra month a year.

This, then, was the set of mental tricks that helped Nancy reconcile believing one thing and living with another.

HOW MANY HOLTS?

In one key way the Holts were typical of the vast majority of two-job couples: their family life had become the shock absorber for a stalled revolution whose origin lay far outside it—in economic and cultural trends that bear very differently on men and women. Nancy was reading books, newspaper articles, and watching TV programs on the changing role of women. Evan wasn't. Nancy felt benefited by these changes; Evan didn't. In her ideals and in reality, Nancy was more different from her mother than Evan was from his father. Nancy had gone to college; her mother hadn't. Nancy had a professional job; her mother never had. Nancy had the idea that she should be equal with her husband. In her mother's youth, that had seemed like a strange, dreamlike idea. Nancy felt she and Evan should have similar responsibilities. Her mother hadn't imagined that was possible. Evan went to college, his father (and the other boys in his family, though not the girls) had gone too. Work was important to Evan's identity as a man as it had been for his father before him. Indeed, Evan felt the same way about family roles as his father had felt in his day. The new job opportunities and the feminist movement of the 1960s and '70s had transformed Nancy but left Evan pretty much the same. And the friction created by this difference between them moved to the issue of the second shift as metal to a magnet. By the end, Evan did less housework and child care than most men married to working women—but not much less. Evan and Nancy were also typical of nearly 40 percent of the marriages I studied in their clash of gender ideologies and their different ideas about sacrifice. By far the most common form of mismatch was like that between Nancy, an egalitarian, and Evan, a transitional.

But for most couples, the tensions between strategies did not so quickly tense up. Nancy pushed harder than most women to get Evan to share, and she lost more overwhelmingly than the few other women who fought that hard. Evan pursued his strategy of passive resistance with more quiet tenacity than most men, and he allowed himself to become far more marginal to his son's life than most fathers. The myth of the Holts' equal arrangement also seemed more odd than other family myths that encapsulated equally powerful conflicts.

Beyond their upstairs-downstairs myth, the Holts tell us a great deal about the subtle ways a couple can encapsulate the tension caused by a struggle over the second shift without resolving the problem or divorcing. Like Nancy Holt, many women struggle to avoid, suppress, obscure, or mystify a frightening conflict over the second shift. They do not struggle like this because they started off wanting to, or because such struggle is inevitable or because women inevitably lose, but because they are forced to choose between equality and marriage. And they choose marriage. When asked about ideal relations between men and women in general, about what they want for their daughters, about what they'd like in their own marriage, most working mothers wished their men would share the work at home.

But many wish it instead of want it. Other goals—like keeping peace at home—come first. Nancy Holt did some extraordinary behind-the-scenes emotion work to prevent her ideals from clashing with her marriage. In the end, she had confined and miniaturized her ideas of equality successfully enough to do two things she badly wanted to do: feel like a feminist, and live at peace with a man who was not. Her program had worked. Evan won on the reality of the situation, because Nancy did the second shift. Nancy won on the cover story; they would talk about it as if they shared.

Nancy wore the upstairs-downstairs myth as an ideological cloak to protect her from the contradictions in her marriage and from the cultural and economic forces that press upon it. Nancy and Evan Holt were caught on opposite sides of the gender revolution occurring all around them. Through the 1960s, 1970s, and 1980s masses of women entered the public world of work—but went only so far up the occupational ladder. They tried for equal marriages, but got only so far in achieving it. They married men who liked them to work at the office but who wouldn't share the extra month a year at home. When confusion about the identity of the working woman created a cultural vacuum in the 1970s and 1980s, the image of the supermom quietly glided in. She made the "stall" seem normal and happy. But beneath the happy image of the woman with the flying hair are modern marriages like the Holts', reflecting intricate webs of tension, and the huge, hidden emotional cost to women, men, and children of having to

manage inequality. Yet on the surface, all we might see would be
Nancy Holt bounding confidently out the door at 8:30 a.m.,
briefcase in one hand, Joey in the other. All we might hear would
be Nancy's and Evan's talk about their marriage as happy, normal,
even equal—because equality was so important to Nancy.

The Family Myth of the Traditional: Frank and Carmen Delacorte

✳

As he begins his interview with me, Frank Delacorte is speaking from his personal chair, a lounger with armrests and a footrest that extends when he leans back. In this modest living room, it is the only chair with armrests. Some men I interviewed sat in chairs turned closely toward the television, suggesting a desire for solitary retreat and recovery. Frank's chair faced outward toward the room, suggesting membership, its size and prominence suggesting authority. It is the centerpiece of the room, the provider's chair. I am seated on the sofa, tape recorder beside me, interviewing a man who, as it was to turn out, holds more traditional views on men and women than Evan Holt, but who does more work at home with far less struggle.

Frank is a slender man of twenty-nine with long, ropey, muscular arms, neatly groomed dark hair, and thoughtful brown eyes. In a modest but deliberate way, he describes himself and his marriage: "I look at myself as pretty much of a traditionalist. It's the way I am inside. I feel the man should be the head of the house. He should have the final say. I don't think he should have the *only* say; my father was the head but a lot of times my mother got her way. But I feel like this is my role in life, and I don't see any reason to want to change it." He pauses and gives a small but not apologetic shrug of the shoulders. He has chosen his words slowly—as if saying something so fundamental it is normally beyond words.

Frank earns $12,000 a year gluing together the pressboard sides of boxes in a factory. Pressboard isn't the real wood he loves to work with. He dislikes the powerful smell of chemicals in the glue and worries whether they might be hazardous. By trade, he says, he is a cabinetmaker, but when his father-in-law's small cabinetmaking business where he had worked failed, Frank was forced into factory work. Though he was scanning the want ads these days for a better-paying job, and had even interviewed for one on a lunch break, nothing had come through. But his marriage was happy, he thanked God. He has been married for six years to Carmen, now in the bedroom watching a love story on television.

The third of six children in a Nicaraguan blue-collar family, Frank had moved often, as a child, with his mother and siblings to be near his father, a merchant seaman who worked out of various port cities. He remembers his mother and father—he describes them jointly as "they"—as "stern" and "somewhat cold." He doesn't want to complain, but he feels there had not been enough affection to go around. He considers carefully whether he has the right to complain—because his parents had had a hard life, too—but he tentatively concludes that he wished it had not felt as cold growing up in their home. He wanted to establish a warmer family, and with his marriage to Carmen, he already had.

Frank Delacorte held to the views of most other working-class men I talked to. Middle-class men often expected their wives to "help" support the family while they themselves expected to "help" at home. They often thought their wife's work was "good for her," and that "she had a right to it if she wanted it." Middle-class men often saw themselves as equal partners playing different roles. Although their higher salaries gave them greater potential power, it was a point of male honor not to press this advantage, not to talk about it, just to have it. Some would occasionally crack jokes about keeping the wife "barefoot and pregnant," or commanding her to "fetch my pipe and slippers," their jokes consolidating the fact that women's oppression, at their class level, was a matter of history.

In contrast, Frank used the language of "letting my wife work." For him, it was a point of male honor to show loving consideration toward one whom God had given a subordinate role in marriage. Because the Delacortes needed Carmen's income to live, Frank actually held less economic power than most middle-class men. Nonetheless, or perhaps because of this, both Delacortes wanted Frank to be "the man of the house," and to have the "final say" over whether Carmen worked. These days, Frank's traditional ideal was too expensive for his pocketbook.

He did not link his desire to be "the man of the house" with the need to compensate for racial discrimination, a link I sensed in a few other interviews with minority men. Had Frank been Irish or German, rather than Latino, he might have had a better crack at a union job. Most of his coworkers in the nonunion, low-paid jobs at the box factory were Latino. But Frank did not require his relationship with Carmen to make up for racial injustice.

Frank had anticipated a conflict between his pocketbook and his traditionalism even before he married Carmen. With some effort to be candid, he explained:

> I wasn't that ready to get married. Actually, at that time I was feeling inadequate, since I didn't have the kind of job I wanted to have yet. I guess I'm not the most ambitious person in the world [light, nervous laugh]. Yeah, Carmen was much more anxious to get married than I was. I was really very hesitant for a while. I felt I might disappoint her, probably financially. Carmen was working at the time. She told me, "If you add our salaries together, really there's plenty to live on. Between the two of us, we shouldn't have any trouble." And that was true! I finally gave in. She really asked me to marry her, rather than me asking her.

Frank would marry Carmen when she wanted to marry and she would accept her need to work with good grace, even though she wanted to stay home and be a "milk and cookies mom." The compromise did not take place after the marriage, as it did with the Holts, but before, as a premise of it. The compromise was not, as for the Holts, between a husband's ideas about a man's role and his wife's. The Delacortes agreed on that. Their compromise was between a traditional ideal they shared, and a pocketbook too thin to permit them to realize it.

So from the beginning, it was understood that if the fickle fluctuations of the market in wood cabinets made Frank lose his job or take a pay cut, Carmen would not blame these things on Frank; they would face them together. More important, Frank's inability to earn all the money—to be "male" in that way— would not be *his* moral burden alone. Carmen would not, like some wives, assume the right to resent having to work. Carmen had a sister-in-law and a cousin, both working mothers, who did resent having to work and they made life miserable for their husbands because of it. Not Carmen; to her, the deal was: "We'll need my salary but I won't rub it in." Like most middle-class feminists, Nancy Holt had wanted to work and felt she should want to work. It had never occurred to her to reserve a right to resent *having* to work; she insisted on a different right: that she be honored in leisure out of deference for her legitimate career. But Carmen felt strongly that the only real work was at home. Having divergent views about womanhood, Nancy and Carmen also held to different notions of what were the right and wrong feelings to have about work, child-rearing, and the proper emotional gifts between husband and wife.

The two women had opposing feeling rules. Carmen thought she should dislike her work and feel it as unimportant. Nancy thought she should enjoy her work and find it important. Carmen felt she should feel grateful for whatever extra help Frank gave around the house; Nancy considered 50 percent of the second shift as Evan's rightful job and found it hard to feel grateful for less.

Carmen, twenty-nine, a pretty, black-haired, heavy-set day-care worker, spoke to me with a spirited voice and dancing hands. She wanted me to know that she did not work because she *wanted* to. That was a point of pride. As she explained: "The only reason I'm working is that every time I go to the grocery store the bill is twenty dollars more. I'm not working to develop myself. I'm not working to discover my identity. No way!" She wasn't *that* kind of woman, the new kind, the kind who's off seeking her real self in some office on the thirtieth floor of some high-rise. Ironically, although she didn't want to like her work, she rather did. She chuckled with obvious enjoyment as she described each child she cared for. A few professional women illustrated the opposite dilemma. One struggling feminist writer despondently confessed, "I *want* to love my work, but I don't." Ironically, it was a blessing that Carmen had to work; she got to enjoy her work even if she wasn't supposed to.

Carmen referred to her day-care job as a "business I run out of my home," not to be confused with "being a baby-sitter." Like every day-care worker and baby-sitter I interviewed, Carmen was painfully aware of the low esteem in which the women in America who tend children are held: "They don't think you're anything if you're a baby-sitter." For women in more "male" and middle-class occupations, this issue of self-esteem didn't arise.

Frank tried to save his pride by explaining to people that Carmen was "really at home." This was not exactly a myth, but it was slightly misleading. One notch above him in social class, Frank's foreman, Bill, could afford to keep his wife home and to tout the correctness of doing so with a certain cutting conviction. Frank drove to work with Bill every day, and next to rising prices, the topic of women came up most often. Frank coughed and explained with some unease: "We were talking about needing extra money, and I told him about the business that Carmen has, and I said, 'You know, you've got a house. Your wife could have a business like Carmen's. It's not too bad.' His attitude was 'No! No! No! I don't want anybody to say she's taking care of children.' He feels he lives the way most people should live—the husband working, the wife at home." Frank believed that Bill opposed the idea of his wife working not because it was too low for her, but because it was too low for *him*. It would rob him of the one luxury that distinguished a foreman from a worker—the domestic services of a full-time wife. I asked Frank how he felt about his foreman's remark and he said, "I definitely felt he put me down."

While she cared for their own year-old child, Delia, Carmen earned about $5,000 a year providing day care for four two-year-old children of neighboring mothers who worked. She was one of the many women who have become part of an emergent female underclass of day-care workers, baby-sitters, maids, au pairs, and companions for the elderly—who accomplish for little pay and status the work performed in a bygone era by the woman of the house. Ironically, it was this declining role of housewife that Carmen aspired to fill. She, too, was proud to work at home. Frank never denied that she earned money working at home. But saying "Carmen was home" helped him preserve a notion of himself as sole provider, that was, these days, harder and harder to keep up.

Carmen was an ardent traditionalist. (One woman in my study was so eager to be the traditional wife that she tried to get pregnant "by accident" so she could drop out of college and marry, had the word "obey" put back into her marriage ceremony, worked "because my husband told me to," dressed mainly in pink, and named her cat "Pretty Kitty." But even this woman's traditionalism was less ardent than Carmen's.) Carmen very much looked up to Nancy Reagan and very much down on Gloria Steinem. Even within her Latino blue-collar culture of women trapped in low-paid, dead-end jobs, she was far more deeply convinced of her desire to stay home and submit to her husband. Women in her position often wished they worked shorter hours, at better jobs and pay, but most such women did want to work. Only 10 percent of women in this study could be counted as "traditional" in the sense of not wanting to ever work, although I suspect the numbers nationwide are larger. What so appealed to Carmen about being a traditional woman was being subordinate to Frank. As she told me excitedly: "I *don't want* to be equal with Frank. I don't want to be equal in work. I want to be feminine. I want to have frilly things. I don't want to compete with men! Heck! I don't want to do what my husband's doing. Let him do it. Maybe that's it—I want to be taken care of."

Carmen went on: "I want Frank to know more than I do. I don't want my children to be brought up thinking, 'Oh, Mom knows it all, and Dad's just a painting on the wall.' I take pride in Frank knowing more. Maybe that's wrong, but I take pride in it."

A bright but uninspired student in high school, Carmen had gone no further, but had followed a narrow path of clerical jobs from which day care seemed a welcome relief. She considered her lack of higher education a virtue, for she thought it made her inferior to Frank—who "knew more" even though he had also ended his education the same way. Carmen applied the same principle in bed: the more Frank knew, the more dominant he was, the better. She said: "I don't want to be his equal in bed. I want him to dominate me! I don't want to dominate him. I don't want to say, 'Hey, this is the way you make love to me.'"

Carmen thought that dominating women were committing a serious sin—right up there with homicide and child abuse. One dangerous avenue to female dominance, she felt, was a successful career. Pursing her lips in disgust, she told me of an "overly" ambitious sister-in-law who got a Ph.D. in veterinary science—"a Ph.D. in bullshit," she hissed—and as a consequence bossed people around and never married.

Carmen disliked ambitious women partly because she felt they were pushing her kind of women out of style. It was bad enough that rising prices were forcing women out of their homes; what was worse, the daytime TV soap operas she followed avidly while the children napped were featuring selfish career women who stole the allure from domestic-minded women. Today, Carmen's kind of women were being portrayed as overweight, depressed, abandoned—as losers. Women who believed in being a house-wife were the latest endangered species. Career-minded women were taking over everywhere. She saw the women's movement as an upper-class fad. As Carmen put it, "Betty Ford is for women's liberation, right? But has she mopped the floor yet? Beautiful nails, face lift, hair done, and I'm there nails broken, hair a mess, and I'm thinking, sure, lady, tell me all about it. . . . Instead of parading around, Gloria Steinem should sit down and watch a soap opera. They tell you the way it really is. She should take off her rose-colored glasses and really look."

On the basis of these views it might at first seem that, by temperament, Carmen was a dependent person. But the truth was Carmen believed in the wilting violet. It was part of her gender ideology. She actively pursued it. This was probably be-cause she feared that without some cultural constraint, she could end up dominating Frank.

Why did Carmen hold this view of the sexes and not some other? I think it might have worked like this: in young adulthood, she matched her qualifications with the real world—no college, no typing experience, and few interesting, well-paid, respectable jobs out there for women without these. As she explained in exas-peration: "I'm not prepared to go out and sit on my butt and be a secretary. I know how to type, but not fifty words a minute. What am I going to do? *Scrub floors?* I should have prepared for such a career [typing] but I didn't, okay? My mother gave me a good education but I didn't take advantage of it. It's my fault, okay? But I'm not on welfare and I'm not on food stamps. I'm trying to help my husband." Carmen couldn't support herself alone without dropping into poverty; better to support herself through marriage. If her husband needed her to work, fine. That's how it was for families these days.

Several other high school–educated women in this study who were equally trapped in low-paid clerical or sales jobs did want to like their job and share the work at home. Lack of job opportuni-ties didn't totally predict women's views on gender.

A more internal motive seemed to be involved as well. Like Nancy Holt, Carmen wanted to avoid the fate of her mother. If Nancy was in flight from her mother's self-belittling life as a housewife, Carmen Delacorte may have become a traditionalist in response to her mother's tough life as an "independent woman." Her mother was a model of a self-made career woman, and to Carmen a *dangerous* one. Carmen's mother was a spunky, gifted woman who married at eighteen, got pregnant at twenty, and divorced at twenty-two. The marriage had been a disaster. Her father never sent child support and called Carmen for the first time in thirty years the day he died of cancer. Carmen described her mother's life with empathy: "In that society, when a woman becomes divorced or a widow, there is nothing else to do except 'dress the saints' [put clothes on the statues of saints in the church on holidays] for the rest of your life. You don't get remarried. You don't date. When my mother got divorced, she was a young woman, so her father started to run her life."

Alone with her baby, Carmen's mother ventured to the United States working her way up from assistant file clerk to file clerk to junior auditor to senior auditor in an expanding insurance company. The two lived in a tiny apartment with two other divorced Latino women and their children, until Carmen's mother got remarried (when Carmen was sixteen) to a cabinetmaker who drank too much.

Reflecting on how she would have fared in her mother's situation, Carmen visibly recoiled. "*I would never want my mother's life! Never, never!* I don't think I could be like my mom because my mom didn't have anybody to fall back on."

Gloria Steinem would have drawn entirely different lessons from the struggles of a single mother, and in fact did. The trials of Carmen's mother would have seemed textbook examples of why society should finally prevent wife battery, discourage the double standard, and ensure that divorced men continue to support their children. But sizing up her situation, Carmen drew a cautionary lesson: Don't go out on your own. If her mother had only *submitted* more to her husband, hidden her intelligence, checked her initiative, maybe Carmen's father would have stayed. The equation seemed to be this: it's a cold world for women outside of marriage. So a woman has to marry. If she is to succeed in marriage, she can't be the dominant type. To avoid dominance, she should try to feel subordinate, and if she can, she should project an image that is delicate, fragile, and innocent of much knowledge. If Carmen could manage to feel or to seem this way, she reasoned, Frank would always stay. For her, women were by nature as likely to be bright and powerful as men; but it was their duty as women to press their natural personality and I.Q. into the "wilting violet" mold. For her, female subordination was not sexism. It was a *shield* against it.

Once established, certain things followed from Carmen's line of thinking. One had to do with her relationship with Frank, the other with the second shift. Given her perception of what she could do, she wanted to be traditional. That called on her to be demure, soft-spoken, sweet, passive, and quiet. But, in fact, Carmen was loud, colorful, engaging, active, willful, and bright. In her occasional heated discussions with Frank, neighbors in the apartment below could hear Carmen's loud voice rising with rhetorical flourish, falling, and coursing through long explanations of something. Then they heard Frank's voice: low, mild, appeasing, steady. In the supermarket, Frank politely followed the unspoken traffic rules of shopping-cart life, but Carmen bumped carts that blocked her way. She sometimes took the offensive in family quarrels. She had, for example, pushed Frank to "stand up for himself" when his father chided him for giving up a promising job he once had as a bank clerk. But the morning after such occasions, she scolded herself for having the "wrong" personality for the kind of woman she aspired to be.

In her youth, she told me: "I had a boyfriend everybody loved, and we thought we were going to marry. But I was awfully dominating. He left me and I always thought he would come back, but he didn't. Mother always says, '*Don't forget William.*'"

Married life after the first three years was harmonious, but Carmen and Frank had had one telling showdown. One day, Frank was complaining that Carmen had shown poor judgment in making a payment on a new chair (which could wait) before paying the rent (which could not). According to Carmen, "Frank said to me, 'Since I'm making the most money, I can make most of the decisions.' I said, 'What?! Wait a minute! Forget it! Just because you're making more money doesn't mean anything. I'm still working.' I told him, 'Do you really believe that?' And he said with a smile, 'Well, not really. I just thought I'd give it a try.'"

All in all, for Frank, the veneer of Carmen's submission would do. He liked Carmen, plucky as she was. Her spunk was no big deal; he wasn't threatened in the least. Getting her personality in line with her ideology was her dilemma, not his.

USING ONE SIDE OF TRADITIONALISM TO GET AROUND THE OTHER

Carmen wanted to be submissive. She wanted Frank to earn the bread while she tended the home. When I asked her what she would do with a million dollars, she laughed raffishly and began naming all the pieces of furniture she'd buy and describing the grand apartment house she'd buy for her mother. Then, slowing down, she carefully explained how the money would not affect the *separation* of male and female spheres: "With that kind of money you would have teas, coffees, showers, benefits to go to. Then I'd have the kids over for Kool-Aid. I'd just be Mom." If they had a million dollars, and if Frank didn't have to work, would he stay home? I asked. "Absolutely not! The children would not respect him if he stayed home. He'd hate himself and after a while he'd hate me. And if I didn't want to do the housework, I'd pick on him to do it. At least he should get in the car and play golf for two hours, do something outside the house."

But back in the real world a practical problem arose: How could Carmen manage all of the second shift? After her first baby was nine months old, Carmen started caring for other children in her home again. Despite her views on women, her needs were no different from those of other working moms: she desperately needed Frank's help. But this need aroused strongly contradictory feelings. On one hand, she really *needed* help. On the other hand, the house was supposed to be "her turf." She said she didn't care much about Frank's sharing the second shift—his help might be nice but it wasn't worth a big fuss. Besides, it might seem dominating of her to make him help in the kitchen. Indeed, to the extent that Frank was not in the kitchen, Carmen was proud. When Carmen described their division of housework, it was as if she had to *concede* how much Frank helped. She interpreted his involvement in her housework as her failure, and in this respect differed from other women who *boasted* about all their husbands did at home. Carmen described Frank's contribution to shopping, paying the bills, cleaning up, in the manner of a confession: "Okay, Frank and I are equal in the sense that we do some of the housework together." But she immediately began to talk about the dangers of sexual equality. "Equality" made a wild leap to "competition" and another long leap to antagonism and divorce.

How was she to manage the contradiction between the desire to keep Frank out of the kitchen and the need to have him in it? She left her submissive persona intact by continuing to claim that Frank was "really the boss." But she also solved her problem by putting an old female custom to new use: she played helpless. It was a stroke of genius; playing helpless allowed her to remain the submissive wife at the *front* door while also bringing Frank into the kitchen through the *back*.

The only cost of this strategy might be the low opinion others held of her competence, but that wasn't a problem. She never asked Frank for help directly, so when he did help, it wasn't because it was his role, but because Carmen couldn't do it. Frank cooked the rice when he got home from work—not because he liked to do it, not because he was especially good at it, but because he could cook the rice better than Carmen could. Frank paid the bills because Carmen paid the wrong ones first. Frank sewed (when Carmen's mother didn't sew for them) because Carmen couldn't sew. Frank worked the automatic teller for Carmen because she "always forgot" the account's code number. Frank drove them on shopping trips because Carmen couldn't drive. Responding to one calculated incompetence after another, Frank had come to do nearly half of the second shift. Perhaps Carmen drew the line there, or maybe Frank did. Half would not have seemed right.

The myth that Carmen was "helpless" saved Frank's male pride: he could now enter the kitchen as an act of chivalry "to help a lady out." And it saved Carmen's female pride: she could tacitly request that Frank share her feminine terrain without being any less of a woman. The myth of female helplessness wouldn't have worked for all traditional men, and it would have appalled egalitarian men. But it was useful to Carmen and Frank.

A STRATEGY OF INCOMPETENCE

Incompetence was one way to induct traditional men into the second shift. Sickness was another. Carmen had arthritis that "acted up" and prevented her from carrying heavy things. It wasn't clear that she used sickness like she used helplessness. But curiously, other traditional women I talked with seemed to get sick more often than egalitarian women. And when they got sick, it followed a certain pattern. Insisting that every task at home was theirs, they worked heroically until they finally fell ill with exhaustion. They didn't stop; their illness stopped them. Sometimes it was pneumonia, sometimes migraines, a bad back, arthritis. Then their husbands, primed to help out in an emergency, "lent a hand." Upon recovering, the woman returned to her double load, plunged full steam ahead, and eventually became sick again. Getting sick could have something in common with "getting" incompetent: both were ways of receiving indirectly what many egalitarian women received directly—a man's labor in the second shift. The 11 percent of women in this study who reported themselves as traditional all reported being ill more often than their husbands, and more often than other women.

Like many traditional couples, the Delacortes were a curious mixture of old and new. They thought, talked, and felt in traditional ways, but they had to live with the stubborn realities of modern life. They aspired to male rule, but had backed into gender democracy. Frank wanted to be the kind of man whose wife didn't have to work, but in truth he needed her wage. Carmen wanted to take exclusive care of their home but she actually needed Frank's help. Frank believed the kitchen was Carmen's domain, but he worked there anyway. He enjoyed the idea of separate spheres for men and women, but often found himself beside Carmen picking canned goods off the supermarket shelf or working their hand calculator to monitor the relentless contest between their modest wages and steadily rising prices. Carmen wanted to strip her work of any meaning except financial. But the awkward fact was that she liked her work and it gave her a power she readily used, ironically, to "give" Frank his dominance and to "work" her subordination. As long as they needed Carmen's wage, she would have a troubling power that subverted their shared ideal.

By discrediting cultural models of female assertion, by strictly confining her tendency to dominate to the female sphere, by "remembering William," by raising Frank above her—Carmen pursued submission. She squelched her assertion outside the home and magnified feelings of dependence.

Their traditionalism fit neither the outer nor inner realities of their lives. The outer reality was that Frank needed Carmen to earn money and Carmen needed Frank's help with housework and child care. The inner reality was that Frank was not dominant and

Carmen was not submissive. What contained both contradictions was the family myth that "Frank did little around the house."

Both the Delacortes and the Holts jointly shared a belief about how they divided the labor of the home, and in both cases, the belief was a myth. The Holts said that their upstairs-downstairs arrangement was equal. The Delacortes said theirs was unequal. Both stories reflected what the couple wanted to believe, which clashed, in turn, with some important reality and created a tension that their "cover story" hid and managed.

By itself, a gender ideology doesn't tell us how much of the second shift the husband of a working mother does. In general, the traditional men in my study actually did slightly *more* around the house than transitional men who supported the idea of their wives working but felt those wives should also care for the home. Most strongly egalitarian men did share.

What tells us more about how much the husband of a working mother does at home is the interplay between the couple's particular gender ideologies, the economic realities of their lives, and the gender strategies through which they reconcile these. Carmen was a tradition defender whose strategy of playing helpless got an untraditional result—a busy man in the kitchen. On the other hand, after her fierce feminist battle, Nancy ended up with a traditional result. In the Holt family, of course, it was Evan who played helpless.

Unlike Evan, Frank didn't dissociate "fairness" from sharing the second shift—he wasn't trying to be fair in Nancy's sense. He didn't, like some men who had committed themselves to fifty-fifty, try to get out of it by pretending to share. Nor did Frank claim to be in the grips of his career or to suffer more on-the-job stress. Without fanfare, he pitched in.

Nancy's strategy was to push for a change. When that failed, she resorted to female wiles she didn't believe in. Her sexual disinterest and her overabsorption with Joey were also daily reminders to Evan of the emotional costs of his refusal.

Nancy Holt's experience tells how a woman tries to get a failed strategy behind her and feel all right about it. Carmen didn't have that work to do. But both stories suggest ways in which early experience creates the emotional steam behind a certain version of womanhood and manhood. Both stories show ways of maintaining the façade of a gender identity when such things as the resistance of a spouse or the limits of a family budget undercut the essence of it.

As economic pressures force more reluctant, home-centered women into low-paid jobs in the expanding service sector, the Delacortes' way of reconciling tradition with modern life may become more common. But what happened to Frank and Carmen may also happen to others. The last I heard, Frank had a falling out with his foreman and lost his job. As they drew together against this rough luck, they often said to themselves, "Thank God for Carmen's job."

A Notion of Manhood
and Giving Thanks:
Peter and Nina Tanagawa

❋

PETER Tanagawa, a dark-haired man of thirty-three with twinkly brown eyes that express exuberance, leans forward in the leather chair of the small office attached to a technical books store. Speaking in a low voice, he sums up something small but key: "Nina wants me to do more with the kids, to be more concerned with their education and development, be more of a family person. And I am! But not as much as *she* is."

The issue of how much of a "family person" he should be was not new for Peter. Early on in their vibrant courtship, riding bicycles, talking for hours on end, Peter and Nina had explored their ideas about "men" and "women," as couples do. Nina had wanted to anchor her identity at home, to ground only what was psychologically left over at work. In this she stood between Carmen Delacorte (who wanted to stay home and put Frank out in the world) and Nancy Holt (who wanted to balance herself and Evan equally between home and world). When Nina and Peter first met, each was attracted to the way the other felt about the roles of men and women. Peter's career in book sales, they agreed, would take priority over any job Nina would pick up, but she'd want to pick up something. They were right for each other, both transitionals.

But tension developed. Like Nancy Holt, Nina Tanagawa pressed Peter to do more at home, and like Evan, Peter resisted. But because Nina started on more traditional footing, she was to turn to an irresistible job offer as the reason she was venturing further into the world, and as the reason he should do more at home.

As a child growing up in a close-knit Japanese community in Hawaii, Peter had been his mother's favorite and distant from his father, who worked long hours and came home tired and distracted. Now, as a father himself (his two children, Alexandra and Diane, were five and three), he felt more engrossed in their lives—like a mother—and more discontent with his book business than his views of manhood would allow. He seemed to need Nina *between* himself and the children for things to feel right.

Nina, a stunning, slender blue-eyed blonde of thirty-three, is slightly shy in manner. When I interviewed her in the evening at home, she seemed still ready for the office, dressed in a white skirt and jacket—a fairy princess in a business suit. Like her father, Nina is resourceful and practical. Her mother, a lifelong housewife and busy volunteer, had been intermittently restless with her husband's refusal to allow her to work. Nina had long expected to be the center at home. Yet she was now inadvertently drawn by her own success toward a desire to be the linchpin of Telfac's personnel department. Gradually she was shedding the feminine identity she'd had when she was twenty—or was she?

PETER'S STRATEGY: EMOTIONAL SUPPORT INSTEAD OF INVOLVEMENT

Peter believes that Nina should tend the home not because her anatomy is her destiny, not because God intended men to dominate women, nor because Peter earns more money. Peter believes she should tend the home because she is more interested and competent in it and has freely chosen to put her time and energy into it. Nina agrees. Accordingly, she does 70 percent of the child care and about 80 percent of the housework. (They agree on this estimate.) Nina stays home if the children are sick; she retrieves a child's forgotten jacket from a friend's house; she waits for the new sofa to be delivered. Although Peter describes his daughters as "daddy's girls" and he seems to me to do quite a bit around the house, they both agree that he has little responsibility for the daily work of caring for them.

One evening when I was visiting their home, Nina took the children upstairs to bed to say their prayers; Peter whispered to me, pleased and proud, "*Now* they're getting *quality* time." Then, since I had asked both parents to go through the evening as they normally would, he settled down with the newspaper. He saw his parental role as supporting *Nina's*. He mothered Nina; Nina mothered the children.

This did not mean Peter was not an able, interested father. Both agree he is more intuitive about the children's feelings. For example, he is quick to sense just what favor to Diane had made Alexandra feel slighted. He knows when Alexandra is really hurt and when she is faking it. Often he tells Nina, and Nina does something about it. Nina tends the children's physical needs, organizes their social lives, and in a kindly way administers them. An absence of warm communication with her own mother had left Nina slightly anxious about being a good mother herself, so she welcomes Peter's appreciation, and Peter appreciates Nina's mothering.

At one remove from the children, Peter is enormously interested in them. When he talks to me about himself, he weaves in extraneous reminders of his wife and children. Unlike many men, he describes his typical workday morning with a consensual "we"—as in "We get up at six." When he describes a typical day, his work seems an interlude between more emotionally charged periods of time with his family:

> Nina will get up first and take a shower. When the door closes, that's my cue to get up. I go downstairs and make coffee for both of us, and while the water is heating, the paper arrives. I glance at the front page, the sports page,

then read the business section, make the coffee, bring the paper and two cups of coffee upstairs, as she's coming out of the bathroom. She and I both drink coffee. Then Nina brings out Diane, our youngest child. I start to change her clothes, and put her on her little potty seat. Then I towel her off so she's fresh and put on her day clothes. Alexandra is getting up and I dress her in her school uniform—she needs the *attention* when she sees me doing it for Diane, it's not that she needs the assistance. So I do it with *that* understanding.

In contrast, Peter's description of his workday is brief and perfunctory: "I arrive at work at eight-thirty or nine. Then once I get there, it's just another daily routine. I leave around five or five-thirty." Once home, Peter disappears upstairs to change into his jeans (after work, Nina remains in her white business suit). He describes mealtime, bath time, and quality time all in spontaneous, appreciative, and loving detail, recalling just what Nina had packed in Alexandra's lunchbox, exactly which clothes she had laid out for Diane.

In Nina's account of her typical day, the morning is short, a matter of warmly, efficiently dispatched routine. The detail begins when she gets to the first morning meeting, the calls and appointments over an impending crisis at the company. She slows down to talk at length about the challenging issues that would come before an important committee next week, and about a bristling rivalry between two members of her staff. Just as Peter lives less intensely at his office than he had intended, Nina lives more intensely than she had intended at hers.

Far more than most men who did not share, Peter could visualize clearly just what sharing would be like. Recalling the preparations for Alexandra's fifth birthday, he describes a vast array of tasks he has not done:

I've done nothing for Alexandra's birthday party this weekend except wrap a few gifts. Nina's the one who has

had to write out the invitations, order the cake, buy
Alexandra all her presents, figure out where we're going,
figure out the lunch menu for the kids. That has all been
her responsibility, and I think she would like me to
participate more in this. I did the decorations, blew up the
balloons, threw the confetti all over the place. And I made
all twenty-two sandwiches and set up the Betamax. But
Nina still does 70 percent to my 30 percent.

Like Frank Delacorte, Peter probably did more to make the
children have a good time than he wanted to imagine. One
evening when I was having dinner with them, Diane began to
whimper and suddenly threw up some purple chewing gum. The
two parents spontaneously leapt to their feet; Peter rushed to Diane, and Nina rushed for the mop. Peter comforted the child: "It's
okay, Diane. Your tummy's okaaaay." After cleaning up the floor,
Nina took Diane's clothes off to be washed. Nina seemed like the
maid of the house—putting in a load of laundry, changing a
lightbulb, packing the lunches, calling the sitter. Peter was the
nanny, the understander and comforter. To reconcile the conflict
between their views about men and women and the inner reality
of their personalities, they developed a family myth: Nina was
"naturally more interested in and better with children."

NINA'S COLLISION COURSE

In 1973, Nina Tanagawa was one of five women in her entire college class to go on to earn a master's degree in business administra-
tion. In the early 1970s, when just a few companies were beginning
to see the profit in female talent from top business schools, Nina
was hired to work in the personnel department of Telfac, a large
and expanding computer company. The job was enjoyable, challenging, and it paid enough to put Peter through business school.

Nina leapt with astonishing speed through the managerial ranks from one promotion to another, until her salary put her in the top half of 1 percent of women nationally. She was five years younger than the youngest employee at her level in the company, and one of the top three women in the entire company; the other two had no children. By either female or male standards, she was a fabulous success.

After Nina had worked for five years in the company, the Tanagawas began their family. First came Alexandra. Nina took a year off to stay home with her. Looking back, she felt it had been the right thing to do. She sang songs to Alexandra, wallpapered her room in candy stripes, and sewed her tiny jumpers. But Nina also admitted to feeling bored taking care of the baby alone at home; she shouldn't have felt bored, she thought, but she did. She also thought she was becoming boring to Peter. So her reason for going back to work, as she told me, was to "be a better wife." Then, when her boss called to ask if she wanted to come back to work part time, she hired a housekeeper/baby-sitter and, despite her reservations, jumped at the chance.

When there was a fall in the computer market, Nina was put in charge of the company's "unhiring" program in several offices, and her hours increased. In the evenings, after Alexandra was in bed, she would read reports and write memoranda about her "unhired clients." To maintain her managerial image, she arrived half an hour earlier than her staff in the morning and stayed half an hour later at night. When staff members stayed late, she bit her tongue and left first. Under the watchful eyes of conscientious coworkers and subordinates, her work hours steadily increased. As Nina recalled: "I came back to work three days a week, then four days a week. But the job grew too rapidly. I was running—go, go, go! I'd drop into bed at night and realize I'd been working for seventeen hours a day."

After about two years of this, their second child, Diane, was born. This time she stayed home for six months before she once again received a call from her boss and once again went back. But this time there was more to do at home and less of her to go around. As Nina put it: "The house got messier. There was that much more laundry with two kids, more dinner action and noise."

She had hired a housekeeper who said, "No windows, no floors and I leave at five-thirty." So after long sieges of work during the week, Nina became the consummate housewife and mother on Saturdays. On Sunday mornings, when Peter played tennis, Nina washed the children's hair, cut their fingernails, and cleaned house. As she put it wryly, "Peter lets me take over a lot." In one sense, though, it was a relief to take over.

All the top brass of Nina's computer company were workaholics, actually or virtually single. At first she tried to pretend to be as involved as they were. But one day, just as Nina was beginning to feel she couldn't pretend anymore, her boss burst into her office with a broad smile: "Congratulations! You've just been promoted!" Well-wishers crowded into her office to celebrate, and Nina felt pleased and flattered. But as she drove home that night, what would prove a lengthy depression was already taking hold. She recalled hearing a speaker at an office seminar on work and family life declare, "I don't know of a working mother who can balance a career, children, and marriage; one of these has to give." Nina remembered secretly thinking, I'm proving you wrong. Now she wasn't sure.

Peter supported Nina's career, in the way transitional men do. He talked with her about her problems at work, he soothed her brow at night. He worried about her health. He did a bit more here, a bit more there at home. But even these bits seemed to take reminders. As Nina put it: "I say to him, 'Do you want to bathe the kids tonight or do you want to clean up the kitchen?' Because if I don't, he'll go watch TV or read the paper."

Nina hinted that she needed help. But she put it in such a way that her job, not she, was doing the asking. Unlike Nancy, she didn't say a word about "fairness." She stuck to the job offer: she didn't want to say yes but how could she possibly say no?

Peter heard the hints, but took them as signs of "Nina's problem." So in time, Nina let her fatigue speak to him. Great rings appeared around her eyes. She had grown almost alarmingly thin. She even began to move and talk listlessly. Finally, she confided to Peter that she was getting close to a certain emotional edge. Instead of having a nervous breakdown, however, she got pneumonia and took the first ten days of pure rest she had taken since Diane's birth. It was as if her illness had said what she herself could not: "Please help. Be a 'mother' too." Although Peter was concerned about Nina, he considered the problem to be a conflict between *her* career and *her* motherhood.

Nina was changing. But had her opinion of *him* as a man altered? In truth, Peter didn't want to change, but he also didn't quite dare especially now that Nina was earning much more than Peter. Nina felt fortunate to be able to add so much money to the family coffers. As she noted: "My salary would make it possible for Peter to get out of technical books, if he wanted, and go into psychology. Sometimes he talks about wanting to become a therapist. He'd be wonderful at it. I've reminded him he can if he wants. We can afford it." By offering to be the main provider for a while so he could get into work he loved, Nina was offering Peter a gift.

Peter appreciated the spirit of Nina's gift, and the opportunity. Her salary also allowed them a new home, a new car, and a private school for Alexandra—even when he was not quite settled in his career. But Peter felt uneasy about Nina's salary. He certainly didn't feel as grateful to Nina as she would have felt to him, had their salaries been reversed. This was not because Peter thought Nina was competing with him. He put it this way: "Nina is successful, but she isn't ambitious. I'm more ambitious than she is. Nina also isn't competitive, maybe just a little, and I am, just a little." So the problem was not Nina's ambition or competitiveness. It was that Nina's higher earnings *shamed him as a man*. Friends and relatives—

especially older males—would think less of him if they knew his wife earned more, he wanted their good opinion.

So he could not gracefully accept Nina's gift. In fact, he and Nina treated her salary as a miserable secret. They did not tell his parents; if Peter's father found out, Peter said, "he would die." They didn't tell Nina's father because "Nina outearns him." And they didn't tell Peter's high school buddies back home because, Peter said, "I'd never hear the end of it." Over lunch one day, Nina told me in a near whisper: "I was interviewed for an article in *Businessweek,* and I had to call the fellow back and ask him please not to publish my salary. When he interviewed me I was proud to tell him my salary, but then I thought, I don't want that there—because of Peter."

Nina was giving Peter the kind of gift that, under the old rules, a man should give a woman: relief from pressure to provide. Peter wanted to give Nina "the choice of whether to work or not." He wanted her to want to work—sure, why not?—but not to need to work. But Nina did not need that particular gift: given her combination of skill and opportunity, she would always choose to work.

With his notion of manhood under new pressure, Peter made one of those unarticulated "moves" that serve the goal of preserving a man's relation to a man's sphere, and his notion of the right amount of marital power. He summoned the feeling that it was not Nina who gave him the gift of her high salary. It was he, Peter, who was giving the important gift. People out there in the world Peter came from and cared about ridiculed men whose wives outearned them. They shook their heads. They rolled their eyes. In order to live with Nina's salary, he had to absorb an assault on his manhood. As Peter said, looking me in the eye, "Only one in a hundred men could take this." Nina was lucky to be married to such an unusual man. And Nina gave him credit: she thought Peter was unusual too. Her salary *was* hard to take. She was lucky.

Curiously, because Peter and Nina allowed them to, it was their parents, the guys in Peter's office, his buddies at home, society out there—not the two of them privately—who defined the value of the gifts they exchanged. What was it that had ultimately lowered Nina's credit with Peter and reduced her side in their balance of gratitude? One thing was their joint appreciation of the injury he had suffered to his male pride—an appreciation based on their feeling that a man *should* be able to base his pride on traditional grounds. And this pride hinged on the attitude of others. In this way, the outside came inside. She owed him one.

On the surface, Peter adapted to her salary; it was "fine"; he wished her well. But, given this concession to his older view of himself as a man, he wanted her gratitude. After all, it was *she* who had passed on the pressure from her irresistible opportunities at Telfac to him and the family.

Through this invisible "move"—to expect Nina to be grateful to him—Peter unwittingly passed the strain of a larger social change (of which the call for female executives at Telfac in the early 1970s was one sign) back to Nina—through their marital economy of gratitude. Now she owed him gratitude for "being willing to take it." Like a great storage closet crowded with objects that would otherwise clutter the house, her indebtedness made the rest of their relationship more tidy. Peter supported and took pride in Nina's work—but only by storing in this hidden emotional closet the tension between his unchanged idea of himself and Nina's new salary. It was like a bite taken but not swallowed.

Nina's sense that Peter was doing her a favor in being that "one in a hundred" guy also had a bearing on the second shift. She told me:

> I've wondered if my salary bothers him. Because if we're
> having a disagreement over something, he sometimes says
> he thinks I'm acting high and mighty—like "Who do you
> think you are?" I said to him once, "You never used to say
> that." And he told me, "I do think you've gotten much
> more assertive than you used to be." Peter might equate my
> assertiveness with my income. I don't know if the money

has anything to do with it, or if I'm just tired of doing all the housework.

Peter made it clear in conversations with me that Nina's salary was painful. He felt he couldn't be the man Nina would still love thirty years from now if he both earned less than she did and also shared the second shift. In his heart of hearts, Peter didn't really care about his career success. What he did care about was his marriage to Nina, and for things to feel right between them, she could not be that far ahead at work, that disengaged from home. Peter wanted to be involved in family life, but only if Nina were *more* involved. He was doing more at home now than when they first married. He wanted credit for all the changing he had done. He felt perilously close to the line that marked the limits of his ability to change, and which he guarded by his move to win credit for sacrificing honor, credit for being the one to adapt when, as Nancy Holt said, usually women do that.

One sign of this line emerged as a surprise in an interview. I had asked Peter to look at a long list of household chores—laundry, sewing, car repairs, and so on—and tell me who did each one. Expecting a series of perfunctory replies, I was taken aback—as he was himself—when we came to lawn mowing. "Lawn mowing!" he burst out suddenly. "*I* do the mowing!" He jabbed the page with his finger and exclaimed:

We share the weeding, but *I* do the mowing! I do not like the idea of a *woman* doing the mowing. I think a father, if he's got the time to mow the lawn and edge it, should not let his daughter do that, or his wife. I think it's lazy! I don't like it. I don't like parents that ask their children to do things when they either could or should do it themselves. I wouldn't want to see my wife mowing the lawn. The logical extension of that is that I don't want people seeing my daughter do that either! And another thing—I don't think girls should drive cars in high school. I wouldn't let Alexandra or Diane drive a car in high school. *No way!*

In the woman he deeply loved, in the home that mattered most, and in the world of work, a whole gender revolution was under way. But old-fashioned customs still held for Peter Tanagawa's lawn and car.

CAUTIONARY TALES OF DIVORCE

Nina felt "lucky." Peter was "one in a hundred men." But behind her sense of luck lurked a cautionary tale. Just as Carmen Delacorte was chastened by the memory of her mother's struggle as a single mother, as Nancy Holt was haunted by her mother's depression, so Nina was chilled by tales of divorce among contemporary friends. Several female colleagues at work had seen their marriages wrecked on the shoals of the second shift and had been thrown down the social class ladder, where some got stuck, and others struggled back up at the expense, Nina felt, of their children. Recently, two close friends exactly Nina's age, both in full-time jobs, both with children the ages of Alexandra and Diane, were suddenly abandoned by their husbands—or so it seemed to Nina and Peter. One of these women stayed with them a week, bringing her devastating story with her. Nina responded with empathy, horror, and a certain fascination. "My friend is gorgeous. But she said she wasn't feeling good about herself," Nina related, "so she got a face lift. She's younger than me! Her husband went out and got a younger woman, even more gorgeous." Outside the safety of their love nest lay this cool marketplace of romantic partners, the men choosing, the women being chosen for youth, looks, the absence of children. It was frightening.

Just as Nina and Peter were speculating about what had gone haywire in their friend's marriage, Peter's father dropped a bomb closer to home. After forty years of marriage, he announced that he was divorcing Peter's mother and taking up with a blond Caucasian twenty years younger than he. What was going on? Had the marriage been that unhappy all along? In the wake of this shock, Peter and Nina turned to reaffirming conversations about how much fun their courtship had been, how their love had deepened.

But Nina vaguely sensed a vital link between these divorces in the outside world and what she was asking of Peter at home. The cold winds outside made the hearth seem warm. As she reflected in a serious tone:

> These divorces have had an interesting effect on our relationship because, of course, you start examining something that's close to home. I do think women—I should say men as well, but actually I mean women—start nagging about little things like picking up clothes. I realize that little things can build up. Peter's father poured out to me things that go back for *years*. His wife would continually nag him about little things, like not hanging up his suit at night. I harp at Peter about helping the kids. He'll let me ask him before he does it, and I don't like to have to ask him to help. If I'm continually harping, maybe I should make some adjustments.

She could ask him more nicely, and less often. They could get more outside help. She could cut back her work hours, do more of the second shift. The "as if" world of divorcees that Peter and Nina would enter if they did divorce also subliminally lowered Nina's credits at home. She was beautiful, well-off, and unusually blessed in chances to remarry. But it was apparently still more scary for a woman like her to be "out there" than it was for a man like him. Life was harder, pickings were slimmer. Divorce was a cautionary tale for them both, but more for her.

So warned, Nina made up for outearning Peter and injuring his male pride by working the extra month a year herself. Peter participated in home life in the spirit of one who leans curiously over a neighbor's fence but avoids getting too involved in the neighbor's affairs. He entered "Nina's sphere," but from the safe vantage point of the active witness, the helpful adviser.

ALEXANDRA'S FRIENDS

Difficulties arose with their dark-haired Alexandra, an observant, somber child who seemed older than her five years. From the first, these difficulties were defined as a "Nina-Alexandra" problem. Peter had routed his own feelings for Alexandra through Nina. Alexandra glumly explained to me one day, "I'm driven to school by Annie's mom, Sarah's mom, Jill's mom. My mom doesn't drive." Alexandra distinguished between school friends (friends she played with at school) and home friends (friends invited home). She had school friends but no home friends. She explained that in order to invite friends home, you needed *a mother* at home. By all three— Nina, Peter, and Alexandra—it was considered a truth that a girl can't make home friends without a mother at home.

If Peter had an urge to plunge more fully into the children's routines, he controlled it. If he had a different urge, to leave it to Nina, he acted on it. He helped Alexandra unreverse her printed *B*'s and *D*'s. He read Dr. Seuss books to her, and buttoned her dress in the mornings. But the rest of quality time, he said with anxious reverence, was up to Nina. In this way he again shaped his inclinations so as to separate himself from the ultimate responsibility for the second shift but to identify lovingly with each family episode through the medium of his wife.

Sensing her father's gaze toward her mother, Alexandra turned to Nina. When Alexandra began to compare her lot to that of school friends with mothers who stayed home, it was to her mother that she addressed a silent protest. It was Nina who felt guilty.

If Mommy wasn't going to be home, it seemed, Alexandra wasn't going to "be home" either—not in conversation, not in weekend play. One day, Alexandra came home with a note in her lunchbox addressed to Nina from Alexandra's teacher. As Nina recalled: "The teacher said that even though this was Alexandra's second year at school, she still had no friends."

On the following Saturday, a week before Valentine's Day, something worse happened. Nina had taken Alexandra to a stationery store to buy valentine cards for her classmates. Alexandra picked the prettiest card for herself because, as she explained in a low voice, "I don't think anyone at school is going to give me one."

Sometimes a way of life collapses because of a small stunning episode. So it was with the valentine card. That night, Nina told Peter, "We have a crisis." The incident had been tiny, but they agreed it wasn't minor. "Handle it the best way you can, honey," he said, "I'm a hundred percent behind you."

THE COMPANY LOYALTY TEST

A week later, Nina asked her boss if she could take a cut in pay and work only three days a week, and he said she could. She broke the good news to Alexandra at dinnertime, hoping for a delighted response. For three days, Alexandra said nothing about it. Then, one evening, she asked nonchalantly if she might invite a girlfriend over the following Friday. As Peter drove Nina to work the next day, he said to her in a warm, excited tone, "Doesn't that make it worth it, honey?"

By telling Nina that she could do "whatever she needed to do" but refusing to become more involved with Alexandra himself, Peter had effectively robbed Nina of the choice he had so lovingly offered, to work full time or not, as she saw fit. Ironically, he worked even harder at extending the market for technical books, work that bored him, while Nina curtailed the work she loved. Neither one saw anything strange about this.

Until this point, Nina had been the showcase woman in top management at a company that prided itself on personnel policies that enabled mothers to work—flex time, part-time work, job sharing. Now Nina had a chance to show the world that workers can be good mothers and part-timers can have real careers. Her immediate boss assured her, "Don't worry, we support you."

But trouble began almost immediately. Nina had handled four departments; she gave up three. Word had it that management was saying, "What Nina does can't be that important if she just works three days a week." Her boss became more "realistic." "I fought for you with the higher-ups, I've been holding them off," he told her. "Now there's only one thing I want from you—to work full time." They had trained and groomed her; now they wanted their money's worth.

Fellow employees gossiped about how "serious" she was. The longer your hours, they reasoned, the more serious and committed you were. Men whose lives ran on traditional tracks had a far better crack at passing this seriousness test than a woman like Nina, who already felt lucky to live with a man who had "taken a lot." Despite its formal progressive policies, the company latently rewarded traditional marriages and punished other kinds. Nina summed up her predicament this way:

> Working three days a week is barely holding them off. I thought that maybe with the four-day weekend, I could at least meet my carpool obligations. And I'd have more time with Alexandra. If I go back to full time pretty soon, I'll be okay. But if I keep this up much longer, I won't be. I may already be out. My boss says, "You're walking alone right now. You're not committed here." Which isn't true. I *am* committed to the company—on a part-time basis.

More and more, Nina was punished for being an uncommitted worker. First she was moved from her large office, facing the San Francisco Bay, to a tiny, windowless office. Then she was told to report to a peer instead of a higher-ranking officer "until she came back full time." Her participation in a company bonus program, all along assured her, was terminated. One older man—whose own marriage to a career woman had come to a stormy end and who had quietly resented Nina's success for years—finally confessed to her, "When you went part time, I realized you weren't serious."

Some of her colleagues in upper management were happily re-married to women who, in second marriages themselves, were more cautiously dedicating themselves to the family. Others were married to wives who worked on timeless graduate degrees, or did volunteer work that offered them a private fantasy of a future public life but did not interfere with their husbands' career. Some of these wives stayed home and seemed to have an easier life. A few men in upper management had career wives, but even they didn't seem to face a dilemma like this one with Alexandra.

Nina was becoming keenly aware of how her male coworkers were, like Peter, protected from the crisis she faced. Were they sacrificing anything to make sure their children got all they needed? She noticed that male coworkers were happy to pin a "mother identity" on her; passing her in the halls, they often said, "Hi, Nina, how are the kids?" She used to give a happy reply. Now she noticed they seldom greeted *men* in this way.

One day when I visited Nina at work, I found her gazing at family photos on her desk. She told me that for the first time she felt like a stranger in her own company. She was taking a hard look at her job: "In my job I lay people off. I have to. We've been going through layoffs. I counsel people and help them solve prob-lems. It hasn't hit me until this year: they're *good* people. They're not poor performers. They're people I can really relate to, people who've worked hard. It wasn't their fault. Their division went under."

As I looked at Nina now, I could see how her delicate, almost Cinderella-like look of innocence, combined with her sharp intel-ligence and high emotional control, could have convinced her boss that she was just the person to give employees bad news kindly. Her helpful manner and mindfulness of corporate purpose had probably saved the company millions in lawsuits. How could a laid-off worker sue after dealing with someone so kind and helpful? I could imagine Nina as the velvet glove on the hard hand of the corporate profit motive. Now, in her spirit of detachment, she saw this too.

She held the company off while she looked for part-time jobs elsewhere. Before long, another computer company offered her a vice presidency, full time. Hearing of this offer, Nina's company suddenly offered her a vice presidency too, with a higher salary and unbelievably high bonuses, again full time. She agonized about Alexandra. She talked and talked with Peter.

Then she accepted the job with her company. She told her boss she would not be able to work late on weekdays or on weekends, but she would work five days a week. As with her last success, she had a sinking feeling. But she told herself that this was a decision "for now"; she could quit if Alexandra's problem got worse.

And it did. Not long after she accepted the new job, she opened Alexandra's lunchbox and found another note from her teacher: "Dear Mrs. Tanagawa, I wanted you to know that Alexandra has made more friends at school. But I have to say that other things still concern me. Recently I assigned the children a story to write and Alexandra wrote a strange story about killing her sister and hating her mother." Nina talked to Alexandra's teacher, and within two weeks, engaged a family therapist. When I last saw them, Peter was still being supportive of Nina in "her" crisis.

Nina's circle of relatives and friends offered no solution. Her "progressive" workplace offered no relief. She had started out a transitional, had pushed softly toward Nancy Holt's position, and like Nancy, met resistance. The Holts' family myth was that they shared the second shift. The Tanagawas' myth disguised the fact that Peter *had* a gender strategy. His move was to push her into playing the supermom. He partly did this to preserve the marriage by shoring up the traditional male role on which he felt it depended. His solution was the problem. Currently, in about 20 percent of the nation's two-job couples (though slightly fewer in my study), women earn more than their husbands. Though the tune may differ a little each time, the beat is usually the same and the problem hardly resolved. For Nina and Peter's marriage is the stalled revolution in microcosm, and like it, their story is unfinished.

Having It All and Giving It Up:
Ann and Robert Myerson

✳

AROUND a walnut table in a small conference room of a rapidly growing electronics firm, a group of working mothers are gathered for a bag-lunch meeting. They are the "moms' group" of a larger organization of women managers from the largest computer companies in Silicon Valley. Among themselves it is safe, it seems, to talk about the antifamily atmosphere of their workplaces, about the pull away from work at home, and about raising a small child. The subject of quitting first arises jokingly. "I might as well quit," volunteers one mother of two in a jovial tone, "I'd probably turn into a mush brain and gain twenty pounds." "What would we do staying home, if we didn't have kids? Eat bonbons in the morning, work them off at the gym in the afternoon?" There is a round of easy laughter; if it weren't for children, no one would want to stay home. But it is Ann Myerson, a thoughtful, tall, slender, red-haired thirty-four-year-old, and a highly paid vice president of a large firm, who first talks of leaving her job in a serious way:

> I'm on the verge of quitting. Right now my twelve-month-old daughter is very clingy as a result of an ear infection. She was colicky to begin with and now if I don't hold her, she screams. I'm supposed to go on a business trip tomorrow, and I have a strong urge to say, "I'm not going." I told my husband, but I *can't* tell my boss my child's sick. The worst

thing I could possibly do is to acknowledge that my children have an impact on my life. Isn't it ironic; I'm on the verge of quitting the company but I can't even tell my boss I don't want to go on this trip because my child's sick.

There is a round of sympathetic nods and no sign of surprise. "It's alright to take time off to baby a client, just so long as it's not your *own* child," says a divorced mother of two. Another mother tells about the time her boss invited her and her husband for dinner: "I asked if I could bring my daughter, explaining she was quiet and would probably sleep. He said no. He has a teenage daughter himself; he should know what it's like to have a child. But I think his former wife brought her up." Heads shook as if to say, "Boy, what a world." After a pause, one woman observed, "I think they hand-pick management for their antifamily attitudes."

When I visited Ann at home, I met the Myersons' oldest daughter, three-year-old Elizabeth, an outgoing child dressed in a ruffly skirt, with long red curls and a bad cold. She quickly recruited me to a game of cooking chicken paprika. The Myersons' second child, Nora, a twelve-month-old, was wide-eyed and fuzzy-haired, toddling, falling, and squealing with delight at her new walking legs. The phone rang: it was a woman who worked for Ann at the office. When Ann hung up she commented, "That woman calls almost every other day, around dinnertime, or on Sundays, about something to do with work. Or else she catches me at work at five-thirty just when I'm packing up to leave. She'll say: 'Oh, I forgot you have to take care of your kids.' She's thirty. She's single, no kids. I've asked her to stop calling me at home but she won't. Maybe she *can't*. It's annoying but it's also sad." Looking at her two young children, Ann said with feeling, "I wouldn't trade my problems for hers."

At the same time, caring for two small children and working full time has become an unbearable strain. When I visited Ann at home one evening, Robert was away on a trip, as he usually was two or three days a week. Ann had raced in the door at 5:58, "because my baby-sitter turns into a witch at six." Ann explained, "Sometimes I bargain with her, 'I'll ask for sick leave on Thursday if you let me come home half an hour late this week.' But she works an eleven-hour day as it is, I've had a series of disastrous baby-sitters, and I need to hold on to her."

As Ann prepared dinner, she patiently addressed a series of slightly anxious requests from Elizabeth: "I need Kleenex. I want to take my leotards off. I've pooped in my pants." Since the last baby-sitter left, Elizabeth has begun acting like a baby again, soiling herself and waking at night. Ann said, "Last night I counted eight times. And the baby wakes up twice a night too." Utterly exhausted at the end of her day, Ann only answered Elizabeth's requests without initiating much play or talk. The more Elizabeth sensed this, the more she thought of something to ask for: "I need a drink. This isn't the right book."

Ann was a gentle, loving mother and right now she was doing her best. But for the moment, she was only giving Elizabeth a promissory note of better things to come later. Their request-answer conversation reminded me of other end-of-the-day, emotionally thinned-out times when a tired mother hurried her eager children through their bath—"Quick. Quick. Let's see who's the first out!" Such moments reveal the emotional cost of fitting family life into a second shift in an era of social transition. Ann was looking for a way to avoid this cost.

Later, when the baby was asleep and Elizabeth was getting to stay up late in her bed, listening to a story on her tape recorder, Ann reflected: "I don't know what I did wrong, but I don't like what's going on at home. My husband is terrific. He's generous. He's cooperative. I've had all the help money can buy. I've had a fifteen-minute commute and it *still* hasn't worked out. I feel like a failure. How do single mothers cope when someone with my advantages can't?"

Over the past three years, Ann had tried nearly all the strategies working mothers use. She worked a 7:45 to 6:00 workday and then kept Elizabeth up until 8:30 to spend time with her (a supermom strategy). She'd turned over a great deal of care to the baby-sitter, reducing her notion of how much time her children needed with her or her husband (redefining "needs" at home). She'd cut back her mental commitment to work (curtailing work). She cut back time with old friends, seeing them only in the friendly chaos of children's company (redefining personal needs). Even so, life couldn't go on like this.

Yet it wasn't easy to quit; her career had long been basic to her identity. A brilliant and hard-driving student, Ann had worked since she was fourteen, developed an ulcer by eighteen, and worked her way through college and graduate school by twenty-six. Work had been a refuge from a lonely social life and a source of great pride. So when she had taken maternity leave to have her first child, she felt suddenly uncomfortable at home. She mused, "Even though I had a newborn, I was still ashamed not to be working. Carpenters were remodeling the house. I had boxes of my mail delivered to my house because I didn't want the construction workers to think I was just a housewife."

By the time I visited her a month later, Ann had quit her job without betraying to her employer that she needed time with her children. She explained: "I would lose every shred of credibility with my male colleagues if I told them. In their world, needing time with children doesn't count as a real reason for any decision about your job. So I told them my husband got a more lucrative offer in Boston. They understood that. They said, 'Oh, Boston. That sounds good.'"

ROBERT: "FIFTY-FIFTY AT HOME" AND TIME FOR READING AND MODEL TRAINS

At our first meeting at the moms' group, Ann told the other women: "Robert easily does half the work at home, with one exception—

I plan. I like the control. But he keeps doing errands as long as I hand them to him. He's very unusual."

Yet when I met Robert he described their arrangement differently and, I think, more accurately: "We've achieved a balance— three to two in Ann's favor, just because I work away so much of the time. But when I'm home, I do more than half the cooking."

Even this description slightly misrepresented the extent to which Ann carried the second shift. Robert was a handsome man of medium height who walked briskly and talked with gusto. When I met him (I was on the floor by the playhouse making "chicken paprika" again with Elizabeth), he thrust his hands in the pockets of his green trousers, rolled back on his heels with a proprietary air, and said, "How about some chocolate sauce on that chicken?" After the morning errands, and a moment of rest, he explained to me:

> If you subtract my travel, I have slightly more leisure than Ann has, partly because I sleep less and partly because she does more at home. I'm on the road two or three days a week. When I'm home, I get up at four to work on my model trains for an hour. Then I exercise for an hour. I eat breakfast at six. At six-thirty, Nora wakes up, then Elizabeth. By seven-thirty our Swiss baby-sitter has arrived and we're out the door. In the evening I try to come home with Ann at six-thirty, although sometimes I come home later. Nora goes to bed an hour later and Elizabeth at eight-thirty. Sometimes I wash the dishes, or do bills and go to bed between ten-thirty and eleven. Other times, I'm so tired I go to bed earlier.

Robert spent longer hours at work than Ann, and his work mattered more to them both. Ann did more at home. Each contributed to the overall well-being of the family, but in different ways. Robert found more time for model trains and exercise than Ann and read more. "Sometimes," Ann said, "Robert gets into a good book, takes it into the bathroom, and emerges forty-five minutes later, unable to put it down." Ann had a list of books she had no time to read. But she did not in the least begrudge Robert his good book—at least not on her good days.

Ann thought that one reason she took primary responsibility in the home was because she naturally noticed things:

Even before children, I had a sense that our house should be orderly, meals should be prepared, our life should be less frantic. We hadn't bought any furniture. Robert would be happy to sit on pillows in the living room or to have wonderful furniture I would buy, either way. He just won't bother with it. It is the same with meals; he'd be happy to eat tuna every night. I'm the one who wants real meals.

Though Ann and Robert had lived in this two-story ivy-covered house for two years, it looked like they'd moved in last week. Few pictures hung on the walls. The living room was bare of lamps, chairs, plants. They'd bought no furniture—the couch and two chairs were borrowed. "It bothers me but it doesn't bother Robert," Ann explained. Yet Ann was so preoccupied with the children and her job, she'd ordered such things as curtains but hadn't kept after the person from whom she ordered them. The house told a story of Robert's friendly detachment and Ann's continual overload. Having moved a great deal as a child, Ann wanted a "homey" house that she could live in a long time. She even referred to this nearly empty house as their "retirement home." She guarded her sense of a real home, real meals, almost the way an ethnic group in danger of assimilating to the dominant culture protects a language or cuisine in danger of disappearing. A mobile, urban life and demanding career system was fast beating that old-fashioned female culture into retreat. In the meantime, the Myersons intended to move into their house—to claim it, to hang a hat, to make a home—when Ann got time.

Their arrangement was a common and honorable one, but it didn't involve sharing the second shift. I began to wonder why Ann so genuinely felt she and her husband did share this shift. The picture of their domestic life didn't seem unusual to me— only the fact that Ann *thought* Robert shared.

Ann's belief that Robert shared was a minor and commonly shared myth, not on the order of Nancy and Evan Holt's myth of the equitable "upstairs-downstairs" arrangement, but a myth all the same. Ann believed her husband shared because she wanted to be part of the "vanguard" of couples liberated from tradition. But she also felt it was "natural" that, as a woman, she manage the house, and suffer a greater conflict between work and family than her husband did.

Despite the fact that Robert had the time Ann herself lacked for model trains and reading, Ann genuinely *felt* that Robert shared the second shift for another reason: her deep gratitude for the many *other* ways Robert was more "advanced" than other men out there.

For one thing, when Robert was home and not tired, he participated wholeheartedly. One Saturday, I went along with the Myerson family as they shopped for a baby jogger, a bureau, and jogging shoes for Robert. I watched as they danced in their bare living room to "Rock Me Amadeus," made espresso in the kitchen, played in the park, and had dinner with close friends who had young children. Throughout this round of activity, Robert chatted exuberantly to each child. As he drove their Jeep from errand to errand, he reached back a hand to pat the baby each time the car stopped at a red light. Throughout the day he hugged them, petted them, and engaged them in a warm, energetic way. When Ann said Robert did 50 percent, one thing she meant was that when he was there, he was fully there.

Of the two parents, Robert was also more indulgent, perhaps because he was away so much. When he was waiting in line to pay for his shoes, Elizabeth dashed excitedly around a rack of skirts. At first he was amused, then for a while slightly anxious as others in the checkout line began to notice a little girl ducking in and out of the hanging clothes. Only when customers began to openly stare did he run after her. When they returned, he confessed, "She wouldn't do that with her mother."

Parenthetically, Robert also exhibited a slightly different style of parenting. When they were buying a bureau, he joked to Nora, "I'm going to shut you in this drawer and leave you there." When Elizabeth started to climb a ladder to get to a tent set atop a bunk bed (they shopped in stores with children's play areas, so that they could combine errands with fun), Robert unzipped the tent and joked, "We'll lock you in!" Ann was the one who reminded Elizabeth to take her shoes off, smiled at her in the tent, price-checked the bureaus, and decided which to buy. Later, when they visited their friends, Robert went exploring in the backyard with Elizabeth, while it was Ann who noticed that a neighbor's child—who had wandered into their friend's home to join the children's play—had chicken pox.

Another reason Ann probably felt Robert shared the second shift was that he was more progressive than such men as Evan Holt or Peter Tanagawa about women's entrance into the upper reaches of the workplace and took pride in not being a "typical male." When his wife earned more than he, he prided himself on that fact—and was pleased he did. As he said with a twinkle:

When my wife started to earn more than I did, I thought I'd struck gold. One time, when we'd first moved here, I had to wait for our bedroom furniture to arrive. When I told my office manager I had to stay home to wait for it, he said, "Why can't your *wife* wait?" I told him, "Look at it this way. In terms of foregone income per hour, *I* should wait for the furniture." My boss didn't understand my attitude.

Robert was very proud of his wife's career. "Now that I've quit my job," Ann confided in our third interview, "I'm worried Robert won't like it. He doesn't want me to be a typical wife. I'm convinced that when we get to Boston, he's going to introduce me by saying, 'This is my wife. She's not working *now* but she *used* to be vice president of a large electronics company, and before that . . .'"

Just as Robert didn't want Ann to be a "typical wife," so he didn't want Elizabeth to be a typical girl. When Elizabeth occasionally wandered down to the basement, where he was working on his model train, he gave her an engine to play with. When Elizabeth started playing with dolls and talking about Snow White, he bought her an Erector set. On the Saturday I joined them in doing errands, they all browsed through a bookstore. Elizabeth brought him *Madeline and the Gypsies*. Robert thumbed through impatiently, then held out a book on trains, saying—in a perfunctory way, as if the battle were lost—"Why don't you look at books on trains like Dada likes?"

Robert was unusual in his desire to share the traditional world of men with women, to offer women the male "advantages." But he was less enthusiastic about wanting to preserve the traditional world of women or share it. He preferred to pay a maid and a baby-sitter to do all that. The most important reason Ann felt Robert shared was that she felt he was honestly *willing* to share the remaining wedge of domestic work—if she wanted him to.

Robert adored Ann and he wanted to please her, and being willing to share, should she need him to, is one way he pleased her. Robert wasn't an Evan Holt. He wasn't a Peter Tanagawa. It was really okay with him to share. Whether she chose to share or not, Ann enjoyed a certain "adoration shield" that protected her from many disadvantages women suffer. As a result of this, what they did share was power.

But Ann did not want Robert to share the second shift. She wanted to think of him as doing half the work at home. She wanted to know he would share if she needed him to. But, even if he didn't have to travel so much, Ann didn't actually want Robert to do half.

ANN'S FLIP-FLOP SYNDROME

On this question of sharing the work at home, Ann listened to two contradictory inner voices. In her "better moments," as she saw them, she wanted to relieve Robert of the work at home, to do it herself. When this voice spoke loudest, Ann spoke appreciatively about the heavy demands of his career and his need to relax: "Robert's a real tinkerer. He becomes immersed in his trains, and builds radios too. It's a wonderful hobby. When he's absolutely exhausted from traveling, he'll still get up at four in the morning to do his exercise and spend an hour working on his model trains."

In her "worse moments," as she saw them, Ann wanted Robert to share at home. When she wanted this, she would say such things as this: "Over time, Robert has become sloppier about helping at home." Describing another "worse moment" she said: "Sometimes I tell him that he makes self-centered choices about what to do with his time. He spends hours on his trains, hours he could spend helping me with the children." But eventually she saw her perceptions of Robert's "sloppiness" or "selfishness" as lapses from a more "true," sacrificial point of view.

Much to her own annoyance, Ann vacillated between her better moments and worse. As she described:

> I flip-flop all the time. One day I want to be superloving. I honestly feel Robert can contribute more than I can. He's better educated. He's just plain smarter. He's genuinely gifted, and when he's able to apply himself, he can really accomplish something, can make a name for himself. I care about him having time to think. One of the contributions I can make is allowing him to make a valuable contribution before I'm burned out. I tell him, "I want to take the pressure off of you. You don't have to worry anymore about coming home at six, or taking care of the children in the

evenings. You need more time to work on your trains." I go through this long spiel. I'm going to play this incredible role.

Then when I come home at six-thirty, take care of the kids, cook dinner, go to bed, get woken up by the baby, I get totally exhausted. I can't stand it anymore. Then I dump on him for not keeping up his 50 percent and causing me to feel so harassed. He knows now this is just a phase. During this phase, he tries very hard to come home at six, help with dinner, the bath, and make an equal number of household-related calls. Then I feel guilty.

But sometimes my wanting-to-protect-him phase only lasts a day. Then I flip back. I say, "I'm well paid. I have authority. Just because I don't take my work as seriously as you do doesn't mean other people don't take it seriously. So I only have to do 50 percent at home."

When Ann was in the "flip" stage, she took the vantage point of Carmen Delacorte. When she was in the "flop" stage, she took the vantage point of Nancy Holt. But to Ann, Carmen's view ultimately felt more admirable, and even if she couldn't hold it for long, she aspired to. She felt exasperated with herself for not being able to stick to it. She also surprised herself: "I never would have thought I'd want to take a backseat to Robert's career. I never used to have this view of marriage."

A BRILLIANT HUSBAND
AND A JOB THAT FEELS UNREAL

Why did Ann feel like Carmen Delacorte, that her husband's job—and really his life—came first, when Frank and Robert, though very loving, did not talk in the same way about their wives? Carmen's belief in male superiority is more easily understood as cultural programming: Given her strict Catholic upbringing, her lack of training and career opportunity, it was un-surprising that she held these beliefs. But Ann had all along been groomed to be the highly successful career woman she had be-come, and her belief in male superiority didn't so neatly fit her cir-cumstances.

When I put this question to her, Ann gave two answers. First, Robert was more intelligent, she said. He had been at the top of his college class. Now perhaps Robert was, in fact, more intelli-gent than Ann. It is still true today that most women marry men who are more educated and accomplished than themselves, while men marry women who are less so. Women marry "up" and men marry "down," a pattern that the sociologist Jessie Bernard calls "the marriage gradient." As a result of this pattern, there are two pools of unmarried people—highly educated and accomplished women and uneducated, low-status men. Perhaps the same pat-tern holds for intellectual development: If Robert is a genius, given this "marriage gradient," he didn't marry another genius. In the realm of intelligence, Robert may have been looking down and Ann looking up.

On the other hand, maybe Ann was just as smart as Robert. After all, she had earned straight A's through college even while working thirty hours a week. Who knows what she might have done with thirty hours more study each week? Maybe Ann can't bring herself to honor her own potential.

The second reason Ann gave for why Robert's time mattered more was that her work felt unreal to her.

I fool people into thinking I take my work seriously. It's not that I think males around me are more capable, or that their jobs are more meaningful. I just think it's amazing that they take their work seriously. The work is not really helping anyone. It's just a pile of paper with numbers.

I envy people who are committed to what they're doing. It's almost like envying people with religion; they seem happier. It's strange; I *expect men* to go around taking their work very seriously, but when I meet a woman who takes a business career seriously, I can't relate to her.

So having children almost provides me with a convenient out. I have to take *something* seriously. And I do take seriously what we're doing this Saturday [shopping for the bureau]. I don't question that. I might be afraid that my sense of unreality will creep into my life at home.

Ann's sense that only home was real even caused her to want more children, to make them into her achievement. She explained: "If I'm going to be the parent at home, well, I want to have a real challenge. If I have half a dozen children, I can show that I can really do it well. Anybody can raise two."

Why, I wondered, did her career feel unreal? As a child, Ann had moved a great deal. Living in a different town each year of high school, she found it hard to make friends; and from age fourteen on, work became her refuge from friendlessness. Her involvement in work became a sign of personal failure. Perhaps the unreality of her work also had to do with her fear that she was not "feminine enough." All through her twenties and early thirties, Ann hadn't wanted children. When she confessed this to her father, a Catholic father of six, he had stormed out of the room, throwing at her the remark, "One would question your femininity." "I took that seriously. I said to myself, 'Maybe that's right.'" Then, too, maybe her work represented outdoing her father, a man with whom she strongly identified and who had done less well in the same profession. If work meant being unable to make friends, if it meant outdoing her father and being unfeminine, then she might have felt afraid of seeing her work as real.

Whatever the cause, Ann's sense that Robert's mind and work were more meaningful than hers led her to do the second shift while she worked full time, and eventually led her to quit. One episode seemed to say this very thing. During a visit to the Myersons', I found Elizabeth and her mother sitting in Elizabeth's walk-in clothes closet playing grocery store. Ann was passing a series of empty spice jars across the "counter" and Elizabeth was telling the "grocery clerk" what was in each one—marinated artichoke hearts, condiments, Hungarian paprika, raspberry conserves. Since her mother was already the grocery clerk, and since I was sitting on the floor apparently unemployed, Elizabeth made me into the nanny. "I hope you can carry my baby," she said winsomely. Maybe because she saw herself in her daughter, Ann interjected with feeling, "But you're the mother. *You* carry her."

All in all, Ann was less interested in sharing the work at home than Nancy Holt, Nina Tanagawa, and most of the women in this study. Most women wished their husbands did share the work at home, but didn't put that wish first, or didn't dare push. Due to a complex set of motives, Ann Myerson's man wasn't getting out of the second shift. She wasn't letting him in.

At the end of our last visit, I asked Ann if she had any advice for young women about to enter two-job marriages. She mused for a while, then concluded that since she had given up having it all, she really had none. She moved in a perfunctory way over the agenda of liberal reforms—part-time work, flex time, job sharing—that would make it possible to have more time at home. Then she shared this parting thought.

It's really sad that I have two girls. They're going to be pulled into the same world I've coped with. They're going to have to care about what I've had to care about. They'll never have a chance to really make a contribution to anything unless they fight against the odds all the time. No matter how smart they are, how driven they are, they will ultimately feel the same conflict. I don't think things are going to change so much that my girls won't be torn. They might be able to succeed if they shut out the idea of having children and family. But then they would miss something. Society would react negatively to them. But if they do have children, they can't manage to do it all and not be torn. I wind up thinking that my husband is an incredibly gifted person and it's almost a shame he didn't have a son. It would be nice to have a boy who didn't have to face this conflict, who could just benefit from being a man, who could use all those brains. I suppose it's sad I feel this way.

A Scarcity of Gratitude:
Seth and Jessica Stein

✳

A<small>T</small> thirty-six, Seth Stein has been a husband for eleven years, a father for five, a practicing lawyer for eight, and a litigation attorney for the last six. He is tall, with broad, slightly stooped shoulders, and a firm handshake. We sit down for our interview at eight in the evening; normally at this hour, he tells me, he would be unwinding from a ten-hour day, beer in hand, slouched and unmoving in his TV chair, moving his thumb over the buttons of his hand-held remote TV channel control almost randomly. He would have had dinner with his wife and two small children at six-thirty or seven, perched himself on the periphery of his children's activities for three-quarters of an hour, and this, now, would have been the first stretch of time he'd had to himself all day.

His unwinding, I discovered, was usually solitary. Once the children were in bed, his wife, Jessica, a lawyer specializing in family law, found herself free at last, and returned to her legal papers. ("Sometimes," Seth said later, "I look over the papers in her study and think, 'We're *both* caught up in our professions.'") The living room, with its modern Danish chairs and bright Indian tapestries standing out against white walls, is his private recovery room, a place where he "comes to" after the daily operations of his demanding career. For the first time all day, he takes off his glasses and loosens his tie.

I ask Seth to describe a typical day:

I get up at six-thirty. Into the bathroom, shower, get dressed, out of the house by seven-thirty. I might see the kids in passing—"Hi, how are you?" and give a kiss good-bye. Then my morning begins with meetings with my clients, and depending on whether we're in the middle of a big litigation case, I'll meet with the other lawyers on the case, check with the paralegals. I'm at the office until six, and I'm generally home by six-thirty at the latest to sit down and have dinner. Then I'll go back at eight or eight-thirty for a few hours. I started coming home for dinner at six-thirty a year ago after realizing I'd missed the first two years of Victor's growing up.

Jessica, a tall, willowy woman of thirty-six, who often dressed in graceful peasant blouses and long floral skirts, had reached that stage in her career, she felt, where she was sure enough of herself as a professional woman that she could abandon the "strong" dark suits she had worn to work earlier, and still wore in court. She grew up the daughter of a widowed waitress in Texas, and worked her way through the University of Texas law school. But there were few clues to the determination it must have taken to do this in the shy, expectant manner with which she approached my questions.

She and Seth had begun marriage intending to honor both law degrees equally. But after many reasonable discussions, Jessica had agreed that Seth's career came first because "litigation law was more demanding." These discussions did not seem like moves in his or her gender strategy, but attempts to "do the best thing" for each person and the family. Seth was happy about the outcome to these discussions but vaguely unhappy about his marriage. Jessica was unhappy about both.

If Evan Holt resisted his wife's pressure to help at home but gave in on the "upstairs-downstairs" cover story, and if Peter Tana-gawa resisted but gave in on his role as the main provider, then Seth Stein resisted and gave up nothing except, gradually, his wife.

Like Nancy Holt, Jessica had begun with a dream of sharing

50–50 and had been forced to give it up. Like Nancy, she remained married, but, unlike her, Jessica gradually began to detach from her husband.

Curiously, Seth had none of the traditional man's attitudes toward "women's work." If he'd had the time, he could have done the laundry or sewing without a bit of shame. His manhood was neither confirmed nor denied by what he did at home, for what he did there didn't matter. Instead, his sense of self and of manhood rose and fell with the opinions of his legal community. Loaded as his career was with this meaning for his manhood and self, Seth's career told him what he had to do.

Yet, this connection between manhood and career was hard for Seth to see. He actually had little to say about what it meant to "be a man." "People are people, that's about it," he would say about these matters. All that occurred to him consciously, it seemed, was how nervous it made him on those rare occasions when he took time off. Meanwhile, fellow lawyers were saying that Seth "had a lot of balls" to break into the fierce competition among litigation lawyers in such a crowded urban market.

While Seth's obsession about his career did not seem desirable to either him or Jessica, it seemed normal and acceptable and had three effects on his family. First, what occurred at the imperial center of his career determined what happened out in the "colony" of his home. Second, although neither of them quite articulated this, Seth's dedication to his career led him to feel he deserved her nurturance more than she deserved his. Because he worked the longest hours, and because long hours seemed a manly way of earning nurturance, Seth felt he had "first dibs." Third, his career led him to suppress his emotional attachment to his children, although not his ultimate concern for them. He loved them, but day to day he left it to Jessica to think about what they needed and felt. As he saw it, these were not a result of a gender strategy, but the normal attitude of a top-notch professional. And indeed, his gender strategy was built into the very clockwork of male-dominated careers. It was not simply Seth's personal attitudes that were at issue, but the normal hours of work in his office, the calls, the gossip that reminded each worker of the overwhelming importance of work to self-esteem, and a whole urgency system based on the exclusion of life at home.

Seth and Jessica had married when they were law students. They share the memory of studying together in the library for exams and being interrupted by a fellow student and friend asking, "Shall we go out for Chinese? Italian?" Six years after their marriage, Victor was born, and two years after that, Walter. As with the Tanagawas, the Steins' firstborn strained the couple's energy, but the second-born provoked a crisis.

Quietly but inexorably a conflict arose between Seth's capitulation to the clockwork of his career and the enormous demands of his young babies and anxious wife. Seth felt Jessica had to handle the second shift. The problem was to prevent her from *resenting* it. To lighten her resentment, Seth dwelled on his sacrifices of leisure: it wasn't so easy to work eleven-hour days. For Jessica, the problem was how she could get Seth to want to share. To make a case for sharing the second shift, Jessica focused on the sacrifices she made of her hard-won career: it wasn't that easy to do. Their notions of "sacrifice" began to clash. Neither one felt much gratitude toward the other.

I asked Seth whether he'd ever considered cutting back his eleven-hour day while Victor and Walter were young. "It's not a question of what I want," he explained patiently, "I can't. I couldn't share my work with a group of incompetent lawyers just to get a night off. It would blow my reputation! When you come to a desirable area like this, the legal competition is fierce." His conversation moved spontaneously from lawyers who cut back their hours to be with family to a top lawyer friend who one day abandoned law to play second trumpet in a third-rate orchestra, and a brilliant friend who became a cosmetic surgeon at a Beverly Hills "fat farm" for rich socialites. To Seth, these men were spectacular dropouts from their reputable worlds, a reminder of how low a man could fall.

I had begun by asking how he felt about taking time off to be with his children, but the topic had slid over to disreputable lawyers. Taking time off to be with his child at a play gym seemed to fit into the same mental category in Seth's mind as working at a "fat farm." Both discredited a man's career, and so the man himself. Seth said he didn't know any *good* lawyers who worked reduced hours in order to spend time with their young children: none.

He explained:

> I'd like to get rid of the anxiety I have about being a lawyer.
> Jessica suggested a long time ago that we could both go into
> public law. Or we could travel and do the things we enjoy.
> If I could get rid of my anxiety about being a lawyer it
> would open up a lot of other opportunities. But I *have* to
> be doing what I am doing. I have to be that guy they turn
> to when the case is really tough. It's a neurotic drive.

Among his legal colleagues it was almost fashionable to be a "neurotic, hard-driving, Type-A guy" and personally a bit unhappy. Fellow lawyers quietly shared tips about how to resist their wives' pleas that they spend more time at home. Seth told me that one doctor friend had advised, "Promise her you'll take the kids to the zoo this Sunday." Another had said, "I've put my wife off by promising her a four-day vacation this spring." I could imagine these lawyers' wives—Jessica among them—calling out from the wings, like the chorus in a Greek tragedy, "Your children will only be young once! Young once. Young once. . . ." Inside Seth's legal fraternity, the career men sometimes joked about fantasies of taking time off for themselves; but they never talked about it seriously. They talked about it like cutting out coffee or mastering French. Curiously missing from Seth's talk about his long hours was talk about his children.

Given that his children were so young, why did he abdicate to the demands of his career with so little struggle? Perhaps a clue could be found in his boyhood in a highly achievement-oriented Jewish working-class family and neighborhood of New York in the 1950s. He described his sisters as "housewives who weren't brought up to have careers." He described his mother as a housewife and his father as a zealous Russian Jew who threw himself into one cause after another. As he explained, "There was a long period when he would have dinner and then go to a meeting every night. He was the chairman of this and that—Russian war relief, food, clothes to the Russians. Later he was a super-duper Zionist. He was always out there every night."

JESSICA: IF THAT'S HOW YOU WANT IT

Even if Seth's childhood had readied him to be an active father (which it had not), even if his legal colleagues had encouraged him (which they did not), in the end it may have been the very unhappiness of his marriage that kept him out of his children's lives.

Seth wanted to see his long work hours as a sacrifice to his family. One day when he was feeling especially unappreciated, he burst out to Jessica: "I'm not sailing a yacht. I'm not on the tennis court. I'm not rafting down the Colorado River. I'm not traveling around the world. I'm working my goddamn ass off." But Jessica listened coolly.

From the beginning Jessica had been prepared to *balance* her law practice with raising a family. The only legal specialties she seriously considered were those she felt were compatible with taking time for a family; that excluded corporate law. But she did not want to be marooned in solitary motherhood, as her widowed mother had been while raising her. As she made compromises in her career, she wanted Seth to make them in his.

After their first child, Victor, was born, Jessica established two patterns many women would consider desirable "solutions": she cut back her hours at work and she hired a full-time housekeeper. Five years later, when I met her, she would talk cheerfully at dinner

parties of having "the best of both worlds"—an adorable three--
year-old, a five-year-old, and work she loved. She dropped Victor
off at nursery school at nine and went to work. Then she picked
him up at noon, gave him lunch, and left him at home with
Carmelita, her housekeeper, while she returned to work until five.
But there was a certain forced cheer in her account of her day that
Seth was the first to explain:

> Jessica has been very disappointed about my inability to do
> more child-rearing, and about my not sharing things fifty-
> fifty. She says I've left the child-rearing to her. Her career has
> suffered. She says she's cut twice as much time from her
> career as I've cut from mine. She complains that I'm not like
> some imaginary other men, or men she knows, who take
> time with their children because they want to and know
> how important it is. On the other hand, she understands the
> spot I'm in. So she holds it in until she gets good and pissed
> off, and then she lets me have it.

Jessica didn't need Seth to help her with housework; Carmelita
cleaned the house and even did the weekend dishes on Mondays.
Jessica didn't need Seth for routine care of their children either;
Carmelita did that too. But Jessica badly wanted Seth to get more
emotionally involved with the children. Even if he couldn't be
home, she wanted him to *want* to be.

Jessica did not adjust to his absence in the way nineteenth-
century wives adjusted to the absence of husbands who were fish-
ermen and sailors, or the way twentieth-century wives adjust to
the absence of husbands who are traveling salesmen. She kept
expecting Seth to cut back his hours and she led the children to
hope for this too. She kept wanting Seth to feel that he was missing something when he went back to the office in the evening, as
he sometimes still did. She acted as if she were co-mothering the
children with a ghost.

A SCARCITY OF GRATITUDE

The Steins' different views about their responsibilities at home led them to want to be appreciated in ways that did not correspond. Seth wanted Jessica to identify with his ambition, enjoy the benefits of it—his large salary, their position in the community—and to accept gracefully his unavoidable absence from home. The truth was, Jessica did understand the pressures of his work as only a fellow lawyer could. But he didn't seem to want to be home, and he wasn't. For her part, Jessica wanted to be appreciated for the sacrifices she made in her career, and for her mothering. She worked twenty-five hours a week now, fifteen billable hours, but had been keen to develop a larger family law practice and perhaps write a book.

Seth ignored this sacrifice—indeed, was it a sacrifice? Wouldn't a twenty-five-hour-a-week job be *nice*? He was also too tired at the end of the day to notice much of what had gone on in his absence. A man like Peter Tanagawa may not have done much of the second shift, but he cast an appreciative eye on all his wife did; Seth was too exhausted to notice.

The clash of ideas about what deserved appreciation led each to resent the other. As Seth put it, "We both feel ripped off." For example, Jessica had recently complained that she'd passed up a chance to go to a family law conference in Washington, D.C., because Seth couldn't stay with the kids. On a different occasion, Seth had been too engrossed in a litigation case to take the chance to go sailing on the bay with friends. Jessica didn't imagine this was *hard* for him; she figured he was "sneaking in more work."

Small events sometimes symbolize bigger ones. So it was with a birthday gift Seth bought Jessica. As he explained: "For her birthday I bought her this gold chain, because I know she likes gold chains. But she felt I hadn't gotten her the *kind* of chain she really wanted, so she was mad. And I was mad that she didn't appreciate the trouble I'd gone to in order to get it. We were both furious." Which was the real conflict—that over the gift of the gold chain with the round links that Seth was able to find on a lunch break or the one with the oblong links that Jessica had had her eye on? Or was it a conflict over getting too *much* of your career, or getting too *little*? Having to be away from home, or getting stuck there?

THE NURTURANCE CRUNCH

The Steins' misunderstanding over gifts led to a scarcity of gratitude, and the scarcity of gratitude led to a dearth of small gestures of caring, especially from Jessica to Seth. Increasingly, they were feeling out of touch. When I asked Seth what he was not getting from Jessica, he replied in a surprising way, slipping in and out of lower-class grammar:

> Nurturing. She don't take care of me enough. But the deal was so straightforward from day one that I'm not bitter. But when I do reflect on it, that's the thing I reflect on: I ain't got a wife taking care of me. Every once in a while I'll be upset about it and long for someone who might be sitting around waiting to make me comfortable when I get home. Instead, Jessica needs her back massaged just as much as I do. No, she don't take care of my MCP needs—which I can't help having, growing up in this kind of society. I'm just a victim of society—so I can have those needs and not feel guilty. I just can't express them!

Why the sudden ungrammatical English? Did he mean to make a joke? To mock himself? Or perhaps he was conveying a feeling there was something *wrong* with him for wanting what he wanted. With a neat little acronym—MCP (male chauvinist pig)—he was summing up the accusations he felt Jessica might throw at him for insisting on his terms of appreciation, his view of manhood.

From time to time, Seth fantasized about having the "right" kind of wife—Jessica without the career motivation. When I asked him, later in our interview, if he ever wished that Jessica didn't work, he shot back: "Yes!" Did he feel guilty for wishing that, I asked. "No!" He wanted Jessica the person, and he felt willing and able to appreciate her enormously, on his terms.

In the meantime, each one felt unappreciated and angry: Seth's acquiescence to career demands that left no emotional energy for his children angered Jessica. Jessica's withholding of nurturance angered Seth. Now they avoided each other because they were so angry. The less Seth was around, the less they would face their anger.

WEARING MOTHERHOOD LIGHTLY

Eventually Jessica accepted Seth's long hours and more whole-heartedly colluded in the idea that he was the helpless captive of his profession and neurotic personality. This was her cover story. But as she did this, she made another emotional move—away from the marriage and family. She did not bolt from motherhood into a workaholism of her own, as some women I interviewed did. But neither did she embrace motherhood. Instead, she wore it lightly. She bought new educational games for Walter and she helped Victor with his piano lessons. But there was a certain mildness in her manner, an absence of talk about the children, an animation when she spoke of times she was away from them that suggested this "solution" of halfheartedness.

If Seth's unconscious move was to remove himself in body and spirit from his children, Jessica's move was to be there in body, but not much in spirit. She would accommodate his strategy on the surface but limit her emotional offerings underneath—give some nurturance to the children, little to Seth, and save the rest for herself, her separate life.

GETTING HELP

This took some arranging. Jessica had had a history of bad experience with help. First she'd hired a nanny who was a wonderful baby-sitter but refused to do anything else, like pick up toys or occasionally wash breakfast dishes. So Jessica hired a housekeeper to do the housecleaning. Then the two began to quarrel, each calling her at work to complain about the other. At first, Jessica tried to unravel the problem, but she ended up firing the housekeeper. Then she hired a wonderful but overqualified woman for the job, who left after three months. Now she had Carmelita, an El Salvadoran mother of two, who worked at two jobs in order to support her family and send money back home to her aging parents. Carmelita did this by arranging for her sixteen-year-old daughter, Filipa, to cover for her mornings in the Stein household while Carmelita worked her other job.

Because neither Carmelita nor Filipa could drive a car, Jessica hired Martha, an old high school friend, as an "extra driver-housekeeper." Martha shopped, took Victor to classes, and did Jessica's typing and bookkeeping. Jessica also hired a gardener. Beyond that, she hired another "helper," Bill, a nineteen-year-old student at a local junior college, as a "father substitute." He played ball with Victor, age five, and in general did "daddy-type things." Jessica felt this was necessary for Victor because "Victor suffers the most from Seth's absence." Bill, a cheerful and reasonable young man, had a cheerful and reasonable girlfriend who sometimes stayed overnight. It was Bill's barbells that Seth tripped over in the hallway and Bill's girlfriend's sweater that sometimes lay on the kitchen table. Sensing that Bill was a "bought father," Victor chose to treat him "just like my brother. He can go with us everywhere." On Saturday afternoons, Jessica wrote checks to pay Carmelita and Filipa; Martha; Bill; the gardener; and other occasional helpers such as plumbers, tree trimmers, and tax accountants.

When I remarked to Jessica that she seemed to have quite a bit of help, she replied, "Well if you want to have children and have a career, I can't think of any other way to do it except to live in a foreign country and have tons of people taking care of you."

In many ways, she had as many servants as a British colonial officer's wife in prewar India but still she was missing something. As she explained in a flat monotone:

I think I didn't look hard enough for a housekeeper that would really talk to the kids when they got home, would be sure they remembered their permission slips from school, would remember birthday parties or to sign the children up for field trips so that they're not late—like Victor was this morning. I came home and found he hadn't been signed up for a field trip. I *thought* my housekeeper would handle that stuff, but she just doesn't.

Jessica had hired many parts of the attentive suburban mother; but she could not hire the soul of that person—the planner, the empathizer, the mother herself. Nor could she hire someone to nurture her.

Jessica had now given up on Seth. Indeed, three years after our first interview, when I asked her again how she felt about Seth's being home so little, she answered with assurance: "Partly it works out so well for me this way because Seth doesn't demand much from me. I don't have to do anything for him. He takes care of himself. Other husbands might do more for the kids, but they would also ask more of me." When I asked what she wanted from her husband, she seemed surprise: "What do I want from him? I think he should let me do what I want to do. Go to New York, Washington, conferences."

A politics of emotional absenteeism had set in. Jessica had stripped down her needs, retracted her demands. Seth should let her "do what she wants." And she offered little in return: "just enough" mothering of the children and very little mothering of him. In a dejected tone, she explained: "Last year, I started being home less and less myself. I still shop and tell Carmelita what to make for dinner, but then if I go away for a conference or some-where else, I don't pay any attention to it. Seth has to do it." Jessica also created for herself a separate world of interest and leisure, where she found nurture for herself:

> I try to do what makes me least dissatisfied, which is going to Seattle on Fridays. I fly there after I put the kids to bed on Thursday evening. I have Friday free for shopping, going to the library, and seeing a psychiatrist I really like who's there, and whom I went to when we lived there. Then I come back that evening. I worry about the kids and my job if I'm here, but going there I have real time to myself. Also, the psychiatrist I am seeing there is really exciting to talk to. I can be fanciful and regressed with him and I'm enjoying that. Plus I have lunch with old friends. That's my perfect day.

With this "perfect day" to make up for the rest of the week, Jessica no longer found Seth's absence so oppressive. After all, Bill was taking Victor to his piano lessons, and Filipa was playing hide-and-seek with Walter. In the past, when problems with Seth came up, she pried them open, worked on them. Now she'd re-signed from that job and withdrawn to another world of perfect days.

YOU CAN'T STONEWALL THE CHILDREN

Certain vestiges of Jessica's earlier strategy remained. Although she often articulated her words hesitantly, as if trying to see clearly through a dense fog, the fog vanished suddenly when she spoke of her children's feelings about Seth: both children felt *cheated* of time with their father. In this the Stein children differed from neighboring children whose fathers were also often gone but whose mothers had prepared them for such absences. Victor settled into a quiet, withholding resentment not so different from his mother's. Walter reacted to his father's absence by stirring himself into a state of agitation. When called to bed, he would suddenly shout, "I've got to put away my blocks!" or "I've got to finish the drawing!" or "I need a drink of milk!" He would run frantically from one activity to another. When Jessica tried to drag him to bed, he struggled violently. Explaining the matter as if it were entirely out of her hands, Jessica said, "He won't go to bed for me but he will for Seth." So Walter was allowed to stay up until Seth came home and coaxed him to bed.

Now when Seth came home, it was to Walter's chaotic frenzy and Victor's stone-faced disregard. With Jessica coolly withdrawn in her study, home became even more a place for Seth's solitary recovery from work.

HOLDING IT TOGETHER

"I used to think of us as a couple of really bright, attractive, well-liked people," Seth said softly, at the end of my interview with him, "but the last three years have been tense. When I'm doing an eleven-hour day, I'm sure I'm no fun. When Jessica is bummed out, she's awful to live with."

But at least, they felt, they had their sex life to hold them together. Both Seth and Jessica complained of lack of sexual interest, but thought it was due mostly to fatigue. In a way beyond sadness, Jessica added slowly: "I would never consider withholding sex, no matter how angry I am. I think both of us realize that if there's no sex, there's no marriage. There's enough else going wrong. If I wasn't sexual with him, he'd find somebody else and I wouldn't be surprised at all. I would assume he would and I would move back to Seattle."

Something had gone terribly wrong in the Steins' marriage. Was Seth too anxious about his self-worth to nurture Jessica, and Jessica too afraid of intimacy? If so, perhaps the Steins would have run into problems regardless of the contradictory pressures of work and family, and regardless of their views of manhood and womanhood. But Seth nurtured his clients and his ailing father (for whom he prepared a salt-free lunch each weekday for an entire year). And Jessica was able to develop a close relationship with her psychiatrist and dear friends.

Again, perhaps the marriage suffered from a clash of ethnic traditions. Seth Stein came from a closely knit, intensely emotional, first-generation Russian-Jewish family. Jessica came from cooler, more restrained, Midwestern Swedish parents who resembled the parents of Diane Keaton in Woody Allen's film *Annie Hall*. In their book *Mixed Blessings*, Paul and Rachel Cowan suggest that the Jewish man who marries a Gentile woman often seeks a wife who is less intrusive and controlling than his mother, while a Gentile woman seeks, in her husband, the warmth, intensity, and excitement of upward mobility lacking in her cool and collected father. By middle age, the Cowans suggest, the wife may find her husband full of badly expressed needs and the husband may find his wife too cool. Perhaps this happened to the Steins. But I found this pattern between workaholic husbands and professionally ambitious wives who combine other ethnic and religious traditions as well.

A third interpretation—that there was a clash of gender strategies—may tell us more. With regard to the second shift, Jessica was not a supermom; she had bought herself out of what she could, and cut back her career to do the rest herself. Seth didn't do the "downstairs," like Evan Holt, nor cheerlead his wife's domesticity like Peter Tanagawa. Seth had joined that group of men at the top of much of the business and professional world, men who are married and heterosexual but to whom women and children are not what's basic. In a way, Jessica felt Seth had "died," like her father.

Seth supported the idea of his wife's career but embraced the heavy demands of his own. He should accommodate Jessica's career, he told himself, but how could he? He should engage his children more, but how could he? The "shoulds" came up in his head on the commute home. The "can'ts" ruled the day.

To the extent that Seth was involved in his family, he expected to *receive* at home and to *give* at work. Jessica wanted Seth to *give* at home as well as at work. They differed from other couples in the early motives they attached to their gender views and in the moves—mainly outward—they made on behalf of them. If at first Seth stayed late at the office in order to become a successful man, later he stayed there to avoid conflict at home, all because, the myth went, he was a "hard-driving Type-A guy." Under the guise of balancing motherhood and career, Jessica had withdrawn somewhat from the children, oriented their frustrations toward Seth, and withdrawn almost totally from him.

It is worth asking why Seth and Jessica didn't sense the potential clash of these "moves" *before* they married. When Jessica met Seth, in her first year of law school, she was attracted to his look of success. He was a good-looking, surefooted, intense man on the rise. Jessica had that look of success too. Seth saw in her the elegant, beautiful, slightly restrained woman of his own dreams.

On the face of it, Seth had quickly adjusted to the prospect of Jessica's career:

> There was a very clear contract when we were both students
> as to what Jessica was about, and why she wasn't going out
> with me one weekend. Her exam was more important.
> There has never been any doubt that Jessica was going to be
> a professional lady all her life. You knew that some women
> in law school would drop out for ten years to raise their
> kids. Not Jessica. Work is her whole life. She's not

interested in an afternoon of tennis. Screw tennis. She'd rather be working.

However, this was not the same Jessica whom Seth imagined would become his wife. He had a secret idea: Jessica had not really meant it. An educated woman's commitment to her career, he felt, was like an attractive woman's commitment to her virginity—if a man makes the right moves, she will give it up. The virgin says, "No, no, no . . . yes." The career girl says over and over, "I'm serious about my career," but ends up saying, "Really, a family comes first."

For her part, Jessica ignored the early signs that Seth would put his career ahead of hers. She did not harbor the idea that he would change his mind, but she all along expected potentially contradictory things: that they would mainly rely on his salary, but that he would be just as involved at home as she was.

If we see in the Holts, the Tanagawas, and the Steins three still-life portraits of strain in two-job couples, each represents a different kind of myth, and underlying tension. The family myth of the Holts misrepresented the *fact* that the wife, Nancy, did the second shift. The Tanagawas misrepresented the *reason* why the wife did it (Peter wasn't as interested). The Steins misrepresented the facts, again. Officially, Seth wasn't home; but unofficially Jessica wasn't either.

All three women felt a tension between their hopes and the realities of their marriages. For all three, this tension was exacerbated by the birth of their first child, and became a crisis with their second. In all three cases, the women ended up doing what got done of the second shift.

But differences appeared in each one's expression of gratitude. In the Holt family, Evan and Nancy appreciated enough *other* qualities about each other to compensate for their displeasure about the division of labor at home. Except for the issue of Nina's higher salary, the Tanagawas, too, agreed enough to appraise each other's gifts in the same light. But the strain in the Stein marriage more completely inhibited their exchange of credit and thanks. Missing this, they gave less love and moved apart. The most strained marriages I found were generally between two people more centered on career than family, and in dispute over their roles at home. In no other kind of marriage was gratitude so scarce, the terms of its exchange so much the object of dispute, and the marital heartbeat so precariously slow.

An Unsteady Marriage
and a Job She Loves:
Anita and Ray Judson

※

Ray Judson is a lean black man of twenty-nine who in 1982 earned $30,000 working the early morning shift as a forklift driver, loading and unloading bags of cement in Crockett, California—a two-hour barge trip across the bay from San Francisco. At home in the study of his small suburban home, he relaxed in a large chair, his guitar hanging on the wall behind him. As with other men and women I talked to, I thought I could always tell a little something by how and where a person sat. Ray was in his study, where we wouldn't be disturbed. He had changed out of his work clothes and was dressed now in a blue silk shirt and slacks. Maybe he had dressed up a bit for the interview. For the six years of their marriage, Ray and Anita had lived in a modest tract home with Ruby, Anita's pensive ten-year-old daughter by a previous marriage, and their son, Eric, a bright, mischievous boy of two. A third child was on the way. Ray enjoyed talking about people's motives; in playful respect, his coworkers at the plant called him "shrink-man." He was looking forward to this interview; perhaps, he confided, it would help him understand his stormy marriage.

The two small tables on either side of the sofa were loaded to the edge with family photographs, magazines, and knickknacks. The living-room walls were covered with posters of Jimi Hendrix album covers, which Ray had recently nailed up, Anita had objected to, and whose fate now hung undecided. The television flickered and chattered on at low volume—as if to add background excitement, like the tropical aquariums and fireplaces in wealthier living rooms.

If the Steins are more typical of two-job couples in the upper white-collar world, the Judsons tell us more about those in the solid blue-collar one. The lower on the class ladder, the less stable marriage becomes, but divorce has increased at each rung. And so many couples may come to live with the hidden dynamic I found in the Judsons' marriage—the unsettling effect of being prepared to leave "just in case" while carrying on married life as if everything were fine.

Ray earned $13.50 an hour, while Anita earned $8.00 an hour at a full-time job typing address labels into a computer for a billing agency. This wage difference was typical in the 1980s, but it had a personal importance for Ray. Anita, a short, stocky woman who dressed for our interview in jeans and a bright green T-shirt, wore a friendly but somewhat anxious smile. She lit her cigarette, exhaled slowly, and put the matter this way: "Ray isn't the antifeminist type. But he has to let you know 'I'm the *man* of the house.' Ego is real important to him. He's got to be respected as a husband and a man. He says, 'I pay the house note [the mortgage]. I work hard every day.' And I always stick in 'I work hard too, you know.'"

When Ray talked about "being a man," the topic soon came around to money, and when he talked about money, the topic often moved to being "man of the house," boss. More than Evan Holt, Peter Tanagawa, or Seth Stein—all of whom earned more—Ray talked about money as a passport to manhood, and at home it was a passport to leisure.

Ray liked to grill steaks outside on the portable barbecue. He played with Eric when he felt like it—"an hour or so most evenings," he said—and he did things like fixing the bathroom shower head when he "had time." That was his share of the second shift, a share that did not go unchallenged.

The links in Ray's mind between money, manhood, and leisure were precarious, because they bound Ray's identity to the fluctuations of an unpredictable marketplace. So long as the price of the bags of cement hauled by his barge company remained high, Ray's company, his job, and his sense of manhood were secure. But if the price of cement fell, it could threaten his job and his manhood. Given the history of black people in America, equating money with manhood was doubly dangerous. It was already an exceptional bit of luck that Ray had landed a stable union job that paid $30,000 a year. Now he was pinning his relation to the woman he loved on a tiny opening in the economic system. How long would the company prosper? How long before it automated or went offshore?

The same relation between money and gender identity in no way applied to Anita. She did not base her womanhood on earnings. This was not because she earned less but because, despite the fact that most women in her family worked, there was not quite the equivalent tie between money and womanhood. Money could give her power but it couldn't make her more "feminine." She could not, like Ray, convert money into an exemption from work at home, because she didn't earn as much as Ray, and because her money didn't carry cultural weight. She was "culturally poorer" because she was a woman.

Ray's childhood seemed to give earning power several meanings for him. For one thing, his father never held a steady job and had little authority at home. When Ray was two years old, his father left him in the care of his mother; when he was four, his mother moved away, and left him in the care of his aunt, a kind but strict and highly religious woman, who raised him along with the last two of her own seven children. After going to live with his aunt, he did not see his mother regularly until fifteen years later. Ray did not remember his father, and felt he had taken this loss in stride. But when his mother left, he remembers missing her for a very long time. If the emotional drive behind a view of manhood has roots in childhood, then perhaps this loss of his mother offers a clue to what might lie behind his insistence that the first shift come first for him, and the second shift come first for his wife.

Important people can leave unless you find powerful ways of keeping them with you. Perhaps by focusing on what he had that she needed—his salary—he could hold enough power over Anita to keep her from leaving too. Something about Anita's skittishness, her feistiness, did remind him of his mother, he said, and something of her motherliness reminded him of his aunt. Ray was a "transitional" man, then, but unlike many other such men, he openly used money to bolster his claims at home, and certain past losses added emotional fuel to it.

ANITA'S STRATEGY:
LOVE OF JOB AS SELF-DEFENSE

As I interviewed Anita, she was standing at the kitchen table, chopping carrots, potatoes, turnips, and meat to make a stew large enough to last several meals. She interrupted herself from time to time to tend Eric or take a quick pull on her cigarette. What she seemed to want to talk about was her volatile marriage to Ray and her recently diagnosed stomach ulcer. (She had not told Ray about the ulcer for fear that he would force her to quit her job.)

Anita's childhood had been as difficult as Ray's, and as important to her later notion of womanhood. Her father, a North Carolina farmer, had been crippled by polio at the age of twenty-two, two years after he married her mother, and four years before the Salk vaccine was broadly available. After bearing him three daughters, Anita's mother became pregnant with a fourth child by a man who helped around the farm—a fact she revealed in great anguish to Anita only years later. When Anita's father discovered the truth about this fourth pregnancy, he became violently upset and ordered Anita's mother to leave with the children. As Anita recalled: "My father wasn't moving out of that house. He said he was going to stay there and die. He felt like he was nothing. In the end he starved himself to death."

Alone now with her four children, Anita's mother worked at two jobs as a domestic, one mornings, and one evenings. Seven years later, she remarried a construction worker with six children of his own, and she continued to work as a domestic. On the evening of Anita's own first marriage, she remembers her mother's advice: "You're a woman now. You've got to think about yourself, your work. Always keep your *own* bank account. If you have a man around, you don't know if he's going to jump up and leave and you'll be stuck with four or five kids." That was Anita's cautionary tale. She felt her mother's life had hardened her toward men and even children:

> My mother had it so tough, with no man around, and really for me it was pretty bad. Every time I approached my mother I always felt she was ready to jump on me. She was really hard, very strict, and that's affected how I am. I can handle the usual things—being housekeeper, cook, and mother—that's fine. But having a man around, having to share my feelings with him—it's hard for me to adjust to that. Like with my husband right now.

When she was nineteen, Anita married a musician in New Orleans and after a year she had her daughter, Ruby. While her husband worked during the day and played his trombone four nights a week and on weekends, Anita stayed home with the baby. Feeling both dependent and neglected, she went back to work as a secretary, really for the adult company as much as the money. Then, without consulting her, Anita's husband decided to quit his daytime job in order to return to music school. This struck a certain raw nerve. Not being consulted or warned, not being supported, felt a lot like being abandoned. Her response was quick: she took the baby and left.

Five months later she returned to her husband, but could not stay with him long because, as she put it, "I couldn't forgive him for being so irresponsible." She sued for divorce, and only after a legal battle for custody of Ruby was resolved in her favor did she and her ex-husband really discuss what had gone wrong. As Anita described it to me, her husband had said, "I didn't know it was my music that broke us up." She had replied: "No, it really wasn't. It was just that you were ambitious and I wasn't there to help you out. I was just young and wanted you to be there all the time." As she told me: "That was the thing—he wasn't there when I needed him. He was probably the man, the father, I never knew. He was the first man I was ever together with, you know, who filled that emptiness."

Four years after her divorce, Anita met Ray. She was deeply touched by the way he talked to her. He seemed to understand why it might be hard for her to trust a man. She said: "Ray told me that he thought I was very tough and strong, but that I had a sensitive spot. Sometimes I tell him, 'I can do without you,' but deep down inside there's a feeling that has to break out. I do need him. Ray has helped me get to that feeling."

In their own ways, Ray and Anita were trying to heal each other. Ray saw a long racial history behind these personal hurts. He said: "Since the time of slavery, black men have always had a hard time holding on to their women. It's said, 'The black man spills his seed and moves on.' I don't want that to happen to me! *No way!*" But it was difficult for Ray and Anita to act on their insights in daily life. Sometimes they drew back from each other in distrust. Sometimes when they quarreled Ray drank too much and fights got physical. Anita's mother, now in her early fifties, lived right next door. She took Anita's side in these quarrels and offered shelter against male unreliability.

Her mother's life and her own inspired in Anita certain contradictory feelings about work. On one hand, she wanted to be economically self-sufficient: after all, your man can always leave. She had also grown up within a long tradition of wage-earning women; her mother, both grandmothers, most of her aunts, and all her female cousins worked. To be a woman was to work. That was the tradition, maybe not for white middle-class women, but certainly for her and for everyone she knew. At the same time her pragmatism sometimes obscured a wistful desire to be taken care of by Ray.

As she talked about it, her wish to be a housewife seemed half serious and half not. In part, "staying home" was a sign of trusting Ray and in part a vacation from the strain of working two shifts. She also associated staying home with being middle class. If she was going to stay home, she said, she wanted her home to have a certain look, "a snazzy kitchen with wall-to-wall appliances." Anita didn't want to be under her husband's thumb like Carmen Delacorte; she wanted time off, a long vacation, and a crack at the good life. If that meant depending on Ray, and if depending on Ray meant subordinating herself to him, well, that might be the cost of getting what you want. The question was how much she dared want it. On tiring days she did, on not-so-tiring days she didn't. Meanwhile, Anita talked about staying home the way Seth Stein talked about cutting back at work. It was a fantasy.

In the meantime, the official truth was that Anita wanted a paid job, and her desire for a paid job led her to want and need Ray to share the second shift. When I asked Ray and Anita, in a joint interview, to describe how they divided the work at home, an old argument flared. Anita complained that Ray didn't help. Ray countered that if Anita would quit working, she wouldn't need help; the key to the problem, he said, was that Anita didn't know *how not to work*. He was offering Anita the freedom he denied himself—the freedom not to work. In return, he said Anita should offer him freedom from housework except for weekend gardening and doing repairs.

Ray didn't claim that his higher earnings excused him from the second shift. He argued that his work had a *different* meaning than hers. As he said: "I don't mind her quitting and starting, quitting and starting. She can do that as long as she wants. I wouldn't care if she never went back to work. But *I* would never consider doing that myself, because it's *my* job that holds us together."

As Ray saw it, he was working the way a *man* works: for the money. Whether he liked his job or hated it, he had to be committed to doing it. He wanted Anita to behave more like a woman. She didn't *have* to be committed to work. She could trust him to do that. However much she actually worked, he wanted her to want to work less, and to like it less. He was offering her the chance to be casual about it.

So why did she reject this chance? Anita defended her right to like work and her right to get Ray's help at home. "I'd pay two hundred dollars a month for child care, just to keep busy." She said she'd feel bored staying at home all day.

> I *like* to work because of the recognition it gives me. I want to make a good impression. That's all. My desk is important to our department. My job is a one-person job. Nobody else knows anything about Customer Service. They've been laying people off, so I've had to do more, so my desk is even more important than it was. I feel good about my work. I'm working because I want to work. I don't think Ray is taking that into consideration at all. I go out to work, and then come home and cook. But whether I work or not, Ray expects his meals on the table!

Ray was baffled. "I can't understand why she feels they'd miss her so much. I consider my job very valuable. It's not that hers isn't valuable, because it is; but mine provides the basic income for our house. So why does she feel they'd miss her so much that she can't take some time off?"

"You never worked in an office before!" Anita snapped. "If you found an interesting job that you really liked, then you'd dedicate yourself to that job." Ray retorted, "I don't see how a group of women working in an office could be any different from the men at my job. What does your job have that mine doesn't?" Anita's job had a middle-class veneer. Ray conceded that. But it was still "just a clerical job." His job was more stressful, hers less so. His was outside, hers was inside. His was dirty, hers was clean. He dressed down for work, she dressed up. She read and typed and sat at a desk, but he steered a forklift all day and lifted heavy bags of cement. His, he felt, was the *harder* job.

Turning to me, Anita explained:

Ray always says, "You don't work hard. You sit behind that desk and punch out numbers and come home." He sees the physical part of his job, sitting on the jitney, driving every day. He sees the dust all over him and he feels that's the hardest job a person can do. But he doesn't think about what I do. I work twenty-four hours a day! I come *home* and I work. And there's the children on top of that! He doesn't see that.

In light of this dispute, I compared their workdays. Ray described his typical day:

If I'm working days, I've got to be up about five-thirty. I get up and sometimes I iron some clothes to go to work and put gospel music on the radio. I don't eat breakfast. I'll mess around the house and get in my truck and get to work by six-thirty or six-forty on a good day. Then we load the freight cars. We load them up and then take a break around nine o'clock. Then we work until eleven-thirty and we're off until twelve-thirty. Me and my buddies usually go down to the park and either get half gassed or sit around and talk about each other. Then we come back to work and finish between one-thirty and two. I come home, grab me a beer out of the box, and start messing around with my guitar or lay down and sleep until Anita gets home with the children. Then I've got to get up. If the weather's nice I work in my yard—I love flowers. Or maybe I'll take a piece of meat out to the barbecue pit and do that. Usually after I'm through doing that, Anita's through cooking [the rest of the meal] and we'll eat dinner together while we're watching TV. Then I'll go off upstairs and start playing my guitar again or try to mess with the keyboards, and by then it's usually time for the kids to go to bed, so we'll say our prayers together.

Anita described her typical day in less detail:

I get up about six-thirty and get the two kids up. I get my son dressed. My daughter dresses herself. They eat breakfast while I'm getting myself dressed. I leave about seven-fifteen. I drop off Eric, and then Ruby. I go to work and do my seven and a half hours and come back. I have to stop at the grocery store, come home, cook, and then feed them. I watch TV for a while, go to bed around nine-thirty or ten, and do the same thing the next day.

At work Ray had more control over the pace of his cargo loading than Anita had over her flow of bills. Ray's foreman did not ride his men. In fact, he allowed a spirit of play: Ray and his coworkers wore cowboy hats and joked and razzed the boss, softening his orders in these ways. But Anita's supervisor often questioned her if she was away from her desk for more than twenty minutes. In this way, their workdays reflected different supervisory styles that exist in most "male" and "female" jobs. A 1972 study by Robert Karasek, for example, showed that men and women report roughly equal workload demands in their jobs. However, women are likely to experience high demands for work performance while exercising less control over the pace of that demand. A telephone operator and a waitress typically have less control over the pace of their work than a meter reader or a telephone repairman. For this reason, Karasek concluded that women's jobs are more stressful. In addition, women in service jobs like Anita's actually suffer more stress-related coronary disease than the group popularly supposed to be at risk—top male executives.[1]

In addition, Ray had more leisure *during* his workday than Anita had during hers. He could, after all, spend an hour getting "half gassed" with the boys, while Anita could not. The sociologist J. P. Robinson has found that, in general, working men enjoy about half an hour more leisure during their workday than do working women.[2]

But to Ray, what mattered was the weight of his responsibility to provide. One family, Ray reasoned, didn't need two who work like that. Just one. He was that one.

Anita didn't back down, and this dispute about the second shift dogged them like it had the Holts, the Tanagawas, the Steins. Nancy cut back her hours. The Tanagawas and Steins hired a housekeeper. Ray brought ten-year-old stepdaughter, Ruby, in as a possible solution. Ruby, he said, could do the dishes and vacuum. She was old enough. It was good training. Besides, he said, he had helped his aunt with a lot of the housework when he was growing up.

But Ruby, already feeling low on the family totem pole, interpreted this assignment as a sign she wasn't valued. She refused to do the dishes and vacuuming and proposed instead to weed the garden—maybe with Ray? The logic Ray had already applied to Anita when she asked him to share the housework, he now applied to Ruby: "I'm sure not going to wait hand and foot on somebody I'm working for already." Ruby sought support in her grandmother next door, who prodded Ray further: Why couldn't Rudy weed the flower beds instead of cleaning house? He felt pressured by his mother-in-law. Anita herself was next door more and more these days. And the kinswomen were ganging up on him.

As he became increasingly alienated from Anita and his children, Ray began to drink too much, and the drinking precipitated some bad fights. Anita and the children moved next door into her mother's house. Now Ray was forced to confront the one thing he had all along dreaded most: the possibility that Anita would leave. And indeed, Ray and Anita were to separate and reunite, separate and reunite, over the next years. The last I heard, they were apart.

The official reasons Ray gave for not sharing the second shift were that he provided most of the income, took his job more seriously, and worked harder. The first statement was true, the second hard to say, and the third was false. But his official reasons also seemed to coincide with a private agenda: to dampen Anita's desire to work, to increase her dependency on him and try to reduce the chance that she might leave.

For her part, the drinking and the fights made Anita feel unsafe. She fought Ray continually over the value of her work. Hers was not a glamorous career, but she clung to it tenaciously, because her mother had warned her, "You've got to think about yourself, your work," and at heart Anita was unsure of her union with Ray. If the marriage was to continue, she felt, her work would help Ray "respect her." Earning money kept Ray "on his toes," which in turn improved their marriage. If the marriage was not to continue, she would need her job even more than she needed it now.

In their views of manhood and womanhood, the Judsons were a mismatch. Ray was transitional; Anita wavered between traditional and egalitarian—knowing only that she *didn't* want the transitional woman's responsibility for both spheres. This clash caused them trouble in the exchange of marital gifts. Anita offered Ray the "gift" of her wage for her family. Sensing she might be preparing to leave, Ray turned it down. For his part, Ray offered Anita the choice to work or not. Disliking the double shift if she worked and sensing a danger in staying home, Anita challenged this choice. Their public myth—though not one they privately believed—was that the second shift was simply an issue of Anita's badgering Ray because she had "too much to do." Certainly this was true, but it was not the whole truth. The issue had an umbilical link to the meaning for each of Anita's work.

Anita's job gave her the modest financial independence she would need if her marriage deteriorated. It was an insurance policy: she worked in self-defense. Early in their marriage, she had tried to trust Ray, tried to avoid divorce. It had been impossible to openly confess that she wanted to work "just in case."

But the possibility of divorce had all along entered the life of their marriage. In this, Anita's dilemma may speak to an increasing number of women. As a black woman she could not look back to a long tradition of marriage as a woman's path to financial security, for most black men have long been barred from higher-paying jobs. For at least a century, the experience of white women in America was different because marriage to a man, almost any man, could lift them to a class higher than that in which their own job would place them. But more and more working- and middle-class white women now face the situation black women have long faced. Now they, too, cannot rely as much as in the past on marriage.

Gradually over the last century, the economic footing that marriage has provided women and their children has become less secure. Half of all marriages in America end in divorce, and despite a short-term dip in that rate, experts expect it to remain as high as it is now. In addition, after divorce, the income of most men rises while that of women drops. A third of divorced women never remarry. Of the two-thirds who eventually do, many divorce again. For most women, then, a shaky marriage raises the prospect of economic insecurity, and for many, outright poverty.

According to the U.S. Bureau of Labor Statistics, women earn 83 percent of the median wages of men. Women age 35 to 44 earn about $200 less a week than men, but their wages rose 12 percent in the last decade, while those of men rose 1.2 percent. And in 2008, young, childless women in most of America's biggest cities actually earned 8 percent more than comparable men.[3]

Still there remains what Joan Williams calls a "maternal wall." Compared to their male counterparts, mothers earn 27 percent less. Partly they earn less because they take jobs more compatible with family, work shorter hours, take more time off, and are less willing to move the whole family to a higher-paying job.[4] But women also work differently these days. Male jobs took a bigger hit in the Great Recession of 2008, causing wives' jobs to become a more important part of the family budget. And for women like Anita there is something else. Anita lived a married life but secretly imagined becoming divorced. She resisted pressure from

Ray to quit because she feared the prospect of losing her place at work, divorcing and falling into a financial trap. Yet the official reality was that their marriage "was for keeps." So Anita hid her pragmatic motive for working, claiming instead to work because "she loved it," because she "needed to keep busy," because "they needed her at the office." As divorce has spread, more and more uncertain women are led to seem married but to ponder work and family in unmarried ways.

The "His" and "Hers" of Sharing: Greg and Carol Alston

❋

A T 7:45 one Sunday morning I slowly drive my car up a newly paved street lined with young trees and clusters of two-story homes that form a curving line up a hill overlooking the San Francisco Bay. It has the feel of a new housing development; along each street the shrubs are sculpted with the same taste. Streets have names like Starview, Overlook, Bayside, and though the traffic goes back and forth only within the development, there are ten-mile-an-hour signs every half block, as if an informal understanding could not be trusted. Between groups of every six houses, ivy lawns sprawl into large communal spaces, and mailboxes are clustered under a small, communal mailbox roof. It was a developer's attempt at community.

At this hour the empty sidewalks are strewn with Sunday newspapers. Other times of day I see only employees—a Chinese gardener trimming, a Chicano handyman fixing floodlights, two white workmen carrying rolls of carpeting from their truck to a home. Half the units are filled with retired couples, Carol Alston tells me later, and the other half with two-income families. "The elderly don't talk much to the young, and the working couples are too busy to be neighborly: it's the kind of place that could be neighborly, but isn't."

Greg Alston answers the door. At thirty-seven, Greg is a boyish, sandy-haired man with gold-rimmed glasses, dressed in well-worn jeans and a T-shirt. Also at the door is Daryl, three, with a dimple-cheeked grin. He has bare feet, and shoes in hand. "Carol's still asleep," Greg tells me, "and Beverly [their three-month-old baby] is about to wake up." I settle in the living room, again the "family dog," and listen as the household wakes up. At 7:15 Greg has risen, at 7:30 Daryl, and now, at 8:00, Beverly is up. For a while, only Greg and Daryl are downstairs. Greg is talking to Daryl about tying shoes, Daryl is discussing the finer distinctions between Batdog, Spiderbat, Aquaman, and Aquababy. Soon, Carol has dressed and calls out to me; I help her make the bed. She breastfeeds Beverly and puts her in a swing that is hung near the dining-room table between two sets of poles; the swing is kept in motion by a mechanical bear, whose weight, as it gradually slides down one of the poles, drives the mechanism that moves the swing. As Carol cleans off the dining-room table and does the dishes, she tells me about a wild two-year-old child of friends whom they had taken to Marine World Saturday, and who had thrown a metal car at the baby. She begins making pecan and apple pancakes for breakfast. Greg is repairing a torn water bed downstairs. Each parent has one child.

Carol, thirty-five, is dressed in a jogging suit and sneakers. She has short-cropped hair, no makeup, tiny stud earrings. There is something pleasantly no-nonsense in her look and a come-on-and-join-me quality to her laugh. She and Greg have shared an extremely happy marriage for eleven years.

Carol is not trying to integrate family life with the demands of a fast-track corporate career like that of Nina Tanagawa. Three years before, she had quit what she called her "real" job on the fast-track as a systems analyst and begun freelance consulting for twenty-five hours a week. As a child, Carol had always envisioned having a career, and, as an adult, she'd always had one. She says she's always divided the work at home 50-50. "I don't know if I'd call myself a feminist," she tells me, as if studying the term from a distance, "but yes, Greg and I have always shared at home, no discussion about it, up until I went part time, of course."

From the beginning, Greg wanted Carol to work and, in fact, told me he felt "upset" when she went part time since he missed her income. For seven out of their eleven years together, Carol earned as much as a systems analyst as he earned as a dentist. In fact, she now earned part time almost as much as Greg earned full time. "The more income she makes," Greg said, "the earlier we can retire."

For the past three years, since having Daryl, Carol's strategy has been to reduce her hours and emotional involvement at work, and to do most of the second shift. But the couple would share again after next November, she said, when they planned to fulfill an eleven-year dream of escaping the gridlock traffic and drugs and racial violence of the urban schools to move to a tiny town in the Sierra mountains called Little Creek. There Greg, too, would take up part-time work. The Alstons have always loved boating and camping; in Little Creek they could enjoy the outdoors in a 50-50 version of a Rousseauist retreat from modern life. They are among the lucky few who could afford this. In short, the financial and ideological stage was set for them to really share the work of the home.

Apart from *work* at home, Greg and Carol shared the *life* of the home. If a home could talk, the Alstons' place would say a lot about their closeness and the importance of their children to them. Theirs is a comfortable, unpretentiously furnished, ranch-style home, designed so that if you close all the doors, Greg in the kitchen can see Carol in the dining room or living room. A picture over the mantel shows a dreamy child blowing at a balloonlike moon. Beneath it are porcelain ABC blocks, a German beer stein, and wedding photos of brothers and sisters. Each sitting area throughout the house shows some material indication of the presence of children: a crib in a circle of living-room chairs, a tiny rocker in an alcove, Daryl's pictures taped to the refrigerator, and a hook to hang his Batman cape on. Upstairs, above Carol's desk, hangs her framed college diploma, her CPA certificate, her state board of accountancy certificate; and beside these are corresponding documents for Greg, a picture of Daryl, and a photo of Carol and Greg white-water rafting. Hanging in the garage are two homemade "dancer" kayaks. ("We made them with a group of boating friends," said Carol. "A girlfriend and I made meat loaf and we just kept painting all day.") Daryl's room is a cooperative effort too. Carol had hung a "star chart" on computer paper on Daryl's door; he had earned one star beside BRUSH TEETH, three beside PICK UP CLOTHES, and none beside PUT NEWSPAPER IN BOX, CARRY BEVERLY'S BAG, or GET UNDRESSED. Greg had designed Daryl's walnut built-in crib and ladder, and set up the electric car tracks. Carol had bought the elephant lamp with the party hat between its ears and the colored beanie on its rump. Everything seems integrated with everything else.

There is only one sad note: hanging in the hallway is a framed, glass-covered composition of the wedding invitations of four couples, their closest friends. In the middle, as if joining the couples together, is a $20 bill. It captures a moment of whimsy and exuberance, and expresses the idea of a gamble. "We made a bet that whoever got married last had to pay the others twenty dollars," Carol explained. Then she grew quiet. "Tim and Jane—the ones in the right top—are divorced, and Jim and Emily, on the bottom left, are in trouble." The Alstons' move to Little Creek would certainly solve the traffic problem, but perhaps they also hoped it would remove them from today's strains on marriage.

Either member of the couple was often doing something for the other. If Carol was holding Beverly she might ask Greg, "Could you feed the cat the dry food?" When Greg was hammering on a fixture in the bedroom and the phone rang, he said, "Can you get it?" One adult was as likely as the other to answer the phone or chat with a neighbor.

They handled the usual tensions at dinnertime in a similar way. Whenever his parents cast out a line of marital communication over the dinner table, Daryl would grab it. "Michael hasn't signed the contract yet," Greg would say to Carol. "The Michael from my school?" Daryl would butt in. "No, a different Michael that Daddy and Mommy know," Carol would answer. At dinner, it was as often Carol as Greg who answered Daryl's questions.

When he was home, Greg spent as much time involved with the household as Carol did; and he tried to maximize his time at home. On the weekends, whatever each was doing, they invested the same amount of time in their work. In all, Greg contributed more time to the second shift than Evan Holt, Frank Delacorte, Peter Tanagawa, Robert Myerson, or Ray Judson. Both Carol and Greg felt the arrangement worked well.

On the other hand, in some ways they did not share. Carol cut back her hours of work and changed her philosophy of work after Beverly's birth, whereas Greg told me that not much changed for him. If real sharing means sharing the *daily* or *weekly* tasks, then again, they didn't really share. Whether she worked full time, time and a half, or half time, Carol was responsible for the daily and weekly chores such as cooking, shopping, and laundry in addition to such nondaily chores as shopping for children's clothes, remembering birthdays, caring for house plants, and taking family photos. Greg's housework list was mainly made up of nondaily chores: household repairs, paying bills, and repairing both cars.

Carol was not a supermom like Nina Tanagawa. Nor did she passively renegotiate marital roles, as Carmen Delacorte did "playing dumb." Nor did she stage a "sharing showdown" as did Nancy Holt through her Monday-you-cook, Tuesday-I-cook scheme. But, over a period of time, Carol pursued several other strategies. First, when the demands of work went up, her production at home went down. As she explained, "When I worked full time, we both ate a big lunch at work, and Daryl eats at day care, so I didn't cook." Carol also cut back at work, and from time to time renegotiated roles with Greg. These were her three strategies, and Greg had a fourth. He evened out the score, it seemed, by seeing how long Carol was taking with the cooking, cleaning, and tending the children, and kept at his woodworking until she stopped. That way, Greg was working "as long as" Carol, only on his projects. These were not hobbies like Evan Holt's projects "downstairs."

Greg often checked his projects with Carol, did them in an order she would suggest, or consulted her on the colors, sizes, and shapes of the things that he made. What Greg did profited them both, but it was not sharing the daily chores and did not take the pressure off Carol.

INSIDE "EQUAL TIME" ON SUNDAY

Compared to Carol, Greg did less with the children and more with the house. He was the handyman. He looked at the mantel-piece with a carpenter's eye; he thought about repairs on the sep-tic tank in the backyard of the house in Little Creek. Carol was the parent who noticed a developing hole in Daryl's trousers. At one point, as Greg pulled out the vacuum cleaner, he quipped, "Carol's just a woman. She hasn't vacuumed for so long, she'd have to relearn. A man better handle this." But, in fact, 80 percent of his tasks that day put him on the male side of the gender line.

Too, Carol was more child-centered than Greg when she was with the children. For example, when each parent stopped occa-sionally during the day to talk with me, usually Daryl was there, trying to join in (he loved talking into my tape recorder) or to get his parent's attention. Carol would give Daryl time. ("Yes, Daryl, I think that Superman can fly higher than Batman. What do you think?") But Greg would tell Daryl, "Daddy has to talk with Arlie," or "If you don't stop making that noise, you'll have to go to your room," or "Go see Mommy."

Carol's breast-feeding of Beverly gave her a natural advantage in forming a close bond with the baby. Some fathers of nursing in-fants gently rock them, burp them, change them, and do every-thing they can until the baby drinks from a bottle, at which point the male disadvantage disappears. Other men seem to avoid their infants, focusing on older children, if they have them, until the baby is weaned. Greg took a middle path. He focused his attention on Daryl. It was he who usually helped Daryl put his pajamas on, had a "peeing contest" with him in the toilet (Daryl loved that), and tucked him warmly in bed.

Greg would take care of Beverly when Carol needed him to; but he held her like a football, and when she cried, he sometimes tossed her in the air, which made her cry more. Now when Greg picked her up, half the time she was calm and half the time fussy. The family explanation for this was that "Beverly doesn't like men." As Carol told me flatly, "Beverly fusses when men pick her up, except for her grandfather." But the only men who picked Beverly up were Greg and her grandfather.

Was this constitutional with three-month-old Beverly? Or was it "natural" male ineptitude on the part of Greg? I was wondering this when a telling episode occurred: Beverly was in her rocker in a pink dress and booties. Carol was cooking. After a while, Beverly began to fuss, then cry. Greg unbuckled her from the bear swing and held her, but she still cried. He sat with her at the dining-room table, trying to read over a dentistry magazine. She wailed. Greg called out, "Mom, come!" and explained to me again that "Beverly doesn't like men." I recalled a certain way I used to comfort my sons, bobbing slowly up and down as well as forward and back (we called it the "camel walk"), asked if I could try, demonstrated it, and she calmed down. Greg replied, "Oh, I know about that one. It works fine. But I don't want to have to get up. See, when Carol teaches night class Tuesdays, I have her all night and I don't want her getting used to it." To relieve Carol, Greg very often took care of Beverly "anyway." But however unconsciously, he seemed to resist the extra effort of taking care of three-month-old Beverly in a way she liked.

Parents can offer contact to the child in the very way they talk. Carol could be saying, "You have your gray pants on today," or "Do you want your apple cut up?" Her voice conveyed a sense of welcoming attachment. She used a "primary parent voice." Along with making one's lap available for sitting, or rotating one's head to keep sensing where a child is, it is this primary parent's voice that makes a child feel safe. Greg used it intermittently in the course of the day; Carol used it all the time.

One Tuesday, when Carol was teaching an evening class in a business school, I could hear the garage door closing, and the sound of Greg in the kitchen scraping the pizza pan in the kitchen sink. Soon Daryl came into the kitchen and the two went to watch TV. Once *Mousterpiece Theater* was over and an absorbing documentary about an expeditionary team climbing Mount Everest had caught Greg's attention, Daryl moved to imaginative play with a car. He began to tell a long tale about a frog going "fribbit, fribbit" in the car. The documentary was now at a dramatic moment when the team had nearly reached the top. The expedition's doctor was telling an indispensable team member that his lungs could not take the climb. Greg was listening to "fribbit, fribbit" with half an ear. He tried to draw his son's attention to the program with fatherly explanations about yaks and snow caves, but no dice. Daryl brought out some cards and said, "Dad, let's play." "I don't know how," Greg replied. "You can read the directions," Daryl suggested. "No," Greg said. "Wait for your mom. She knows how."

During the season when she was working longer hours than Greg, Carol said, "There have been nights when I've come home and Daryl's dinner was popcorn." "Does he do that as a treat for Daryl?" I asked. "No, just lazy," she said with a laugh.

Greg was a very good helper, but he was not a primary parent. Many of his interactions with Daryl took the form of inspiring fear and then making a joke of it. For example, one evening when Daryl had finished dipping his dessert candies into his milk, and was waiting to be taken out of his high chair with milky hands, Greg playfully wiped his hands with a cloth, took the boy out of his high chair, and held him upside down. "I'm going to wash you off in the dishwasher." "No!" "Yes! You're going to be shut inside to get all cleaned off." "Haah." The boy half-realized his father was joking, and was half-afraid. Only when a sound of alarm continued in Daryl's voice did Greg turn him right side up and end the joke. Again, when Greg was fixing the water bed with some pliers, he held the pliers up to Daryl. "These are good for taking off eyelashes." "No!" "Yes, they are!" Only when the boy took the pliers and held them toward the father's eye, did Greg say, "That's dangerous."

There were safer jokes that Daryl always got. "Daddy's going to take off Daryl's nose and eat it." Or, "I'm going to throw your nose down the garbage disposal." But another often-repeated joke was a less sure bet: "Ow. You kicked me. I'm going to kick you back." As often as not there was a scuffle, serious protest from Daryl, and serious explanation from his father that it was "just a joke." All these were gestures unconsciously designed, perhaps, to "toughen" him up, to inoculate him against fear, to make him into a soldierly little man.

Carol warned me early on that "some people think Greg has a disquieting sense of humor." When I talked to him alone, Greg said spontaneously, "Sometimes Carol doesn't understand my sense of humor. Daryl doesn't either. But it's how I am." Greg's "humor" was unusual among the families I studied, but only in degree. Fathers tended toward "toughening" jokes more than mothers did.

Some fathers answered children's cries less readily, and with a different mental set. One father worked at home in a study looking out on the living room where a sitter tended his nine-month-old son. When asked whether his son's cries disturbed his work, he said, "No problem, I actually want him to fall and bang himself, to get hurt a little. I don't want him to have a fail-safe world." When we'd finished the interview, the husband asked his wife (who also works at home) how she would have answered the same question. She said immediately, "I hate to hear him cry."

Many parents seem to enter a cycle, whereby the father passes on the "warrior training" he received as a boy, knowing his wife will fulfill the child's more basic need for warmth and attachment. Knowing she's there, he doesn't need to change. At the same time, since the husband is rougher on the children, the wife doesn't feel comfortable leaving them with him more, and so the cycle continues. Greg carried this warrior training further than most fathers, but the cycle was nearly obscured by the overall arrangement whereby Greg and Carol "shared" the second shift.

Primary parenting has to do with forging a strong, consistent trusting attachment to a child. For small children, a steady diet of "toughening" is probably not good primary parenting. But Greg could afford his "jokes," because Carol would come forward with her warm, outreaching voice and watchful eye, to neutralize their effect.

Ironically, Greg felt more confident about his parenting than Carol felt about hers. For Greg compared himself to his father, who was less expressive than he, while Carol compared herself to the baby-sitter, whom she thought more patient and motherly. Neither drew a comparison to the other.

"I HAVE AN MBA!"

The main strategy that either Carol or Greg pursued was Carol's quitting her full-time job, and this had important consequences for her. As she explained: "After Daryl was born, I stayed home for six months, and I discovered how much of my self-esteem was wrapped up in money. Being out of work, I felt really inferior. When I went out to the supermarket in the morning, I felt fat [she hadn't lost the weight from her pregnancy] and dumb. I wanted to go up to the people in the aisles and say, 'I have an MBA! I have an MBA!' I didn't want to be classified as a dumb housewife."

Like an urbanized peasant might feel returning to a land he had ambivalently left behind, Carol now felt a mixture of scorn, envy, and compassion for the housewives shopping in the market. She mused: "I learned not to judge. Whereas before, if I saw a woman with a kid, I would think, 'What is she *doing*? Why isn't she doing something productive with her life?' I think I was partly jealous, too. You go into the store in the middle of the day, there are all these thirty-year-olds shopping. I mean, where do they get the money? It made me wonder if there's some easier way to do this."

After a while, Carol began to feel an affinity with women who didn't work outside the home:

> I don't know whether I'm rationalizing in order to feel good about myself while I'm not working, or whether I'm on to the innermost truth. But I've changed my perspective. I've missed the sexy part of business, going out to lunch, talking about big deals, talking about things that "really mattered." Only over the past few years have I realized how superficial that life really is. In the long run, what's important is Daryl, Beverly, Greg, and my friends—some of those friends are work friends whom I will carry in my heart to the grave.
>
> I have a different identity now. I don't feel like I have to have a job. Greg shouldn't have to have one either.

Meanwhile, Greg's routine didn't change much, nor did his perspective.

BEHIND THEIR GENDER STRATEGIES

Carol would have preferred for Greg to go light on the "pliers jokes," the "you-hit-me" jokes, the fatherhood of toughening. She would have preferred that Greg give Daryl something more than popcorn for dinner. In short, Carol wanted Greg to act more like a primary parent. But she didn't press him to change his ways. She was grateful that he woke up with Daryl Saturday mornings, and worked the second shift as hard as he did.

Carol and Greg present a certain paradox. Both believed in sharing both housework and child care. This is the first side of the paradox. On the other hand, in the psychological fabric of home life Carol was far more central. Each side of this paradox poses a question. First, why did they believe in sharing? After all, the Delacortes, the Tanagawas, and indeed 40 percent of the women and three-quarters of the men in this study did *not* believe in it.

In Carol's background was hidden an important experience that may have fueled her strong desire to be an independent career woman, and to adopt the view of sharing that, in the late 1980s in her professional circle, went with it. Carol remembers her mother—a navy wife left alone for six months at a time to care for two small children—as an example of womanhood to avoid. As Carol realized: "I remember her dressed all day in her nightgown, sighing. My sister says our mother was suicidal. I don't remember that. But she did try to leave us. My sister and I were into normal mischief and wouldn't go to bed. My mother said, 'Well, I'm leaving.' And she walked out the door. I can remember telling my sister, 'Don't worry. I know how to make soup.'"

Through her early twenties she had few thoughts of marriage or children, and Greg won her heart only by gallantly declining a big job offer in another city in order to be with her. (Many happily married women described some early gesture of sacrifice that convinced them this was the right man for them.) "I was strong-minded," she said, "and I wanted a man who would never let me down." Part of "never letting her down" was probably connected to Greg's continued involvement at home.

For his part, Greg wanted Carol to work and to share the second shift. Carol speculated that it was because Greg's mother had worked full time from when he was five years old. "I thank Meg [Greg's mother] for setting him an example of how independent a woman can be." After Greg was five, his father retired from the army, got a teaching credential, taught math and wood shop in middle school, and was home when Greg returned from school. His mother worked overtime as a secretary in order to make ends meet and his father shared the second shift.

The other side of the paradox is that, despite their modern belief in sharng work at home, Carol and Greg implemented this belief in a traditional way. Some traditional men such as Peter

Tanagawa actually parented their children in a more "motherly" way than Greg did. Again, why? Greg commented:

My dad never touched me much. He was probably afraid. Plus, my dad is quiet, like I am. He doesn't express himself. I have reflected upon the fact that I don't embrace my dad. About six months ago, when he was here, I accidentally embraced him. I'm glad I did. He commented on it. He said that I hadn't hugged him for years. He used to wrestle with me a lot but that stopped after I started to beat him at fourteen. After that we didn't really touch. I don't know whether it was him or me, but it stopped.

Perhaps Greg's awkward way of holding his daughter and his aggressive joking with his son expressed a fear of getting close. Perhaps his jokes were a verbal stand-in for the old boxing matches. But time had brought change.

Greg would plant many small kisses on Daryl's cheek each night, and from time to time hug Daryl in the course of tussling with him. Greg was, he felt, far more physically affectionate with Daryl than his father had been with him.

Greg was not as much a primary parent as were some men nor was Carol as ardently committed to getting him to become one as some women were. Part of the reason seemed to be that Carol discovered she enjoyed parenting. After all, she had completely put off thoughts of children until her thirties, and a few months after her son was born, she'd put him in the care of a baby-sitter for ten hours a day. (Even now she urged Greg's mother to live near them in Little Creek to help "raise the kids.") Unlike some women, Carol had not been attached to the idea of being the main parent until her second child was born. Now parenting was more important, perhaps because she found in it a way to reparent herself.

The greater importance of parenthood for Carol may illustrate the theory Nancy Chodorow offers in her book *The Reproduction of Mothering*.[1] Chodorow argues that women develop a greater desire to be a mother than men do to be fathers. This is because as children most boys and girls are both brought up by mothers. Socially speaking, this need not be; after a child is born, fathers can care for children as well as mothers, she argues. But as long as it is *women* who mother, boys and girls will develop different "gender personalities," which alter their later motives and capacities. Both girls and boys first fuse with the mother. But when girls grow up, they seek to recapitulate this early fusion with the mother by becoming mothers themselves. When boys grow up, they try to recapitulate that early fusion by finding a woman "like mother." The reason girls and boys recapitulate this early fusion in different ways is that girls are females, like their mothers, and can more readily identify with her than boys can. According to Chodorow, because mothers are the object of the child's earliest attachment, boys and girls differ in another aspect of "gender personality." Girls are more empathic, more able to know how others feel than boys, though they are less able than boys to maintain a clear boundary between themselves and others.

Chodorow's theory deals with the familial origins of men's and women's motives for becoming parents. By her mid-thirties, motherhood was a more central identity to Carol than fatherhood was to Greg, and perhaps this was one reason why.

But in Chodorow's theory, all women come out pretty much alike. Her theory doesn't explain why some women like Adrienne Sherman felt no urge to be the primary parent, while Carmen Delacorte had always felt a strong urge, and Carol Alston only came to feel it in her middle thirties. Carol didn't want her husband involved at home as ardently as Nancy Holt did, but she clearly didn't want to "protect" her husband from the burden of parenthood like Ann Myerson, nor did she want him in the picture mainly to exert authority, as did Carmen Delacorte. Clearly women's motives *differ* enormously because of other things.

In Chodorow's theory, all men are pretty much alike too. So we don't know why Evan Holt and Seth Stein are so disinterested in fatherhood while Art Winfield and Michael Sherman have immersed themselves so passionately in it. Clearly, other factors—the quality of a person's early bonds with their mother and father, and broader cultural messages about manhood and womanhood—enter in. The concept of gender strategy adds to Chodorow's theory an interpretation of the remarkable differences we find between some men and other men, and between some women and other women.

To understand why Carol and Greg Alston's approach to parenthood is different from that of other couples, we need to take account of other kinds of motives—Carol's desire to be different from her own mother, unfused with her, joined instead with Greg. It is probably true that, for better or worse, Carol's mother was a more important figure to her than her father. She criticized her mother. She didn't like her. But she talked about her mother far more, and with greater feeling, than she talked about her father. So, in that respect Carol fits Chodorow's theory. But because this fusion was problematic for Carol, she had invested a great deal of energy in her early adulthood avoiding motherhood. Now that she was trying it out, it was not so easy for Carol to become a mother-not-like-her-mother; it was frightening. Every bit of Greg's support helped; and perhaps that was why she wanted Greg by her side at home and believed in 50-50 parenting.

By happily sharing the job of earning money, by not caring much about material things, she freed Greg from worry about being the provider. By expressing gratitude for all he did around the home, she encouraged him to do more. Consciously or not, Carol pursued a strategy of bringing Greg to her side to support her in the task of being a mother-not-like-her-mom.

To understand Carol and Greg, we need something else missing from Chodorow's theory: culture. Carol's mother didn't offer a good example of mothering, but even as a small child Carol had some idea about what "regular" mothers do; there was a culture of motherhood outside her home, and she grew up in it. For some periods of Greg's boyhood, Greg's father was a primary parent to him—and thus an exception to Chodorow's theory—but a primary parent who could hug his son only in a boxer's clench. This way of being a dad surely has much to do with Greg's father's notion of manhood.

Although the cultural shifts and opportunities of the 1980s had led Carol and Greg to a life ideologically and financially removed from patriarchy, that older, entrenched system influenced them anyway. Because conditions were worse for women in general than for men in general, Carol felt more grateful to Greg than he did to her. The love ran both ways, but the gratitude ran more from Carol to Greg. Although Carol had for years earned more money than Greg and taken most of the heat off the second shift, Greg did not spontaneously talk about being grateful for this.

Carol had catalogued a series of "miserable boyfriends" she'd met in college whose laundry she'd washed and whose weekend dinners she'd cooked. Compared to these other possible men, Greg was wonderful. Greg hadn't washed any girlfriend's laundry; for him the pickings weren't so slim. Again, Carol explained: "My God, these single mothers whose husbands don't see the kids or pay child support. I don't know how they do it. I couldn't. Being a single mother is the worst thing that can happen to you, next to cancer." Greg would never leave; Carol was grateful for that. But Greg didn't feel haunted by a dread of abandonment, by the sense "that could happen to *me*." He didn't picture himself as a single dad. The general supply of male commitment to shared responsibility was far lower than the female demand for it. Through this fact in the *wider* society, patriarchy tipped the scales *inside* the Alston marriage. It evoked Carol's extra thanks.

And her extra thanks inhibited her from making further demands on Greg, who was already doing comparatively so much. Carol had a "wish list" on which sharing primary parenting was probably fourth or fifth after the desire that Greg be healthy, faithful, mentally sound, and able to help provide. Greg had a wish list too, with many of the same wishes. But given the generally worse lot for women, Carol's extra sense of gratitude and of debt inhibited her from going as far down her wish list as Greg went in his. In this different rate of climb up each wish list, Carol

and Greg were like nearly every couple I met. Greg really was unusual, and given the scarcity of such men, Carol was "right" to be
grateful. She had fewer options. Equal as they felt they were, the
burden of the second shift fell mainly on Carol's shoulders. And it
was the larger, societal support of inequity between the sexes, a
system outside of their stable, happy marriage, that indirectly
maintained the "his" and "hers" of sharing.

No Time Together:
Barbara and John Livingston

✳

CONSUELA finally opens the door a crack, looks me over, and lets me in. She leads me up to the second floor of the Livingstons' friendly, weather-worn Victorian home to a family room with overstuffed chairs, family photos, and an excitable parrot in a large cage, all of which seem to face the cluster of toys on a blanket in the middle of the room on which Cary, two and a half, sits drawing trolls.

Mary Poppins is on the video machine, and has been all day. Just now, Mary Poppins, the nanny, is announcing dinner to the upper-middle-class British Mr. and Mrs. Banks and their children, all primly seated at the dinner table. As I settle in, start drawing trolls with Cary, and talk with Consuela the baby-sitter, Barbara Livingston returns from work. She asks Cary for a kiss, then changes into jeans. Half an hour later, John Livingston returns from work, gets a big running hug from Cary, and sits down to chat. In a while, he rises to drive Consuela home, saying to his wife, "On my way back should I pick up some carry-out?"

Unlike Mary Poppins, so free and—at least symbolically—"on the rise," Consuela, at twenty-two, has a seven-year-old child of her own living in El Salvador with Consuela's mother. As Barbara explained to me later, the baby-sitter shared a small two-bedroom apartment with two workers and her husband, a salad waiter at the Toreador Restaurant. As an undocumented worker, Consuela fears the immigration authorities. "She never goes to the park with Cary because she's afraid they'll find her." Unlike Mrs. Banks on the video screen, Barbara has just returned from a ten-hour day at the office, and unlike Mr. Banks, John is picking up carry-out from the deli down the street. Consuela's life and the Livingstons' in the United States today seem at least as far apart as those of Mary Poppins and the Banks family a hundred years ago in England. If anything, Consuela's life is more different from the Livingstons'. Social class differences seem to have lived on, while relations between men and women slowly change for both Consuela and Barbara, but here I tell Barbara's story.

When I entered the Livingstons' home, I noticed a half-empty trellis standing ready to support a frail, outreaching bougainvillea with leaves of brilliant crimson. A window was cracked. The paint was peeling. As Barbara said, "We haven't had time for the house." It occurred to me later that the house was a little like their marriage, the last entry on a long list of things to fix up. At the moment, they were negotiating with a workman to refloor the kitchen. The dining-room table was heaped with lamps separated from their shades, stacks of books, piles of linen. Only Cary's room looked finished. John and Barbara had painted it themselves, green walls carefully edged with red, yellow, blue, and orange hearts at the top, which matched the hearts decorating Cary's pillow cover. A hat collection hung behind her bed, next to a clown puppet. Their bedroom, the living room—these awaited attention. With ten-hour workdays and Saturday fractured into a dozen errands, many things had to wait, but not Cary, not Cary's room.

At thirty-four, Barbara is a youthful, lively woman with soft brown eyes, short, dark hair, and—considering the eight times the phone rang that evening—a consistently friendly telephone voice. She manages a large health club and beauty shop in Daly City. John is thirty-seven, tall, thin, with sandy hair; his crinkly eyes betray the quiet sense of humor that has recently gotten him through tough times at work and home. He works in the billing department of a plastics wholesale company.

Both began their interviews by describing hard times in their childhoods. Barbara described growing up in a gaggle of girls in a working-class Catholic family in Wisconsin, an alcoholic father, and a strong mother who died when Barbara was fifteen. John told me about a taciturn father who moved away to an empty room of the house when company came. For as long as John can recall, his mother worked as a waitress, even taking an extra job selling ice cream on weekends. "All I can remember is their criticizing me," he said. "It made me a quiet person myself." For most couples, marriage is a chance to heal and restore each other emotionally, but for the Livingstons this healing was vital. They had been married for nine years.

In strategy, Barbara was a supermom, and to a lesser degree, John was a superdad. Barbara left the house at 7:45, returned at 5:30. (The last four months had been unusually busy in her office: "I've eaten dinner and gone back to the office for two or three more hours, and worked ten hours a day on Saturdays.") What made Barbara a supermom was not her long hours at work but the four hours of concentrated time she devoted to Cary after work. She encouraged Cary to take two-and-a-half-hour naps during the afternoon so that she could stay up until 9:30 or 10:00 (according to Barbara), 10:00 or 11:00 (according to John), to play with her parents in the evenings. Also, as John explained, "Cary doesn't sleep on weekends. She makes up the sleep on weekday afternoons." These days, Cary often woke up two or three times a night, and usually Barbara got up to "march her back to bed." This meant Barbara subsisted on an interrupted seven hours of sleep a night, although, as she explained with a laugh, "I'm not one of those people who feel just fine with five hours a night."

Barbara split the housework and child care 50-50 with John and had not struggled for this. John had always shared in the sense Greg Alston had shared the second shift—in time but not in responsibility. Consuela helped with some of the cleaning, and Barbara was the organizer and Cary's primary parent. As John noted, "On weekends, Barbara mainly takes care of Cary. I would if she'd ask me, but she doesn't." One evening at dinner, as John moved his chair closer to Cary's feeding table, just as Cary slithered down from it, Cary's toe accidentally got caught under John's chair and she cried hard. John took her in his lap, soothed her with soft, explanatory talk, and cradled her warmly. But Barbara stood up to lift Cary out of her daddy's lap and to comfort her in the same way, herself. John handed her over.

Like many couples, Barbara and John also cut back on housework. On the cooking, John declared, "About forty percent of the time we buy take-out, eat out, or don't eat." They cut back on clothes shopping: "Except for Cary's things, we don't shop. We don't need anything," Barbara said. They no longer walked their nine-month-old German Shepherd, Daisy, but left her to pace their small backyard. Guilty over neglecting Daisy, they were wondering whether to give her away. They also cut back on letter-writing. ("Five years ago we found our Christmas cards in the glove compartment of our car in June. They'd never been mailed, and we haven't sent any since.")

John told me that Barbara's job "matters as much as mine," and Barbara agreed. As with the Alstons, neither spouse had much leisure, but the responsibility for the home was mainly Barbara's. She decided what needed doing and asked John to do errands, which in a considerate spirit he always did. Although John was often "on board" as much as Barbara, as fully interested in Cary and as fully skilled in primary parenting, Barbara wanted to be more primary to Cary. She, not John, had stayed home on "parental leave," and that had seemed to set a pattern they both allowed to remain.

They felt the problem was not their *division* of labor. It was the huge amount of time that housework, Cary, and careers were taking from their *marriage*. Barbara commented with a sigh, "I can't remember the last time we went out alone." And she found it hard to talk about their marriage.

In fact, Barbara had talked for nearly two hours in a relaxed way about how her father had remarried, to a wonderful woman, but was living in a trailer now, watching TV all day and drinking heavily. She had chatted about the day-to-day events of working and raising Cary, when she came upon the fact that she and John were "seeing a counselor. . . ." Suddenly she burst into tears, paused, then continued softly, "Because we felt like our marriage wasn't working out."

It Started with the Birth of the Baby

There are certain ways during an interview that a husband and wife show how they are related. They will sigh or gesture together. (This evening Barbara and John had spontaneously laughed together at John's microwaving Daisy's meat bones.) When I interview one, he or she will spontaneously talk at length about the other. And this will be because when I ask a question about one spouse's feelings about work or children, the response will naturally reflect a bond with the other. Often the answers to the housework checklist (who cleans the dishes, makes the beds, etc.) reflect the telltale "both . . . both . . . both. . . ." The interviews will describe different lives but reflect experience in common and genuine empathy for any experience that remains unshared. All of this was true of Barbara and John. Whatever problems they had, I felt, were in spite of the fact they loved each other very much.

I asked them if they wanted to talk about the problem in their marriage. They said they did; it might help. What was the problem? The problem was not their child. They were profoundly pleased with their exuberant, bright, winsome, curly-headed daughter and wanted another child just like her. For different reasons, both were unhappy in their present jobs, but neither lived for career, anyway. They never fretted or quarreled about money, and neither one spent much. ("Barbara will call from the store and ask me whether she should buy a blouse, and I'll tell her, sure, but why are you asking?") Many of the usual causes of trouble didn't bother the Livingstons.

They said the problem was partly that they lacked time together. Softhearted people, they opened their home to dozens of kin and friends in need. Barbara's father stayed with them for six months when Barbara was pregnant with Cary, gradually gaining weight and getting off the bottle. Shortly after that, they invited Barbara's mentally retarded cousin to live with them. On a regular basis two or three nights a week, they invite friends or out-of-town colleagues to dinner.

In addition to the continual rounds of hospitality, they heaped loving attention on Cary, and this, too, effectively prevented them from talking to each other. As Barbara explained: "We were in a bad habit for a while. One of us would lie down with Cary and then fall asleep. Whoever was awake would drag the other to bed half-dozing. Now we're trying to get Cary to sleep earlier so we can have some time together. But it's a slow process, and scary, because we got so far apart."

They both recognized a pattern of avoidance. But what were they avoiding? Barbara said: "I'll say something critical. He'll withdraw. We're afraid that we won't know what to say to each other, and we'll have to face some things. I felt that he was holding things back from me. But he wasn't. He's just like that. And in my hurt, I developed a shell that just got thicker and thicker. I lost touch with what makes me happy. I just knew something was wrong."

I asked John, "How much do you feel the problems you've had communicating and feeling close with Barbara are related to having two careers and a family?" He answered:

It probably *all* stems from that. The problem started with Cary being born. The sex part of our relationship diminished a lot after Cary was born, mostly on my part. It was nil for a long time. Maybe I was jealous of Cary, because for the six years Barbara and I were married before the baby, I was the most important person to her. Maybe I just depended on Barbara too much and then when she had to share herself with Cary, the problem started.

When Cary was four months old, Barbara went back to full-time work at her old job, and Consuela came from eight-fifteen until six o'clock. At this point, John got some time with Cary but not under the relaxed condition he would have liked. And now the pressures on Barbara had slowly escalated as well. As John put it:

> I don't know if I resented it, but for several months while Barbara was working those long hours I would come home and spend most of the night with Cary, which was okay. But I resented Barbara not being there because I wanted a few minutes to myself. Then I felt that Cary was being cheated by her not being here. And I wanted Barbara to spend more time with me. I think I withdrew, then. I didn't want to complain, to make her feel guilty about working long hours.
> Sometimes when I get angry I don't talk. And when I don't talk, that makes her mad. It led to our not communicating.

John had found in Barbara the one person who could communicate with him in a way that his mother and father never had, and now depended on her for that. When Cary was born, Barbara focused on the baby. John focused on Barbara, feeling excluded, hurt, and angry.

At the same time, John felt these weren't the "right" feelings: he wanted to have as much paternal feelings toward Cary as Barbara had maternal ones. But perhaps because Barbara unconsciously crowded him out, perhaps because he didn't know how to feel paternal, that's not how it worked out. On the surface, the idea was "we are equally involved in parenting Cary." But in reality, it didn't feel that way. Given John's belief that his wife's career should be as important to her as his career was to him, John felt too *guilty* to complain about her long hours. In the face of this conflict, he withdrew and began working longer hours at his own job:

> The first year after Cary was born, I worked sixty, seventy hours a week. If I walked out [of the office] before seven o'clock, I'd get dirty looks. I really got involved in advertising for our products. The first year they said I was the greatest thing. Blah blah blah. Don't let us down. Blah blah blah. I felt insecure; I wanted to please them. But I also felt this anger building inside me, like I *could* have been spending more time with Cary.
>
> My bosses were jerks, workaholic lawyers. I wasn't an attorney, and to them you were nothing if you weren't an attorney. When the market for our plastics declined, they completely lost interest in me. Later, when I quit, they hired two people to replace me.
>
> Both my bosses had babies Cary's age. Their wives had part-time interests. One was a potter. The other sold Mary Kay products. After seven o'clock each night, each wife would start telephoning the office. One guy was devastated for months because he had a girl instead of a boy. What a jerk!

Finally, John quit his job and was quickly hired by another company, where once again his work situation was difficult: "There are three vice presidents. None of them trust me, because I'm not Japanese. I'm getting nasty telexes from my boss in Tokyo asking 'Where's this?' and 'Where's that?' Then my boss in Los Angeles is talking to the people who work under me about my Tokyo boss's complaints."

Feeling abandoned at home and criticized at work, John began to suffer anxiety attacks. As he described:

> The first attack I had was at work. I was on my way out of the office to go to lunch and all of a sudden I just got dizzy and passed out. When I woke I was on the floor. I thought I'd had a heart attack. From then on, it happened just about

every day, for almost a year. My hyperventilation starts when I wake up in the morning. It happens when I'm getting up, taking a shower, getting dressed. Sometimes I sit down for an hour before I can leave, because I'm hyperventilating. It hasn't happened for a number of months. But like yesterday morning, I just sat here for twenty minutes. I was on my way out the door, ready to go, but I felt the anxiety building up. I shake. I can't breathe. I just thought, "No, I can't drive."

For his anxiety, his doctor prescribed Xanax, but now John had gradually become dependent on it: "They do control my anxiety, but they're downers. They make me lose sexual interest. I used to take about two a day. I wanted to get off them; every time I'd call for a refill I'd hope they'd say no. I'm still taking them, but not nearly as often."

Desperate for a nonchemical solution to his anxiety, John went to a biofeedback institute, where his instructor told him he was suffering from "male menopause." But John was doubtful: "I don't think that was it. I felt my anxiety had more to do with my home life and my work. I didn't go back."

Never in his life had he so needed someone to talk to and never had it seemed so hard. Barbara was trying her level best to take care of Cary and her job; beyond that she felt trapped in the heavy silence between them.

In the eighteenth century, young parents like John and Barbara might have been faced with a bad crop of corn, a fire in the barn, a child's colic. And one might have suffered a "nervous disorder," said to be caused by diet and damp weather. Each might have found it hard to communicate. Each might have felt alone. But they wouldn't have dreamed of divorce.

As a late-twentieth-century couple, the Livingstons required of their marriage a higher standard of human happiness. A marriage without talk or sex is, by modern measure, a marriage that need not be. The question of divorce was haunting Barbara and John when they thought of seeing a counselor.

The counselor suggested that they ask the mentally retarded cousin to leave the house, that they put Cary to bed earlier, that John wean himself from the Xanax, and that they both give more time to their marriage. But where would the time come from? The first shift, or the second? John thought this:

> I think Barbara should consider a part-time job, or—yes, quitting. I know she enjoys working. I don't know if she wants to be home. Maybe I'm placing too much of a burden on her to ask her to quit. I'd be willing to stay home. It's not necessary that she be here, just that one of us be here to spend more time with Cary. I think deep down Barbara would like not to have to work so much. But she won't admit that. I guess we don't know what she wants to do.

I asked him, "You'd be willing to quit your job?"

> Yes, it seems less natural for me, but if Barbara decided she wanted to work full time, and if we could arrange it financially, I'd quit my job and stay home with Cary, and if we have another child, stay home with both of them. It would take a little time to adjust, but I could do it. I think I would need to have some interest, some part-time work and make some financial contribution too, as little as it might be.

John said he wanted Barbara to quit because of *Cary*. But it was he, not Cary, who was feeling deprived.

I asked Barbara if she would be willing to quit her job to stay home with Cary. She looked vague. "I don't know. I can't feel my feelings." When she gave her reasons for working, she mentioned such things as "wanting to be able to spend twenty dollars for lunch with friends rather than three dollars for a sandwich at Bill's." The work itself, she went on to explain, was a little boring just now. Then, dissatisfied with her answer, she repeated, "I don't know what I'm feeling."

Barbara and John's family myth had been: Barbara can't stop to talk to John because she's a busy working mother. The counselor had begun to show them that Barbara's perpetual motion had also become a way to avoid conflict with John. Now she didn't dare stop.

This fear of conflict struck me during a certain episode that occurred in the kitchen one evening I was with them. John was preparing a delicious baked chicken from his own recipe. Barbara was sitting at the kitchen table, teaching Cary Spanish names for the parts of the body. ("Where are your *manos*? Where is your *cabeza*? Where are your *ojos*?") Consuela spoke little English, and Barbara was trying to create some consistency. They had invited Ann, an acquaintance in town on business from Kansas, to dinner. Ann turned out to be a dog fancier ("rather have a dog than a child") who was two weeks past the signing of her divorce. Daisy, meanwhile, had been banished to the cellar, where she was silently cutting teeth on Cary's old dolls. Occasionally looking toward the cellar door, the guest held a polite smile while Cary tied a chair to the garbage can with a long rope. I was also a guest that evening, talking for the moment with Cary.

Barbara asked me if I'd read the book *How to Be a Better Parent*. I said I hadn't. In what little time she and John had available, she was eager that they learn how to be the best parents they could. In particular, she'd noticed that she was more often the disciplinarian, John more often the "softy." One thing they already did well was parenting; feeling confident, perhaps, that they could build on that strength, she said to John: "You'll want to read *How to Be a Better Parent*. It's really good. We need to work on being more consistent." John looked doubtful. She remarked about another parenting book, which he had liked. "It was okay," John replied. She urged him a bit more to read *Better Parent*. Feeling pressed at work, and perhaps accused of being not quite up to snuff in the one area of life he did feel good about, John turned on her. "Do they have lessons on how to be a bitch?" There was a long, painful silence. "I didn't mean that," he said softly, "I *really* didn't." "There's truth in sarcasm," Barbara replied. They saw no way to undo the harm and, with the two visitors, the embarrassment. Almost against their will, the marital machine had punched out regrettable words that could not be taken back. Finally, the child improvised a new rope game with the guest, amused us all, and the rest of the dinner was fine.

The last I'd heard, the owner had moved Barbara's beauty salon to Stockton, adding a two-hour commute to her workday. Yet, reporting this news, Barbara was curiously relaxed. "So, it will be a long drive," she said. John philosophically added, "We'll have to see what the counselor says."

Two months later, they invited me to dinner again. I said I'd bring dessert. John answered the door. "Nothing's changed," he said right away. "We had twelve for dinner two nights ago. And three friends of Barbara's from New York have been staying overnight." One friend who was moving to San Jose placed an ad in the newspaper for an apartment, listing their home phone number, so the phone rang day and night. I asked if they didn't feel imposed on. "No," John said. "We're happy doing it." Their openheartedness to others, their sociability, their love of commotion was continuing, as John thought it probably always would. "When Cary grows up, I hope she invites friends over."

But despite what John said, something had changed. They had not created more time for themselves; they were beginning to fear it less. I noticed that the house looked more fixed up and settled in. For the first time, John mentioned the idea of a vacation without Cary. On an afterthought, Barbara had decided to keep the dog. Still for the most part the dog was in the yard or basement— set aside, like the marriage. But now they wanted to keep her and she was allowed to frolic excitedly in the kitchen with Cary for a while and urged to calm down before she was sent outside.

Barbara voiced the feeling that, as the grand arranger of the second shift and primary parent to Cary, sometimes she felt like John's mother. Their counselors had assigned John the task of trying to feel and act more like Barbara's father. Before he died, John's father had not put his hand on John's shoulder, had not talked to John about things on his mind. Since John's mother had been uncommunicative as well, there was little in John's childhood he could draw on for this task. But he had a hopeful, exuberant manner as he described trying to feel and act fatherly toward Barbara. It was fun to try. And if Barbara wanted him to, he was pleased to try his very best. It was an "exercise" the counselors had given them, a little embarrassing, but already Barbara looked pleased.

Compared to the time of Barbara's grandmother, Barbara and John lived in an era in which the demands on marriage had increased, expectations of it had risen, and support for it declined. At the very least, one long-range solution for modern marriage probably lies in reducing demands and boosting support. In the meantime, I asked Barbara what advice she would pass on to younger couples. As one who had looked over the brink and returned, she said with feeling, "See a good counselor and work on it."

Sharing Showdown and Natural Drift: Pathways to the New Man

✳

E IGHT out of ten of the men in my study of two-job couples had one thing in common. Like Evan Holt, Peter Tanagawa, Seth Stein, and Ray Judson, they didn't share the care of the home and children. This introduced extra work for their wives and often tension in their marriages. The two men I describe here believe in sharing, and take care of their children as a "primary parent" does. Their starting points differ drastically, as do their means of arrival, but the influence on their marriage and children is the same.

Michael Sherman

As the only son of an immigrant who began work at the age of twelve and rose to the top of the scrap-metal business in New Jersey, Michael Sherman became the repository of all his father's ambition. The reading of Michael's school report cards was a family event, while the cards of his two older sisters received little notice. From kindergarten through high school, he was always first in his class. Now, as a man of thirty, he recalls still with a touch of bitterness how his father would dangle him on his lap, showing him off to admiring old men, and between report cards lose interest in him.

He grew up, therefore, more in the company of his mother, his two older sisters, and a maid. When Michael was eighteen and left for college, his father suffered a nervous breakdown so serious that

he never recovered. Having been alternately idolized and neglected as a child, Michael early vowed that he would never treat
his own children as his father had treated him. But, he told me, he
initially expected his marriage to Adrienne to be like his father's
marriage to his mother: he would get the "A's" at work, she would
raise a lovely family.

He wanted Adrienne to be well educated and, in the phrase
circulating in his parents' circle, a "brilliant mother." Unlike his
own mother, though, she "might also work." When Michael was
courting Adrienne, he made it clear: "It's fine if you work, but my
career will come first." He planned a career in microbiology.

Adrienne had been the adored only daughter of older parents.
Her father had walked her into the parlor after dinner—past the
dinner dishes—to read together from the encyclopedia. A gifted
student, she had intended to have "some sort" of career, perhaps
as an anthropologist. Previous boyfriends had shown polite admi-
ration for this plan; but by comparison, Michael seemed genuinely interested in it. His views were more traditional than hers,
but he seemed more flexible than other men she'd met. She agreed
to put his career first. He agreed she should have some sort of
career, and they married.

Three years later, when he was finishing his last year of graduate school, Michael applied for postdoctoral positions, was accepted everywhere, and chose one at Duke University. Adrienne
quit her studies at New York University and applied to the Ph.D.
program in anthropology at Duke, and to two other programs.
She was turned down by all three. So she arrived in Durham as
Michael's wife, the rejected doctoral candidate. In New York,
where she had done two years of graduate work already, she had
been praised as an outstanding student in her department. Her
mentor had invited her to lunch to discuss her work. She had
close friends and colleagues. Now she sat alone every day in the library staring blankly at a cold stack of books, so miserable she
could hardly read.

After a few months of this, something in Adrienne snapped.

One evening, Michael came home at five o'clock from his "real" job as a postdoctoral fellow. Adrienne arranged to come home at the same time from her "unreal" job in the library as a would-be scholar trying to read. At 5:05, when Michael sat down as usual to read the paper and wait for dinner, Adrienne exploded in a burst of fury and tears. Why did *his* day entitle him to rest? Didn't *her* day count too? It was bad enough that the world was ignoring her career plans; did he have to ignore them too? She had been happy to follow him to Duke; that was fine. But she desperately needed his support for her own fragile career plans, and sharing the second shift was a symbol of that support.

Michael was baffled. Hadn't they *agreed* long ago his work came first? Why this sudden storm? It was so unfair. Maybe Adrienne was still feeling stung by Duke's rejection. Maybe this would pass with time, he thought. But it didn't pass. Adrienne remained distressed and determined. If Michael couldn't bring himself to value her career ambitions as he valued his own, if he couldn't symbolically express this by sharing housework, she told him she would leave. Michael refused, and Adrienne left.

What *had* happened to Adrienne? After all, she had married Michael in good faith on terms they had agreed on. Only a year earlier, among supportive colleagues and planning a brilliant career, she could never have imagined leaving. Part of her also loved being a homemaker and a hostess; before our first interview in her San Francisco home, she served me home-baked nut bread, carefully softened butter, and coffee freshly ground and brewed. She was beautifully dressed and had a stylish hairdo. She was not, it seemed, in flight from femininity or the domestic sphere.

But on the evening she had left Michael five years earlier, she couldn't bear the idea of staying home. As Daddy's girl, the future scholar, she had done so very well. It had felt so good. As she sat alone in the library, rejected and isolated, staring blankly at her book, she wanted even more to do well again. She desperately needed Michael to back her up or she didn't want to be with him.

With Adrienne gone, Michael stopped to consider his choice.

He felt that she knew and loved him far more deeply than any other woman could; and despite how impossible she'd been, he loved her. After two months, he woke up one morning with a decision: he could do without being waited on, could do without his career coming first. He'd rather have Adrienne back. He called to tell her he would share the second shift, and she quickly came back. Raised as a little king, Michael had never done housework before, but now in their modest apartment he did half. Adrienne felt much happier, and so now did Michael. Now on the new terms, Adrienne could brave it at the library.

Adrienne wanted Michael to share not only because it was fair to her but because she wanted equality to be just as important to him as it was to her. In truth, Michael shared the second shift because he loved Adrienne and knew how terribly important it was to her. At least that was his main thought at first.

Adrienne applied to the graduate program in anthropology at Duke the next year, and this time she got in. After her first year there, Michael made another sacrifice in a spirit of genuine support. Although he had finished at Duke, he stayed on for an extra year so Adrienne could collect data for her thesis. For the first time, she applied for an instructorship. One day, her mother telephoned, trying to be supportive according to her own lights. She said to Adrienne, "You have so much to do, dear, I hope you don't get the job." Adrienne collapsed in tears. Michael picked up the phone, indignant at his mother-in-law. "What do you *mean* you hope Adrienne doesn't get the job? She *wants* the job!"

After Adrienne finished her thesis research, she followed Michael again to the best job he was offered. Miracle of miracles, she was offered an excellent job in a nearby city. She spoke with quiet humor about a memo tacked on the anthropology department bulletin board listing all job applicants and the posts they had won: her name was at the top. "First I was seen as the tagalong wife with the chopped-up career. Then they saw that list and suddenly thought I was the hot stuff and Michael was following me!" Now the twists of fate could seem funny.

In the sixth year of marriage—three years after the showdown and one year after beginning teaching—they decided to have a child. When Adrienne got pregnant, Michael spoke proudly of "our pregnancy." Bedridden for the last two months, Adrienne taught seminars from their living-room couch. Michael did all the cooking and shopping and planning. When twin boys were born, Michael came home every day in time for the five-thirty feeding. As he recalled, "It was *very* important to me to be there for that feeding." Adrienne found it hard to handle both twins; for a while, before she finished breast-feeding one, the other was awake and ready. After six weeks they switched to the bottle. Michael fed one twin, Adrienne fed the other.

The twins grew into a rambunctious pair. One would climb on the other's back to try to scramble up the chimney. With conspiratorial giggles, they would push on the garden gate together, open it, and dash up the street. Once they took turns drenching each other in a bucket of motor oil. If Adrienne's showdown had forced Michael to "concede" to sharing, now Michael was having fun with it. As he reflected, "I'm amazed at myself. I hadn't imagined the extent of nurturing feelings I have that I had really played down." He began to feel proud: "I honestly think I'm the best father I know. I'm surprised at how patient I am, and also at how impatient." For their part, the twins responded appealingly to his attentions, and drew him into their play. Crossing the street, each reached up for Daddy's hand. They alternated in the mornings, calling for Daddy or Mommy. In search of more time to spend with his sons, Michael asked for some leave time from his university. Part of the time, he had to travel to give papers, but that was fine with Adrienne.

But, increasingly, Adrienne was under more pressure at work. Now in her fourth year in the anthropology department, she found herself in fierce competition for tenure with six hardworking male assistant professors. How many articles had she published this year? How many more in the works? When was the "big" book due? Her department chairman took fiendish pride in telling junior colleagues how "tough it really was." He admitted that Adrienne put in far more time guiding student research than her male colleagues, but reminded her "as surely she knew" that teaching didn't matter in getting tenure.

When the twins were three, Adrienne was out of the house forty-five hours a week and worked all evening after they were in bed. Even with this effort, she was falling behind male colleagues whose wives took care of their second shift. As Adrienne explained:

> I realized I was going to sink in my mid-career review unless I published. So that fall when I was dashing around madly teaching and doing committee work during the week, I started working weekends. I worked through five weekends in a row, and I'll never do it again. It was a complete disaster. My kids regressed a hundred and one paces. They were upset about being separated from me, because Michael was out of town at a conference. First I tried working in the study at home, but that was too hard. Then I went into my office, and that's where I got a surprise. One of my colleagues said, "What brings *you* in?" And another said, "We haven't seen you in all four years you've been here." These are the guys who've said to me—I must have heard it fifteen times in my four years here—"You've got your husband to support you." And when I meet them in the halls they always say, "How are the *twins*?"

During this period, the Shermans' baby-sitter grew depressed, began to drink heavily, and one day disappeared completely. Michael could do his share, but no more. For the first time in years, Michael yelled at Adrienne: "I'm happy you have a career, but I don't think you should have a career *like this*. There's an upper limit."

She knew he was right. Adrienne asked her chairman to delay her tenure review but he refused ("If I did it for you, I'd have to do it for everyone"). She felt she'd reached a dead end and thought of quitting. She could combine an old interest in sculpting with child therapy, a job outside a hierarchy. One comment by a rival faculty member, which she had suppressed to smooth her way before, rang in her head now: "Do you *really* feel like a mother to your children? Or is your housekeeper more their mother?" His tone said, "It must be hard on you," but he meant, "It must be hard on *them*."

Adrienne spoke to a senior colleague about extending her tenure review deadline despite the chairman's veto. Out of sympathy and perhaps guilt over their own struggling wives, the faculty granted her an extension. She asked for a half-time appointment, and, with Michael's support, she fought for it. After more than a year of meetings; letters; calls; and long talks with deans, colleagues, and a network of feminists in other departments, Adrienne became the fifth faculty member on the entire campus to be granted a half-time tenure-track position.

Michael had yelled at Adrienne for withdrawing from the children, but had dissuaded her from falling into a swoon of maternal guilt and retreating into sculpture and flower arranging. He had hung in there. If a sharing showdown had shocked Michael into a strange journey toward equality, now he was discovering who he could be as a father and husband when he wasn't being the showcase kid. He was growing into it. Michael's salary was higher than Adrienne's, but this wage gap—the same issue that loomed so large for others—didn't come up in the Shermans' interviews until I raised it, and then neither had much to say about it. Neither job came first; both came second.

Michael did not struggle with Adrienne; both now struggled against the pressures of their careers. Twins or no, their professional worlds spun on; colleagues wrote books, won prizes, got promotions. Both loved their work, and it took discipline to moderate their ambition. Adrienne was now also part of the tiny world of women professors busily scurrying from one committee ("It's an all-male committee, we really need a woman, could you . . . ?") to another, addressing the endless student demand for attention from "concerned" teachers, and finally settling down at night with a cup of tea to the "real" work of writing. Some of these women had children, many were waiting. All were overworked and some generated a workaholic subculture of their own, which put pressure on all of them in turn.

If the Shermans had a "family myth," it was perhaps that Michael's transformation involved little sacrifice. The twins were one surprise after another. It was so much fun, he didn't want them growing up so fast. At the same time, it was hard for a straight-A showcase kid, carrier of the Sherman line, to backpedal his scientific career while others around him were making a run for it, like Seth Stein. Holding back at work was a sacrifice. Changing his view of manhood midstream was a sacrifice. These were sacrifices other men—men like Evan Holt, Peter Tanagawa, Seth Stein— did not make, and in the eyes of women like Adrienne, this made Michael rare and precious. In the present-day relational marketplace, his market value was higher than hers. They were off the "marital market," because they couldn't imagine life apart; this shielded Adrienne from the unfavorable market realities. But she also felt deeply indebted to Michael for his sacrifices. If there was just a tiny bit of unresolved tension beneath their family myth, it centered on just how grateful Adrienne should feel to Michael for getting a "fair deal" in the second shift.

Meanwhile, both gave up the spectacular career success they might have had for the respectable careers their attention to family allowed. To some colleagues, Adrienne's half-time schedule made her seem like a dilettante. To half-disapproving, half-threatened neighboring housewives she was one of those briefcase-and-bow-tie women. By working short hours in a long-hours profession, by taking odd times of the day off to be with his kids, Michael was even more anomalous. Both felt morally isolated from their conventional relatives in upstate New York, who continued to write puzzled letters and from many of Michael's male colleagues who ran through more wives but seemed to get more work done. Neither the old world of family nor their new world of work fit them easily. But they fit each other, and pulled together against the social tide.

During my last meeting with the Shermans, they took turns laughing and telling me this story. The previous summer when they were visiting Michael's parents, Michael began clearing the dishes off the dining-room table. His mother, who now approved of their arrangement, remarked to his father, "Look how Michael clears the table. Why didn't *you* ever do anything like that?" Michael's father replied solemnly, "Adrienne is turning Michael into a homosexual." "Oh, Jacob," Mrs. Sherman cried, "don't be ridiculous!" Adrienne and Michael looked on, laughing and incredulous as Michael's mother began a sharing showdown of her own.

Art Winfield: Natural Drift

Art Winfield, a thirty-five-year-old laboratory assistant with a high school education, had only the barest acquaintance with the women's movement, and, unlike Adrienne Sherman, his wife had never pressed him to do more at home. But Art has a natural interest in children and a passion for being with his five-year-old adopted son, Adam. Art is not the self-consciously celebrated New Man; he is a gentle, easygoing, black man, the New Man disguised as an ordinary fellow.

He was taking night classes twice a week in lab technology mainly at his wife's urging; she had hoped these classes might motivate him to search out more interesting work. But as he drove to and from his lab, Art's mind would wander from his job to the bright smile that would light his son's face when he greeted him at the day-care center door. "My son gets only three-and-a-half hours of my time a day," Art explained, "so the time I'm with him is very important to me." Sometimes when he came to fetch Adam at day care, Art lingered for half an hour or so to see a secret hideout, climb a favorite tree, or organize a relay race. During several months when he was on leave from the lab, he stayed longer.

The Winfields needed two salaries to live, no question about it, so Adam had to be in day care. But Art's feelings about it are mixed: "Adam's best buddy, his number-one main man is there [at the day-care center]. But sometimes he gets tired of being there. It's real hard for a five-year-old kid to spend eight hours away from home. Sometimes I'll take the day off and take him out of day care and spend the day with him."

Wherever people found Adam on a weekend—bicycling, visiting a favorite uncle, collecting rocks—they found Art. Friends and relatives called them "the twins." Basking in the subject of his tie to his son, Art reflected: "We're affectionate toward each other. Sometimes I wonder if I overdo it. But I think a father-son relationship happens pretty easily."

Some fathers reach out more easily to a son than to a daughter, but this didn't seem true for Art. He and his wife, Julia, who is white, are trying to have a child of their own, and when I asked him how he felt about a daughter, he replied:

> I'd *love* to have a little girl. Yeah. I think little girls are
> precious. I'd like to have a father-daughter relationship, and
> I guess I'm sort of nontraditional when it comes to that.
> Regarding sports, or her basic outlook on life. I'd raise my
> daughter just as positively as a boy. My wife is a strong
> woman and I'd like to have a daughter like that too. Girls
> are very smart! They certainly learn a lot quicker than boys
> do. That's quite obvious. Plus it would be special for Adam
> to have a sister.

Art also enjoys children who are not his own, and they flock to him. Tough teenage boys drop by the Winfields' home in a rough neighborhood of East Oakland to show off their pit bull dogs, and talk. When there's trouble in the neighborhood, they protect the Winfields' home. One disturbed boy showed up regularly on Art's porch. As Art recalled:

> It was a challenge to me to get to know him, because I
> knew what he needed. His mother was raising five kids by
> herself, and he needed some attention. We worked together.

He came around and got to be one heck of a kid. His grades improved. Now he's an "A" student. He knew I was really serious about my relationship toward him, that I wasn't trying to prove I could conquer and make him be an exceptional individual. He just turned out to be a real good kid, which he was *anyway*. He's eighteen now and the bond is still pretty tight.

Art's wife, Julia, feels she lacks Art's gift with children:

I love my own son, but I'm not good with everyone's kids, like Art is. I'm one of these people who doesn't know how old a child is. I'll ask, "How old are you?" And they'll say, "Why do you want to know, lady?" But Art knows what level to approach a child on. After a long day's work, it's hard for me to compliment all the little kids at day care on their finger painting the way he does.

Art focuses on children. About tending house he simply feels that "sharing is fair." As he puts it:

I went through a period where I wasn't really involving myself in a lot of housework—like most men, I have to admit. That's conditioning, too, because we're led to believe we're lords and masters of the household [laughs]—that there are certain things we're not supposed to do. Also, I'm kind of stubborn and it's wrong to be like that. Anyway, Julia works as hard as I do, probably a lot harder. She deserves to have me participate. So, for about ten months, since Julia's had to work overtime at her office, I've been doing half.

Art does the laundry, vacuuming, yard work, and half the cooking. Julia, a plump, good-natured woman of thirty, appreciates the help. But she also wishes that Art loved his work more. It seems to make her a bit anxious to be more engrossed in her own job as a legal secretary than Art is in his. She doesn't care about money; between them she feels they have plenty. It was more a matter of her wanting him to be drawn to his job—because it is good for people to like their work, maybe especially if they are men.

For his part, Art feels that $25,000 is pretty good pay, and that the center of a man's life ought to be his family. He wonders at Julia's ambitions for him. Does it mean there is something wrong with him? Does he seem inadequate? He explained to me in confidence that he thought her anxiety might be due to her desire to please her older brother, a conventional man who had never approved of her interracial marriage, or of their house in East Oakland. Art talked the matter over privately with his mother by phone, and finally agreed, without enthusiasm, to let Julia type out a résumé for him and apply for an evening course in laboratory technology.

I asked Art why he thought his bond with his son was so warm, relaxed, and strong. He began his answer with his early childhood. His mother had raised his brother and himself by working as a cook in a child-care center. As he put it, "I could give you the whole black saga—living in a dingy apartment, sleeping in bed with my brother and my mother, rats jumping over it at night." From time to time, his father would appear at their apartment, argue bitterly with his mother, then disappear. "I think my father helped me know what kind of man I *didn't* want to be," Art said. He continued: "He was my biological father. And from the time I was born until I was nine, he was all I had as a father. We didn't really have the fatherly thing when I was coming up. Because my mother was a very strong force, I didn't realize I was missing a father."

When Art was nine, his mother married a longshoreman, a strong, gentle, kindly man with no children of his own. He worked the evening shift and was home days, waiting for Art when he came barreling in the door after school. Coming to trust and love this man was the most important event in Art's life:

When he married my mother, he understood that it would take some time to interject himself into our family. I can recall that he took his time doing that. He got to understand us first. I was a sensitive kid, and the youngest, and it had to be explained to me that my mother was still going to be there, that he was joining the family to make it a little better. He was a *gentle* man, a *good* man.

Art spoke of his stepfather with great softness:

> I don't call him my stepfather. He's my *father*. He's everything a father ever could be. I love him as if I was the biological son. Because he's a good man. He's a gentle man. He's a very honest man. We were always together. I had a father that was always there to help me whenever I needed something. He wouldn't *give* me anything, but he made me realize I had to work for what I wanted. He really did teach us how to love. . . . Through him I learned what I want to do with my own kid. I'm trying to form the same kind of relationship. I want Adam to know that I *really* care about him.

Vacations at his grandmother's farm in Arkansas were vacations "with my father." As he spoke about this his eyes dampened, as if it was *still* hard for him to believe his stepfather loved him. "I hate to keep saying this," he said, "but it's true, he's a *very* warm man."

Perhaps Art's double legacy—a father he did *not* want to be like and a stepfather he *did* want to be like—prompted his gift with children. In his bond with his own adopted son he may be consolidating his own great boyhood victory.

A THIRD STAGE OF FATHERHOOD

Neither Michael Sherman nor Art Winfield told "pliers" jokes like Greg Alston or waited until the end of a wail of a nine-month-old who's tumbled. They had their own styles of hands-on parenting.

Michael Sherman and Art Winfield differ in how they arrived at a comfort with it. Michael backed in, starting with housework and moving to child-rearing. Art stepped forward into it, starting with his feeling for Adam and quietly extending a principle of justice to housework. Fifty-fifty meant slightly different things to each; for Michael it was a way to "be fair to Adrienne," for Art it was a way of "being a number-one Dad to Adam." The results differ too: Michael is as much the primary parent to the twins as his wife; Art seems slightly more involved than his.

Certain motives forged in boyhood made them want to be the "New Man." Both had grown up in largely female worlds; both had reacted against "bad" fathers, and neither had grown up as what they imagined to be a typical male. Even as a teenager, Art had been unusually good with small kids, which past a certain age among teenagers in East Oakland was unusual. Michael had never felt like a "typical boy." He didn't reject things masculine; he got along with the guys at school. But he didn't feel the most interesting things went on in the male world or that the most interesting people were there. In truth, Michael hadn't outgrown a traditional male identity; he'd never had one. In his high school gym class and later during basic training in the army, much of the time he felt he was acting the male role. It was as if he had grown up speaking a foreign language, fluently and without a noticeable accent, but a language not quite his own. As he put it, "I was always the guy hanging around the edge of the football field." Different motives animate a way of seeing manhood and these private motives animated theirs. So when the door of history opened, when the culture lit the way, when the demands of two-job life called out, they wanted to walk in.

In the history of American fatherhood, there have been roughly three stages, each a response to economic change. In the first, agrarian stage, a father trained and disciplined his son for employment, and often offered him work on the farm, while his wife brought up the girls. (For blacks, this stage began after slavery ended.) As economic life and vocational training moved out of the family in the early nineteenth century, fathers left more of the child-rearing to their wives. According to the historian John Nash, in both these stages, fathers were often distant and stern. Not until the early twentieth century, when increasing numbers of women developed identities, beyond brief jobs before marriage, in the schoolhouse, factory, and office, did the culture discover the idea that "father was friendly." In the early 1950s, popular magazines began to offer articles with such titles as "Fathers Are Parents Too" and "It's Time Father Got Back into the Family." Today, we are in the third stage of economic development but the second stage of fatherhood.

Men like Michael Sherman and Art Winfield lead the way into that third stage, but they've done so privately. They are tokens in the world of new fathers. Lacking a national social movement to support them in a public challenge to the prevailing ideal of manhood, they've acted on their own. Not until the other Michael Shermans and Art Winfields step forward, not until a critical mass of men becomes like them, will we end the painful stall in this revolution all around us.

Beneath the Cover-up:
Strategies and Strains
❋

I n the ten marriages I've described, the second shift became a forum for each person's ideas and feelings about gender and marriage. When Evan Holt fixed dinner, Nancy Holt felt Evan was saying he loved her. When Robert Myerson cooked dinner, Ann half the time felt guilty she was failing to protect his more valuable career from family demands. When Frank Delacorte made the pesto sauce for the pasta, it meant Carmen "couldn't." When Peter Tanagawa roasted the chicken, it meant he was "helping Nina." When Ray Judson barbecued the spare ribs, Anita imagined he did it because he liked to, not to help her out. When Seth and Jessica ate the meal the housekeeper cooked, Jessica figured it was her salary that paid the housekeeper, Seth's salary that paid for the food. The personal meanings of the second shift differed greatly, but to most people they either meant "I am taken care of" or "I am taking care of someone."

Some personal meanings leaned toward a traditional ideal of caring, and others toward a gender equal ideal. Indeed, a split between these two ideals seemed to run not only between social classes, but between partners within marriages and between two contending voices inside the conscience of a single person. The blue collar tended toward a traditional ideal, and the white collar tended toward a 50-50 one. Men tended toward the first ideal, women toward the second. And Ann Myerson flipped to the

one and flopped to the other. Most marriages were either torn
by, or a settled compromise between, these two ideals. In this
sense, the split between them ran through every marriage I came
to know.

To be sure, I saw important differences in social class. And in
the world at large there are far more couples who spend their Saturdays doing laundry, like the Delacortes or the Judsons, and fewer
who spend them making out checks to the help like the Steins or
the Myersons. The problems of the two-job family are tougher in the
working class, but they are difficult in a different way among the
affluent as well. What exacerbates the strain in blue-collar marriage
is the absence of money to pay for services they need, economic insecurity, poor day care, and lack of dignity and boredom in each
partner's job. What exacerbates it in the upper-middle class is the
instability of paid help and the enormous demands of careers in
which both partners become willing believers. But the tug between
two ideals of manhood and womanhood runs from top to bottom
of the class ladder.

Regardless of the ideal to which a couple aspires, the strain of
working shifts often affects men nearly as much as women. It affects women who work the extra month a year in obvious ways—
through fatigue, sickness, and emotional exhaustion. But one
important finding of this study is that the strain clearly extends to
men as well. If men share the second shift it affects them directly.
If they don't share, it affects them through their wives. Michael
Sherman shared the emotional responsibility and time it took to
do the work at home. He had to redefine his career ambitions, confront the high hopes of his family, and detach himself from the
competition of his colleagues. Evan Holt and Seth Stein made no
such adjustments, but they paid an enormous price nonetheless—
Evan Holt through the resentments so woven into his sexual life
and bond with his son, Joey, Seth through the disappearance of
his wife and children into lives of their own.

GENDER IDEOLOGY, FEELING RULES, AND COPING WITH FEELINGS

When I began this research, I naively imagined that a person's view of gender would cohere as a cognitive and emotional "piece." I imagined this view would go with how he or she wanted to divide the second shift. Couples who believed in 50-50 would share more, those who believed in 70-30 would share less. But I discovered amazing fractures. Peter Tanagawa supported his wife's career "a hundred percent," but grew red in the face at the idea that she would mow the lawn, or that his daughters, when teenagers, would drive a car to school. Many men like Evan Holt lauded their wives' careers. They pointed out that their wives wanted to work. It made their wives more interesting, and it gave the couple more in common. But when it came to a man's part in the work at home, the underlying principle changed. For Robert Myerson the principle seemed to be that a man should share the work at home "if his wife asks him." For Peter Tanagawa, a man should pitch in so long as she's doing a bit more.[1]

More important were the contradictions between what a person said they believed about men and marital roles, and what they seemed to feel about them. Some people were egalitarian "on top" and traditional "underneath" like Seth Stein or traditional on top and egalitarian underneath like Frank Delacorte.

Sometimes the deep feelings that evolved in response to early cautionary tales *reinforced* the surface of a person's gender views. For example, Carmen Delacorte's dread—that she would face the same struggles her mother had as a disparaged single mother—strongly reinforced her idea that women should find male protection through submission to them. On the other hand, Nancy Holt's fear of becoming a "doormat," like her mother, infused emotional steam into her belief that Evan ought to share 50-50 at home. Ray Judson's childhood loss of his mother and his current fear of losing his wife reinforced his idea that a man needs to get a woman dependent on him so that she won't take off.

For other people, covert feelings seemed to subvert the surface of their gender ideology. For example, Ann Myerson described herself growing up as a tomboy who believed girls were "just as good as boys." A hard-driving career woman who didn't begin to consciously want children until she was thirty-two, Ann felt similar to her husband, Robert, in her needs and desires. Yet for some reason, her role at the office didn't feel real while her role at home did. Rather than reinforcing her surface attitudes, this underlying feeling prompted her ambivalent "flip-flop" syndrome.

Similarly, on the surface, John Livingston had always been for sharing the provider and homemaker role. But when his daughter, Cary, was born, he felt that Barbara withdrew her attention from him, leaving him abandoned, dependent, and angry. When Barbara returned to her job, he resented her working. But, he felt guilty about resenting her work. In this way his ideology established a certain feeling rule—you shall feel good about your wife working. Yet this feeling rule clashed with his actual feeling—anger that Barbara was so unavailable. Since it was John's habit to withdraw when he was angry, he withdrew. This withdrawal and Barbara's upset in response to it spiraled into the conflict which, in their "overbusyness," they avoided.

The first year of Cary's life, John withdrew emotionally from Barbara and established himself as second to Barbara in the care of Cary, and as champion of the idea that "someone" needed to care for her more. Insofar as work permitted, he did not resist sharing the second shift; he did it, but he resisted forgiving Barbara for her emotional withdrawal from him. All the minute ways in which John sought to interrelate what he thought (his gender ideology), what he felt (upset by Barbara's withdrawal), and what he did (to work long hours and to cut back on time for the marriage)—this complex of thought, feeling, and action together—constitute his "gender strategy." And the interplay of his gender strategy and that of his wife determined how they actually divided the second shift.

Everyone I interviewed, in one way or another, developed a gender strategy. In some, the surface of a gender ideology strongly conflicted with underlying feelings, in others they didn't. In some, the feeling rule was "We *should want* to share the second shift," "We shouldn't be angry about *having* to share, or angry at the deprivations it might entail" (for example, the Shermans). In others, the feeling rule was to feel ashamed to "have to" share it (the Delacortes). But what a man or woman wanted to do usually did not completely explain what they did. For always a dance was in motion with another.

WOMEN'S STRATEGIES: THE DIRECT APPROACH

Most women who wanted 50-50 did one of two things. They married men who planned to share at home or they actively tried to change him afterward. Before she had children, Adrienne Sherman took the risky step of telling her husband, "It's share or it's divorce." She staged a sharing showdown and won. After she had Joey, Nancy Holt initiated a major crisis in the marriage but backed away from a showdown. Both women confronted their husbands, and caused great upheaval as a result. Other women initiated a series of smaller prods. When she was eight months pregnant and her husband was working nearly all the time, Carol Alston recalls sitting her husband down on the front stairs as he came home from work and saying, "I won't have this baby if you don't emotionally prepare for it with me." Though she didn't really mean she wouldn't have the baby, she was making an important point. Still other women initiated exhaustive talks, which brought their men around.

Over half the working mothers I interviewed had tried one way or another to change roles at home. One reason the effort is so common among women is that they bear the weight of a contradiction between traditional views about men and women and modern circumstances. Unless they assume the extra work of trying to change a common habit, it is usually they who work the extra month a year. If women lived in a culture that presumed active fatherhood, they wouldn't need to devise personal strategies to bring it about.

INDIRECT WAYS TO CHANGE ROLES

Women also tried to change marital roles indirectly. This was a primary strategy for traditional working mothers who desperately needed help at home but who couldn't call on a husband to share the load because they didn't believe in such a thing. Facing such a dilemma, Carmen Delacorte "played helpless" at cooking rice, paying bills, and sewing. Some women, like Nina Tanagawa, used physical illness as a half-conscious signal of distress. One highly successful businesswoman, Susan Pillsbury (a woman who described herself as "sharing equally" with her husband), told this story:

> When I was pregnant we were trying to think what to name the baby and we couldn't think of a name. My husband, Jerry, wanted to have the baby but he wasn't interested in what to name it. I didn't want to ask him to be interested. So, you know he's a consultant in decision analysis; that's his specialty. I suggested that we set out "decision criteria," like the name should be a family name, or the first name should fit the last name well, it should be a certain length. . . . Once I posed it as a problem in decision making, he got so into it he couldn't stop. I always like to tell that story. Now he tells it.

Even women who abhorred "female wiles" sometimes resorted to them. Nancy Holt felt it demeaned women to withhold sex from their husbands in order to angle for something they wanted. But when Evan persistently refused to share, Nancy did withhold sex, and felt remorse about doing so.

SUPERMOMING

In contrast to strategies designed to change roles, supermoming was a way of doing both shifts *without imposing* on their husbands. About a third of mothers pursued this strategy. They put in long hours at the office but kept their children up very late at night to get time with them. Many believed that the extra month was theirs to work. Others wished their husbands would share but didn't feel they had enough moral credits in the "marital bank" to persuade them to do more.

Supermoming was a way of absorbing into oneself the conflicting demands of home and work. To prepare themselves emotionally, many supermoms develop a conception of themselves as "on-the-go, organized, competent," as women without need for rest, without personal needs. Both as a preparation for this strategy and as a consequence of it, supermoms tended to seem out of touch with their feelings. Nina Tanagawa reported feeling "numb." And Barbara Livingston said again and again, "I don't know what I feel."

CUTTING BACK AT WORK

After trying hard to change Evan, Nancy Holt reluctantly cut back her hours at work. As she'd all along planned to do after her second child, Carol Alston willingly cut back hers. After a hopeless succession of quarrelsome baby-sitters, Ann Myerson quit her job. To some women, cutting back felt like a defeat, as it did to Nancy Holt and Ann Myerson. To others, it felt like a great triumph.

Women often prepared emotionally for cutting back by detaching themselves from work-centered friends, renewing friendships with family-centered friends, and generally gathering support for entering a more solitary life at home.

Especially for women in high-powered careers but really for most women who cut back, one major emotional task was to buoy flagging self-esteem. After taking time off for her first baby, Carol Alston felt depressed, "fat," "just a housewife," and wanted to call down the supermarket aisles, "I'm an MBA! I'm an MBA!"

CUTTING BACK ON HOUSEWORK, MARRIAGE, SELF, AND CHILD

Yet another set of strategies involved cutting back on ideas about "what needs to be done" for the house, the child, the marriage, or oneself, and on efforts to meet those needs.

Cutting back on housework was clear, intentional, and almost across the board for those without maids. Traditional working mothers often began the interview with apologies for the house and felt its state reflected on themselves personally. They either felt badly when the house was messy, or thought they should and it was a wrench to disaffiliate their self-esteem from the look of it.

Egalitarian women did the opposite. They tried hard *not* to care about the house, and proudly told me about things they'd let go. As Anita Judson said with a triumphant laugh, "I'm not the type to wash walls." Others questioned the need to make beds, vacuum, clean dishes, pick up toys, or even make meals. As Carol Alston explained, "We eat big lunches, and I'm trying to diet, so dinner's not a big deal."

On the whole, women cared more about how the house looked than men did. When they didn't care, they exerted more effort in trying not to care.

After the birth of their first child, every couple I interviewed devoted less attention to each other. Most couples felt as if they were "waiting" to get more time together. As Robert Myerson commented: "We have no time together alone. We're hanging on until the girls get older." But when marriage became the main or only way of healing past emotional injuries—as it was for John Livingston—it was *hard* to wait.

In the race against time, parents could inadvertently cut back on children's needs as well. For one thing, they cut corners in physical care. One working mother commented: "Do kids have to take a bath every night? We bathe Jeremy every other night and then otherwise wash his face and hands. Sort of sponge him off. He's surviving." Another mother questioned a child's need to change clothes every day: "Why can't kids wear the same pants three or four days in a row? When I was a girl, I had to change into fresh clothes every day, and my favorite clothes went by so quickly." Another mother shared her philosophy of eating greens: "Joshua doesn't eat greens anyway. So we fix something simple—soup and a peanut butter sandwich. He won't die." Another mother sheepishly complained of housewifely standards for preparing Halloween costumes: "God, these mothers that have their Halloween costumes sewn in September! I go 'Oh no! It's Halloween,' and I dash out and buy something." Another working mother lowered the standard for considering a child sick. "I send James to day care when he has a cold. I don't have backup and the other mothers are in the same boat. All the kids there have colds. So he gets their colds. He might as well give them his."

Sadly enough, a few working parents seemed to be making cuts in the emotional care of their child. Especially when parents received more from their own parents than they are giving their children, they were managing guilt. Trying to rationalize her child's long hours in day care, one working mother remarked about her nine-month-old daughter that she "needed kids her age" and "needs the independence." It takes relatively little to cut back on house care, and the consequences are trivial. But not so the needs of a baby.

SEEKING HELP

Some couples who could afford it hired a housekeeper. Others called on mothers, mothers-in-law, or other female relatives for child care though in many cases these women worked as well. Surprisingly few called on their older children, as Ray Judson did, to share house cleaning or care of younger children.

The main outside help, of course, came from baby-sitters. Sometimes mothers tried to make the baby-sitter "part of the family" or at least to create a strong friendship with her, unconsciously perhaps to assure her loyalty and goodwill. Carol Alston left her six-month-old baby with a "wonderful baby-sitter" for eleven hours a day, and gave the sitter a great deal of credit: "My son should call her 'mother.' She's earned it." Carol often invited her sitter and husband to dinner and on outings and exchanged birthday and Christmas gifts. But it was hard for Carol to allay the sitter's doubts that Carol befriended her only *because* she baby-sat the children.

Finally, most women cut back on their own needs. They gave up reading, hobbies, television, visits with friends, exercise, time alone. When I asked her what she did in her leisure, Ann Myerson replied, "Pay bills." When I asked a bank clerk about her "leisure," she answered "time at my terminal." I interviewed no working mothers who maintained hobbies like Evan Holt or Robert Myerson. It was part of the culture of the working mother to give up personal leisure.

Over time, most women combined several strategies—cutting back, seeking outside help, supermoming. There was a big divide between wives who urged their husbands to share the second shift (like Nancy Holt and Adrienne Sherman) and wives who didn't (like Nina Tanagawa and Ann Myerson).

MEN'S STRATEGIES

In part, men's strategies parallel women's, and in part they differ. Some men are superdads, the full or near equivalent to supermoms—John Livingston, for example. When their children were young, other men cut back their emotional commitment or hours at work—like Michael Sherman and Art Winfield. Many men let the house go more, lowered their expectations about time alone with a wife, cut out movies, seeing friends, hobbies. In these ways, some men's strategies paralleled women's.

But for men, the situation differed in one fundamental way. By tradition, the second shift did not fall to them, and it was not a "new idea" that they should do paid work. In the eyes of the world, they felt judged by their capacity to support the family and earn status at work, and got little credit for helping at home, so most men were not pressuring their wives to get more involved at home. They got pressured. That was the big difference. Of the 80 percent of men in this study who did not share the work at home, a majority mentioned some pressure from their wives to do so.

Most men resisted. But their wives' pressure often evoked a number of underlying feelings. "Underneath" Ray Judson's objections to sharing was the fear of losing control of his wife if he wasn't the number one earner. Beneath Peter Tanagawa's resistance was his fear of losing status as a man with the guys back in the valley. Evan Holt feared Nancy was trying to boss him around and get out of caring for him.

For some men, avoiding work at home was a way of "balancing" the scales with their wives. A man may decline to pitch in at home to compensate for his wife's more rapid advance at work, or in other ways gaining "too much" power. (Women do this "balancing" too.) Underlying all these extra reasons to resist sharing was, finally, the basic fact that it was a privilege to have a wife tend the home. If a man shared the second shift, he lost that privilege.

At least at first, most men gave other reasons for not wanting to share: their career was too demanding. Their job was more stressful. When these rationales didn't go over, resistant men resorted to the explanation that they weren't "brought up" to do housework.

Some 20 percent of men expressed the genuine desire to share the load at home, and did. A few men expressed the genuine desire to share but said their wives "took over" at home. As a teacher, and mother of two, put it, "My husband does all the baking. He'd share everything, if I let him." Some men who shared resisted at first but grew into it later. But most of these men ended up feeling like Art Winfield: "I share housework because it's fair and child-rearing because I want to."

Other men resisted, and in a variety of ways. Some did tasks in a distracted way. Evan Holt forgot the grocery list, burned the rice, didn't know where the broiler pan was. Such men withdrew their mental attention from the task at hand so as to get credit for trying and being a good sport, but so as not to be chosen next time. It was a male version of Carmen Delacorte's strategy of playing dumb.

Many men also waited to be asked, forcing their wives to take on the additional chore of asking itself. Since many wives disliked asking—it felt like "begging"—this often worked well. Especially when a man waited to be asked and then became irritated or glum when he was, his wife was often discouraged from asking again.

Some men made "substitute offerings." Peter Tanagawa supported Nina in her every move at work and every crisis at work, and his support was so complete, so heartfelt, that it had the quality of a substitute offering.

Consciously or not, other men used the strategy of "needs reduction." One salesman and father of two explained that he never shopped because "he didn't need anything." He didn't need to take clothes to the laundry to be ironed because he didn't mind wearing a wrinkled shirt. When I asked who bought the furniture in their apartment, he said his wife did, because "I could really do without it." He didn't need much to eat. Cereal was fine. Seeing a book on parenting on his desk, I asked if he was reading it. He replied that his wife had given it to him, but he didn't think one needed to read books like that. Through his reduction of needs, this man created a great void into which his wife stepped with her "greater need" to see him wear clean, ironed shirts, to eat square meals, live in a furnished home, and be up on the latest word on child-rearing.

Many men praised their wives for how well organized they were. The praise seemed genuine but it was also convenient. In the context of other strategies, like disaffiliating from domestic tasks or reducing needs, appreciating the way a wife bears the second shift can be another little way of keeping her doing it.

How much a working father actually shares housework and parenting depends on the interaction between a husband's gender strategy (with all its emotional meanings) and the wife's gender strategy (with all of its emotional meanings). What he does also, of course, depends on outer circumstances as well—shift hours, commute time, lay-off scares—and the meanings these hold for each.

Many couples now *believe* in sharing, but at this point in history few actually do. A new marriage humor targets this tension between promise and delivery. In Gary Trudeau's "Doonesbury" comic strip, a "liberated" father is sitting at his word processor writing a book about raising his child. He types: "Today I wake up with a heavy day of work ahead of me. As Joannie gets Jeffrey ready for day care, I ask her if I can be relieved of my usual household responsibilities for the day. Joannie says, 'Sure, I'll make up the five minutes somewhere.'"

But what often tips the balance between a wife's gender strategy and her husband's is the debits and credits in their marital economy of gratitude. Ann Myerson, Nina Tanagawa, Carol Alston, and most wives I talked with seemed to feel more *grateful* to their husbands than their husbands felt toward them. Women's lower wages, the high rate of divorce, and the cultural legacy of female subordination together created a social climate that made most women feel lucky when their husbands shared "some." Beneath the cultural "cover-up," the happy image of the woman with the flying hair, there is a quiet struggle going on in many two-job marriages today. Feeling that change might add yet another strain to their overburdened marriage, feeling already "so lucky," many women kept cautiously to those strategies that avoid much change in men.

Tensions in Marriage in an Age of Divorce

✵

The two-job marriages I came to know seemed vulnerable to three kinds of tension. One tension was between the husband's idea of what he and his wife should do at home and work, and his wife's idea about that. Gender strategies clashed—as did those of the Holts and the Steins. Another existed as a shared desire to live an old-fashioned life—the wife at home, the husband working—and the real need for her salary. The Delacortes, for example, did not clash in their vision of life or ways of trying to realize it, but both suffered a conflict between ideal and reality. The third tension is more invisible, nameless, and serious: that between the importance of a family's *need* for care and the *devaluation* of the work it takes to give that care.

ONE BEHIND, ONE AHEAD: COUPLES WHO CLASH

Two-thirds of couples in this study, most of them married for seven to ten years, shared views on how men and women should be. Two-thirds were *both* traditional, *both* transitional, or *both* egalitarian. But a third had important differences of feeling— especially about who should do how much work at home. (And note that couples who disagree violently don't appear in this study since I didn't talk with couples who were currently divorced.)

These marital clashes reflect a broader social tension—between *faster-changing women and slower-changing men.* Because changing economic opportunities and needs influence women more powerfully than men, women differ more from their mothers than men differ from their fathers. The "female culture" has shifted more rapidly than the "male culture"; the image of the go-get-'em woman has yet to be fully matched by the image of the let's-take-care-of-the-kids-together man. Men's underlying feelings about taking responsibility at home have changed much less than women's feelings have changed about forging an identity at work.

Perhaps because couples with dramatic schisms have been purged from the group by divorce, the remaining marriages I saw of this type were usually not between a man who disapproved of his wife's working and a woman who worked. They were marriages between men who were happy their wives worked but wanted them to take care of the home and women who wanted more help at home.

Whether they had to or not, these wives wanted to work. Many professionally trained wives felt their work was challenging, enjoyable, or worthwhile. But even women in low-level service jobs felt work gave them sociability, a sense of usefulness, and respect in the eyes of others, including their husband.

Tensions often showed up in each partner's sense that he or she wasn't getting credit or appreciation, that the other wasn't grateful enough. The exchange of appreciation in these marriages became a sort of "dead letter office," thanks sent to the "wrong address." The question became: Where is my thanks? The big gift Jessica Stein offered Seth was to give up working full time. For Seth, the big gift was to give up leisure to work overtime. Their problem was not, I think, that they could not give. It was that Seth wanted to "give" at the office, and Jessica wanted to "receive" at home—to have Seth play catch with their younger son, play piano with the older one, while she escaped to her desk and perfect day elsewhere. A gift in the eyes of one was not a gift in the eyes of the other. Each felt "taken advantage of." In the end, each was left with a thin pile of thank-you notes. If measured in gifts exchanged, their marriage had quietly ended some time ago.

Countless other self-sacrifices—following a spouse to another city, looking after the ill parents of a spouse, paying college tuition for a stepchild, doing with less money all around—takes on value only as they are seen through a cultural viewpoint. Ray Judson wanted to offer Anita "the privilege of staying home." Anita couldn't accept. Peter Tanagawa wanted to offer Nina the same. Nina appreciated the offer but not as much as Peter would have liked. Nancy Holt wanted to offer Evan the benefits of her work, her salary, participation in her work friendships, any status that might rub off, dubious rewards to Evan. It is through the different appraisals of such "gifts" that the major social revolution of our time enters the private moments of marriage.

Once a tension between partners arises, the couple faces the question—how to resolve it?—or if they can't do that, how to manage the failure to resolve it. Neither the Steins, the Judsons, nor the Holts actually did resolve the tension between them over the second shift. Each managed their unresolved tensions differently— the Steins by separating emotionally, the Judsons by separating physically, and the Holts by sharing a joint emotional life under the umbrella of their myth of the happy "upstairs-downstairs" solution.

Other myths also offered a way of allowing a joint emotional life under conditions of great tension. The Livingstons' myth that "we're not avoiding each other, we're just so busy" obscured the frightening thought that they didn't dare risk the very thing they said they missed—time together. Ann Myerson held to a more private myth: that Robert shared the second shift. This misrepresentation didn't obscure a struggle between husband and wife; Robert didn't think he was sharing at home these days. Ann's belief obscured a subterranean struggle between the side of herself that wanted Robert to share and the less easily acknowledged but more powerful side that didn't.

There are probably as many marital myths as there are motives to avoid conflict. But the conflict between husbands and wives over male participation at home seems the most widespread. The more couples clash in strategy but want to love each other happily anyway, the more they settle for containing their differences without, alas, resolving them. And the less they resolve their conflicts, the wider their unconscious search for the myths that help contain them. Couples pay a price in authenticity for their marital myths, the price they ultimately pay for coming of age in an era of the stalled revolution.

THE TENSION OF BEING "BEHIND THE TIMES"

Even if this first tension between faster-changing women and slower-changing men is resolved, a second one may remain. There were families like the Delacortes whose ideas were "behind the times" in the sense that their ideals were suited to an economy long gone. Both agreed on what each should do at home, and on who deserved credit for what. They had the same exchange rate in their marital economy of gratitude. The strain they felt was due to a clash between a traditional ideal and a thin pocketbook. I found this pattern more common among blue-collar than white-collar couples.

Their traditionalism did not mean that husbands shirked the second shift. Traditional men did slightly more at home than transitional men, partly because they felt guilty they could not be the sole provider. Some husbands also cared for the house because their wives worked a different shift and they were the only ones home. Traditionalism didn't stop such men from helping; it only meant they *didn't feel good* about it and that it counted as more of a favor.

The tension for tradition defenders lay not in the second shift itself but in the fact that their wives worked. And some of their wives felt pushed into working and hated it. Some didn't feel it was right to blame their husbands, but still clung to their "right" to stay home. Like Carmen, most tried not to complain. But in this very effort, they were managing a conflict between the ideals—separate sexual spheres, male rule—and the reality of their lives. These wives wanted to seem more different and unequal than they were. Hence, Carmen's strategy of "playing dumb" to draw Frank into the kitchen while leaving his male identity at the kitchen door.

WOMEN WHO BECOME LIKE TRADITIONAL MEN AND TRADITIONAL MEN WHO STAY AS THEY ARE

Couples unaffected by the first two sources of tension could still be vulnerable to a third—the assimilation of women to the values of the dominant male culture. I have focused on men crossing the "gender divide" to pitch in with work their mothers used to do. But a troubling trend moves in the opposite direction—women pitching in at the office and acting like their work-consumed fathers. Men and women may share the work at home but do altogether less of it. A strategy of cutting back on the housework, the children, the marriage may be on the rise, with corresponding thinned-out ideas about what people "need."

Among couples who shared, some were oriented primarily toward work, both playing "father." Others were more oriented toward the family, both playing "mother." The first were cutting back equally on family life; the second were cutting back equally on career.

Middle-class couples who put family first often felt at odds with the "commitment norm" in their careers, as did Adrienne and Michael Sherman (the parents of the twins who got into the motor oil). Adrienne struggled against her chairman's view of the ideal scholar, Michael with the hopes of his proud parents and priorities of his colleagues. Both struggled with their own inner desire to make scientific discoveries and write great books. They both tried to avoid being total "father."

Other couples seemed to capitulate to a workaholism à deux, each spouse equitably granting the other the right to work long hours, and reconciling themselves to a drastically reduced conception of family life. One thirty-seven-year-old woman lawyer, married to another lawyer, each of whom was trying to make partner in different firms, commented:

> Before we had children, we could work hard and play some too. We used to go out a lot together, sometimes to a different movie every night. We bicycled weekends. But when our practices got up to fifty-five hours a week and Kevin was born, we went into a stage of siege. No one tells you how a child turns your life around. For a while there we were, just surviving, very little sleep, no sex, little talk, delight in Kevin and adrenaline. We just say hello in bed before dropping off. We're still doing this.

To others, such a siege seemed normal. For example, a thirty-two-year-old accountant married his wife with the understanding that the house "didn't matter," they could eat out, cater parties, and engage a "wonderful nanny" for the children. They equitably shared an aversion to anything domestic. Since the "wonderful nanny" tended the children, cleaned house, and cooked meals, the couple had little of the second shift to share.

In their single-minded attention to career, these couples also focused less than others on their children. Their homes were neater; there were fewer paintings stuck to the refrigerator door, fewer toys in the hallway. The decor in the living and dining rooms was more often beige or white. The space where the children played was more clearly separated from the rest of the house.

Such couples shared in whatever family life there was *to* share. Sometimes such marriages degenerated into rivalry. One highly successful businessman and his wife, a lawyer, the parents of a five-year-old son, began to compete for who could be more away from home than the other. As the wife explained: "I found myself doing things all workaholics do—deliberately creating a situation where I had to be at work late. You fritter away time during the day knowing you won't get all your work done. That way, when Jim called, I could tell him I had to work late without lying." Each thought of staying home or caring for the child as a defeat. Caring less was a victory. Not until the couple separated did the wife look back at this competition with regret and begin to devote real attention to her son.

In the first group of marriages—like that between Nancy and Evan Holt—tension focused on a clash between the husband's view of his role at home and his wife's. In the second group of marriages—like that between Carmen and Frank Delacorte—the tension centered on finding an acceptable way for a man to do a woman's work. In the third group of marriages, the tension centered on the gap between the care a family needs to thrive and the devaluation of the work of caring for it.

The first tension could be resolved if the Evans of the world shared the second shift. The second tension could be resolved if the Franks could earn enough so the Carmens could stay home. But beneath these issues lay a basic question—tying a shoe, arbitrating a quarrel, reading a story—how much self should go into it?

DIVORCE AND THE SECOND SHIFT

Over the last thirty years in the United States, more women have gone out to work, and more have divorced. According to the sociologist William Goode, working women divorce at a higher rate than housewives in the former Soviet Union, Germany, Sweden, and France. Indeed, in France, working women have twice the divorce rate of housewives. So some conclude that women's work *causes* divorce. In one national survey, Joseph Pleck and Graham Staines found that working wives were more likely than housewives to say they wished they had married someone else and more likely to have considered divorce. But people who conclude that it is women's work that causes divorce look only at what *women* are doing—earning money, feeling more independent, thinking better of themselves, expecting more of men.[1]

My research suggests something else. Since *all* the wives I studied worked outside the home, the fact that they worked did not account for why some marriages were happy and others were not. What did contribute to happiness was the husband's willingness to do the work at home. Sharing the second shift improved a marriage regardless of what ideas either had about men's and women's roles. A national study of over a thousand married couples conducted by Ronald Kessler and James McRae also found that working wives suffered less distress if their husbands helped with the home and children.[2]

Among the families I've described, a number came close to divorce. Two months after I first interviewed them, Anita and Ray Judson separated. John and Barbara Livingston had been about to separate when they sought counseling. The Steins seemed divorced in spirit. In the study as a whole, one out of every eight couples had at some point thought seriously of divorce. Apart from the Livingstons, in every one of these couples, the man avoided the work at home.

Did they avoid their wives in the course of avoiding the second shift or avoid the second shift in the course of avoiding their wives? It was often hard to tell. But wives often felt their husbands' refusal to help at home as a lack of consideration.

A twenty-six-year-old legal secretary, the mother of two and married to a businessman, said: "Patrick empties the garbage occasionally and sweeps. That's all. He does no cooking, no washing, no anything else. How do I feel? Furious. If our marriage ends, it will be on this issue. And it just might." A thirty-year-old mother of two, who works at word processing, was more resigned: "I take care of Kevin [their son]. I do the house cleaning. I pay the bills. I shop for birthdays. I write the Christmas cards. I'm a single mother already."

Tom O'Mally, a thirty-eight-year-old engineer, described a harrowing marriage and bitter divorce. For seven years of marriage to his first wife, Tom left all housework and care of their four sons to his wife, a school administrator. He said his wife reasoned with him about it, then argued. Then she tried lists. When that failed, she tried therapy. When that failed, she left, and Tom was faced for the first time with the sole care of their four sons. When asked what caused the divorce, he answered, "Lists." As he explained:

> Especially the last several years of my marriage, we had lists of household chores that had to be done. I came to *hate* these lists. We had this formal thing about Tuesday, Wednesday, Thursday—whose turn to do dishes, whose turn to do the laundry. Finally, when it didn't work out, my wife went to a therapist. Then we went to one of those marriage encounters and came up with a definite way of splitting up housework. I have to think that [arrangements to split housework] destroy more marriages than they save.

"So were you doing some of the chores?" I asked.

> No. I wasn't doing any of them. I always felt I'd been railroaded into doing them against my will. I hated that goddamn list. I still remember blowing up and stalking out of the house. I never stuck with the list.

With her Tuesday-Wednesday-Thursday list, his ex-wife reminded me of Nancy Holt. But instead of accommodating to the extra work at home, his wife kept the list but ended the marriage. Tom O'Mally then married a much younger, less-educated woman who stayed home to tend the house and children. He told his second wife, "*Anything* but a list!"

Men's resistance to sharing the extra month a year is by no means the only cause of divorce, but it is often a source of tension underlying the others.

In a few cases, a certain reverse of this story occurred. A twenty-eight-year-old saleswoman, Diane Hatch, told of how a marriage of seven years ended when her baby was nine months old. Her husband had always supported her career, the marriage had been stable and the baby planned, she said. But when the baby arrived, and Diane wanted to stay home for six months to care for him, her husband objected, suddenly worrying—she felt needlessly—about their finances. As she put it, "I went back to a job I didn't want before I was ready."

At first blush, it seemed that Diane's husband, Jim, was replacing the old adage "A woman's place is in the home" with a new one: "A woman's place is at work." But Diane went on to explain matters in a way that cast a different light. She said her husband had suffered a blow at work, and she had criticized him strongly, adding one blow to another. He had been extremely involved with the birth of his son, and wanted to share the care of him. Perhaps if things were not going well at work, he wanted to devote more of his identity to being a father. It was when Diane began to crowd him out of his potential role at home that Jim began to urge her back to work. To the utter shock and dismay of family and friends, Jim walked out on his wife and nine-month-old baby. But this may have been why. Some men seek identity within the second shift.

In a telling 1983 study, Joan Huber and Glenna Spitze asked 1,360 husbands and wives: "Has the thought of getting a divorce from your husband (or wife) ever crossed your mind?" They found that more wives than husbands had thought about divorce

(30 percent versus 22 percent) and that wives thought about it more often. How much each one earned had no effect on thoughts of divorce. Nor did attitudes toward the roles of men and women. But the more housework a wife saw her husband do, the less likely she was to think of divorce. As the researchers noted: "For each of the five daily household tasks which the husband performs at least half the time, the wife is about 3 percent less likely to have thoughts of divorce."[3] (The five tasks were meal preparation, food shopping, child care, daily housework, and meal cleanup.) The researcher also found that if a working wife thinks her husband *should* share housework, she is 10 percent more likely to have thoughts of divorce than if she does not believe this.

In another study, of 600 couples applying for divorce, George Levinger found that the second most common reason women cited for wanting divorce—after "mental cruelty"—was "neglect of home or children." Women mentioned this reason more often than financial problems, physical abuse, drinking, or infidelity. Among middle-class women who filed for divorce, a man's neglect of home or children was the single most common complaint, mentioned by nearly half. Both men and women mentioned neglect of home and children: 39 percent of the women, and 26 percent of the men.[4]

Happy marriage is famously mysterious. But an added ingredient to it these days is some resolution of the extra month a year. As the role of the homemaker is vacated by many women, the homemaker's work has been devalued and passed on to low-paid housekeepers, baby-sitters, and day-care workers. Like an ethnic culture in danger of being swallowed up by the culture of a dominant group, the contribution of the traditional homemaker has been devalued first by men and now by more women.

In the era of a stalled revolution, one way to reverse this devaluation is for men to share the care of their children not simply as a matter of justice but of wisdom. A South African miner forced under Apartheid to work eleven months a year in the gold mines, visiting his family in the Homelands (reservations for blacks) only one month a year, said this: "I need to work to support my family, but I miss them terribly, especially my children. I miss the chance for me to bring my children up."

Men Who Do and
Men Who Don't

✳

ONE out of five men in this study were as actively involved at
home as their wives. Some, like Greg Alston, shared in a
"male" way, doing such things as carpentry; others, like Art Winfield, in a "female" way, as people imagined these ways to be.
Since the men who shared the second shift lived happier family
lives, I wondered what conditions produced such men. How do
men who share *differ* from other men?

They were no more likely than other men to have "model" fathers who helped at home. Their parents were no more likely to
have trained them to do chores when they were young. Michael
Sherman and Seth Stein both had fathers who spent little time
with them and did little work around the house. But Michael became engrossed in raising his twin boys, whereas Seth said hello
and good-bye to his kids on his way to and from an absorbing law
practice. Sharers were also as likely to have had mothers who were
homemakers or who worked and tended the home as non-sharers.

Wives of sharing men eagerly offered complex explanations for
why their husbands were so "unusual." Yet each story differed from
the next. For example, one woman explained:

> Jonathan has always been extremely involved with the
> children. I think it's because he grew up the son of Jews
> who survived the Holocaust and immigrated to Canada
> after World War Two. He never felt a part of Canadian

society, he always felt like an outsider. I think that's why he never bought into conventional sex roles either. His mother worked day and night running a grocery store, so he rarely saw her. She didn't like kids anyway; he was brought up by his grandmother so he didn't believe only a *mother* could raise kids.

Another wife offered a different explanation: "Dwight is unusually involved at home because his father was away so much in the navy, and his mother stayed home to take care of the kids by herself. I think it was seeing her handle all that by herself that made him want to share, and I thank his mother for training him."

The "upbringing stories" of such wives often focused on the impact of their husband's mother. But the only recurring theme I could discover had to do with the son's disaffiliation from a detached, absent, or overbearing *father*. John Livingston's father, as he sadly described him, was a recluse who ignored his son. Michael Sherman's father alternately praised and forgot his. Art Winfield's biological father disappeared entirely. Many men had bad memories of their fathers, but the men who ended up sharing child care differentiated themselves from their fathers; seeing them as bad examples they vowed *not* to be like. The *most* involved father—Art Winfield, the father who played with the children at his adopted son's day-care class—was both disenchanted with his real father, a "bad" model of fatherhood, and ardently devoted to his kindly stepfather, a "good" model. What seemed important was the combination of how a man identified with his father and what that father was like—not how much the father had helped around the house.

But most people believed that it was "upbringing"—how much a man helped around the house as a boy—that made the difference.[1] Evan Holt, who did his hobbies "downstairs" while his wife cared for the "upstairs," said he was just acting the way he was "brought up" to act. But Evan didn't do many other things he was brought up to do, like go to church, avoid using credit cards, or wait to have sex until after marriage. In these areas of life he was his own man. Around the house, he said he was just doing what his mother taught him. The "upbringing" story seemed like a cover for a more illusive psychological predisposition.

Men like Art Winfield and Michael Sherman seemed to have two characteristics in common: they were reacting against an absent or self-centered father, and at the same time, they had sufficiently identified with some male to feel *safe* empathizing with their mothers without fear of becoming "too feminine."

Did the men who shared the work at home love their wives more? Were they more considerate? It's true, egalitarian men had more harmonious marriages, but I would be reluctant to say that men like Peter Tanagawa or Ray Judson loved their wives less than Art Winfield or Michael Sherman, or were less considerate. One man who did very little at home said, "Just last week I suddenly realized that my wife's life is more valuable than mine because my son needs her more than he needs me." Men who shared were often devoted to their wives, but so were men who didn't.

Two external factors also did *not* distinguish men who shared from men who didn't: the number of hours they worked or how much they earned. Husbands usually work a longer "full-time" job than wives. But in the families I studied, men who worked fifty hours or more per week were just *slightly* less likely to share housework than men who worked forty-five, forty, or thirty-five hours a week. In addition, fifty-hour-a-week *women* did far *more* child care and housework than men who worked those hours. Other national studies also show that the number of hours a man works for pay has little to do with the number of hours he put in at home.[2]

At first, I also assumed money would loom large. The man who shared, I thought, would need his wife's salary more than other men, would value her job more, and also her time.

American wives in two-job couples in 1989 and 2006 averaged about one dollar for every three their husbands earn, and this average prevailed among the families I studied too.

In 1980 a wife in a two-job couple, like those in this study, earned thirty-three cents for every dollar her husband earned; today, such women earn seventy-six cents per husband dollar. Earlier many marriages reflected the labor force itself—a pilot married a flight attendant, a secretary married a boss, a dental assistant married a dentist—while today more couples marry those in similar jobs. But when couples' jobs differ, as they often still do, it is usually the wife who has the less-well-paid—but steadier—job, and the husband who has the higher-paid but unsteady one. Men more typically work in the automotive industry or construction trades, for example, which are more vulnerable to outsourcing, automation, and recession. And among men and women in full-time jobs in 2010, women earned eighty-one cents for every dollar a man earns.

I assumed that the man who shares would not earn more. Both spouses might agree that because his job came first, his leisure did too. I assumed that men who earned *as much or less* than their wives would do *more* housework, that being the least valued activity. A woman who wanted 50-50 in the second shift but had married a high-earning man would reconcile herself to the family's greater need for her husband's job and work the extra month a year. By the same token, a traditional man married to a high-earning woman would swallow his pride and pitch in at home. I assumed that money would talk louder than ideals.

If money explained who did what at home, that would mean that no matter how much effort a woman put into her job, its lower pay would mean less husbandly help at home. According to research about on-the-job stress, low-level service jobs, where women are concentrated, cause more stress than the blue- and white-collar jobs men more often do. Although working mothers don't work the long hours fathers do, they devote as much *effort* to earning money as men, and many women earn less for work that's more stressful. Thus, by using his higher salary to "buy" more leisure at home, he inadvertently makes his wife pay indirectly for an inequity in the wider economy that causes her to get paid less. If money is the key organizing principle to the relations between men and women in marriage, it's a pity for men because it puts their role at home at the mercy of the blind fluctuations of the marketplace and for women because if money talks at home, it favors men. The extra month a year becomes an indirect way in which the woman pays at home for the economic discrimination outside it.

THE LIMITS OF ECONOMIC LOGIC

Money mattered in the marriages I studied, but it was not the powerful "invisible hand" behind men who shared.[3] For one thing, this is clear from the family portraits. Michael Sherman earned much more than Adrienne but his job didn't matter more. For years Ann Myerson earned more than her husband but put her husband's job first anyway. John Livingston valued his wife's job as he did his own, but she took more responsibility at home.

A number of researchers have tried to discover a link between the *wage* gap between working parents and the *leisure* gap between them, and the results have been confusing. Among couples in this study, these two factors were not related in a statistically significant way.

An intriguing clue appeared, however, when I divided all the men into three groups: men who earn more than their wives (most men), men who earn the same amount, and men who earn less. Of the men who earned more, 21 percent shared housework. Of the men who earned about the same, 30 percent shared. But among men who earned *less* than their wives, *none* shared.

If a logic of the pocketbook is only a logic of the *pocketbook,* it should operate the same whether a man earns more or a woman does. But this "logic of the pocketbook" didn't work that way. It only worked as long as men earned as much or more than their wives. Money frequently "worked" for men (it excused them from housework) but it didn't work for women (didn't get them out of it).

Another principle—the principle of "balancing"—seems to be at work: if men lose power over women in one way, they make up for it in another way—for example, by avoiding the second shift. In this way, they can maintain dominance over women. How much responsibility these men assumed at home seemed related to the deeper issue of male power. Men who earn much more than their wives already have a power over their wives in that they control a scarce and important resource. The more severely a man's identity is financially threatened—by his wife's higher salary, for example—the less he can afford to threaten it further by doing "women's work" at home.

Men who shared the second shift weren't trying to make up for losing power in other realms of marriage; they didn't feel the need to "balance." Michael Sherman had given up the *idea* that he should have more power than Adrienne. Art Winfield talked playfully about men being "brought up to be kings." But Peter Tanagawa felt a man *should* have more power, and felt he'd given a lot of it up when Nina's career rose so dramatically. He'd adjusted to earning much less, but to a man of his ideas, this was a huge sacrifice. Nina made up for it by putting in more time at home.

More crucial than cultural beliefs about men's and women's *spheres,* were couples' beliefs about the right degree of men's and women's *power.* Women who "balanced" felt "too powerful." Sensing when their husbands got touchy, sensing the fragility of their husbands' ego, not wanting them to get discouraged or depressed, such women restored their men's lost power by waiting on them at home.

Wives did this balancing for different reasons. One eccentric

Englishman and father of three children was a tenured member of the English department of a small college. He taught classes and held obligatory office hours but had abandoned research, minimized committee work, avoided corridor conversations, and long since given up putting in for a raise. He claimed to "share" housework and child care, but what he meant by housework was working on a new den, and what he meant by child care was reflected in his remark, "While I'm working on the house; they muck about by themselves." He was touchy about his accomplishments and nervous, it seemed, about what he called the "limitless" ambition of his workaholic wife. Without asking him to do more, perhaps his wife was making up for her ambitions by carrying the load at home.

One architect, the fourth of four highly successful brothers in a prosperous and rising black family, had lost his job in the recession of the late 1970s, become deeply discouraged, taken occasional contracting jobs, and otherwise settled into a life of semi-unemployment. His wife explained: "Eventually we're going to have to make it on my salary. But it's awfully hard on my husband right now, being trained as an architect and not being able to get a job. I take that into account." Her husband did no housework and spent time with his son only when the spirit moved him. "I do very little around the house," he said frankly, "but Beverly doesn't complain, bless her heart." Meanwhile, they lived in near-poverty, while Beverly worked part time, cared for their baby and home, and took courses in veterinary science at night. As she let fall at the end of the interview, "Sometimes I wonder how long I can keep going."

Other men earned less and did less at home, but weren't "balancing." They were going back to get a degree, and their wives were temporarily giving them the money and time to do this. The husband's training for a job counted as much in their moral accounting as it would if he already had that more important job. For example, one husband was unemployed while studying for a degree in pediatric nursing. His wife, a full-time administrator, cared for their home and nine-month-old baby. The rhythm of their household life revolved around the dates of his exams. His wife explained: "My husband used to puree Stevy's carrots in the blender. He used to help shop, and weed the garden. Now he studies every evening until ten. His exams come first. Getting that 'A' is important to him. He plays with the baby as a study break." She didn't mind doing the work at home and only got upset when he complained the house was messy. She said, "I keep myself going by reminding myself this is *temporary*, until Jay gets his degree."

I heard of no women whose husbands both worked and cared for the family while the wives studied for a degree. For a woman, getting a degree seemed not so honored an act. There was no tradition of "putting your wife through college" analogous to "putting your husband through college." A wife could imagine being supported or being better off when her husband got his degree. Husbands usually couldn't imagine either situation. One husband *had* shared the work at home 50-50 when his wife worked, but came to resent it terribly and finally stopped when his wife quit her job and went back to school to get a Ph.D. A job counted but work toward a degree did not. Feeling deprived of attention and service, one man shouted into my tape recorder—half in fun and half not: "You can't eat it. You can't talk to it. It doesn't buy a vacation or a new car. I *hate* my wife's dissertation!" Women who put their husbands through school may have resented the burden, but they didn't feel they had as much right to complain.

Taken as a whole, this group of men—semi-unemployed, hanging back at work, or in training—neither earned the bread nor baked it. And of all the wives, theirs were the least happy. Yet, either because they sympathized with their husbands, or expected their situation to improve, because they saw no way to change it, or because they were maintaining the "right" balance of power, such women worked the extra month a year. Meanwhile, their lower-earning husbands often saw their wives as intelligent, strong, "a rock." At the same time they enjoyed the idea that, though not a king at work, a man had a warm throne at home.

Some women had other ways of accumulating more power than they felt "comfortable" with. One woman M.D., married to a former patient, an impecunious musician, did all the second shift. As her husband put it, "She never asks." Another woman, a teacher, secretly upset the power balance by having a long-term extramarital affair almost like another marriage. Life went on as usual at home, but she quietly made up for her secret life by being "wonderful" about chores at home.

In all these marriages, money was not the main determinant of which men did or didn't share. Even men who earned much more than their wives didn't get out of housework *because* of it. One college professor and father of three explained why he had committed himself to 50 percent of housework and child care:

> My wife earns a third of what I earn. But as a public school
> teacher, she's doing a job that's just as important as mine.
> She's an extraordinarily gifted teacher, and I happen to
> know she works just as hard at her teaching as I do at mine.
> So when we come home, she's as tired as I am. We share the
> housework and child care equally. But [in a tone of
> exasperation] if she were to take a job in insurance or real
> estate, she'd just be doing another job. She wouldn't be
> making the contribution she's making now. We haven't
> talked about it, but if that were the case, I probably
> wouldn't break my back like this. She would have to carry
> the load at home.

Ironically, had his wife earned *more* at a job he admired less—and worked only for *money*—he would not have shared the second shift.

Other evidence also points away from the logic of the pocketbook. In a 1985 report, Joseph Pleck found that over the last ten years, men married to *housewives* have increased their contributions to housework *nearly as much* as men whose wives do paid work.[4] Such housewives earned nothing ten years ago and earn nothing now. Yet husbands of housewives now help their wives at home more. That isn't money talking, and not a matter of men "keeping the edge." They had the edge, and gave some up.

These husbands of housewives may help more because of a rising standard of male consideration. Just as nonunion industries often try to avoid unionization by keeping wages in nonunion shops comparable to those in unionized shops, so husbands of housewives may be unconsciously responding to the women's movement by helping more at home. Without quite knowing it, some "nonunion" (nonfeminist) women may be enjoying the gains won by "union" agitators. Again, the political struggle behind a cultural shift and not the timeless logic of the pocketbook seems to determine how much men help at home. To push the analogy further, the women who struggle to get their husbands to do more at home and whose husbands divorce them because of it may be like the trouble-makers who fight the company, win the point, but get fired. The outrageous few improve things for the "good workers" who make no noise.

This doesn't mean money has nothing to do with the second shift. In two different ways, it does. In the first place, couples do need to think about and plan around financial need. Most of the men who shared at home had wives who pretty much shared at work. The men earned some but not much more. And whatever their wives earned, blue-collar men like Art Winfield really needed. Second, future changes in the general economy may press more couples to do "balancing." Some experts predict that the American economy will split increasingly between an elite of highly paid, highly trained workers and an enlarging pool of poorly paid, unskilled workers. Jobs in the middle are being squeezed out as companies automate or seek cheaper labor pools in the Third World. The personnel rosters of the so-called sunrise industries, the rapidly growing, high-technology companies, already reflect this split. Companies with many jobs in the middle are in the so-called sunset industries, such as car manufacturing. As the economist Bob Kuttner illustrates:

"The fast food industry employs a small number of executives and hundreds of thousands of cashiers and kitchen help. . . . With some variation, key punchers, chambermaids, and retail sales personnel confront the same short job ladder."[5] In addition, unions in sunrise industries often face company threats to move offshore, and so these unions press less hard for better pay.

The decline in jobs in the middle mainly hits men in blue-collar union-protected jobs. Unless they can get training that allows them to compete for highly skilled jobs, such men will be forced to choose between unemployment and low-paid service work.

The "declining middle" is thus in the process of creating an economic crisis for many men. This crisis can lead some men to feel it "only fair" to share the load at home, and other men—through their wives' balancing—to do less.

Sharing men seemed to be randomly distributed up and down the class ladder. There were the Michael Shermans and the Art Winfields. In the working class, more men shared without believing in it. In the middle class, more men didn't share even though they did believe in it. Everything else equal, men whose wives had advanced degrees and professional careers—who had what the sociologist Pierre Bourdieu calls "cultural capital"—were more likely to share than men whose wives lacked such capital. All this formed part of the social backdrop to the working man's gender strategy at home.

Added to this was the influence of his wife. Nearly every man who shared had a wife who urged—or at least welcomed—his involvement at home. They did not hoard their children, as Nancy Holt came to do with Joey. When Evan had been about to leave to take Joey to the zoo for a father-son outing, Nancy had edged Evan out by deciding at the last minute to "help" them get along. At first awkward and unconfident with children, Michael Sherman might have retreated to the "downstairs" had it not been for Adrienne's continual invitation to pitch in. Often, something as simple as the way a mother holds her baby to "see Dad" indicated her effort to share. Adrienne Sherman didn't just leave her twins with Daddy; she talked to them about what Daddy could do with them. She fostered a tie. She didn't play expert. She made room.

As a result, such men were—or became—sensitive to their children's needs. They were more realistic than other fathers about the limits of what their wives provide, and about what their children really need.

LIMITING THE IDEA OF FATHERHOOD

Involved fathers had a much more elaborate notion of what a father was than uninvolved fathers did. Involved fathers talked about fathering much as mothers talked about mothering. Uninvolved fathers held to a far more restricted mission—to discipline the child or teach him sports. When asked what he thought was important about being a father, one black businessman and father of two said:

> Discipline. I don't put up with whining. It bothers me. I'm shorter tempered and my wife is longer tempered. I do a significant amount of paddling. I grew up with being paddled. When I got paddled I knew damn good and well that I deserved it. I don't whip them. One good pop on their bottom and I send them down to their room. I've scared them. I've never punched them. And I'll spank them in front of people as well as not in front of them.

To him, being a disciplinarian *was* being a father. As a result, his children gravitated to their mother. In a strangely matter-of-fact way, she remarked that she didn't "feel comfortable" leaving the children with her husband for long periods. "If I go out to the hairdresser's on Saturday, I might come back and find he didn't fix them lunch; I don't leave them with him too much." Developing a "longer temper" didn't feel to him like part of a father's job.

When I asked uninvolved fathers to define a "good mother" and "good father," they gave elaborate and detailed answers for "good mother," and short, hazy answers for "good father," sometimes with a specific mission attached to it, like teaching a child about cars, soccer, baseball.

I asked one man, "What's a good mother?" and he answered: "A good mother is patient. That's the first thing. Someone who is warm, caring, who can see what the child needs, physically, who stimulates the child intellectually, and helps the child meet his emotional challenges." "What is a good father?" I asked. "A good father is a man who spends time with his children." Another man said simply, "A good father is around."

It is not that such men have an elaborate idea of fatherhood and don't live up to it. Their idea of fatherhood is embryonic to begin with. They often limit that idea by comparing themselves only to their own fathers, and not, as more involved men did, to their mothers, sisters, or other fathers. As a Salvadoran delivery man put it, "I give my children everything my father gave me." Michael Sherman gave his twins what his mother gave him.

CURTAILING THE IDEA OF WHAT A CHILD NEEDS

Men who are greatly involved with their children react against two cultural ideas: one idea removes the actual care of children from the definition of *manhood*, and one curtails the notion of how much care a child needs. As to the first idea, involved fathers' biggest struggle was against the doubts they felt about not "giving everything to getting ahead" in their jobs. But even when they conquered this fear, another idea often stood in the way—the idea that their child is "already grown up," "advanced," and doesn't need much from him.

Just as the archetype of the supermom—the woman who can

do it all—minimizes the real needs of women, so too the arche-type of the "superkid" minimizes the real needs of children. It makes it all right to treat a young child as if he or she were older. Often uninvolved parents remarked with pride that their small children were "self-sufficient" or "very independent."

I asked the fifth-grade teacher in a private school how she thought her students from two-job families were doing. She be-gan by saying that they did as well as the few children she had whose mothers stayed home. But having said that, her talk ran to the problems: "The good side of kids being on their own so much is that it makes them independent really early. But I think they pay a price. I can see them sealing off their feelings, as if they're saying, 'That's the last time I'll be vulnerable.' I can see it in their faces, especially the sixth-grade boys."

Throughout the second half of the nineteenth century, as women were increasingly excluded from the workplace, the cul-tural notion of what a child "needs" at home grew to expand the woman's role at home. As Barbara Ehrenreich and Deirdre Eng-lish note in *For Her Own Good*, doctors and ministers argued strongly that a woman's place was at home. The child needed her there. As the economic winds reversed, so did the idea of a woman's proper place—and a child's real needs. Nowadays, a child is increasingly imagined to need time with other children, to need "independence-training," not to need "quantity time" with a par-ent but only a small amount of "quality time." As one working fa-ther remarked: "Children need time to play with other children their age. It's stimulating for them. Nelson has enjoyed it, I think, from when he was six months."

If in the earlier part of the century, middle-class children suffered from overattentive mothers, from being "mother's only accomplish-ment," today's children may suffer from an underestimation of their needs. Our idea of what a child needs in each case reflects what par-ents need. The child's needs are a cultural football in an economic and marital game.

An Orwellian "superkid" language has emerged to consolidate this sense of normality. In a September 1985 *New York Times* article entitled "New Programs Come to Aid of Latch-Key Children," Janet Edder quotes a child-care professional as follows: "Like other child-care professionals, Mrs. Seligson prefers to use the phrase 'Children in Self-Care' rather than 'Latch-Key Children,' a term coined during the depression when many children who went home alone wore a key around their necks." "Children in Self-Care" suggests that children *are* being cared for, by themselves. Unlike the term "Latch-Key Children," which suggests a child who is sad and deprived, the term "Children in Self-Care" suggests a happy superkid.

Another article, in the August 1984 *Changing Times*, entitled "When You Can't Be Home, Teach Your Child What to Do," suggests that working parents do home-safety checkups so that a pipe won't burst, a circuit breaker won't blow, or electrical fire start. Parents should advise children to keep house keys out of sight and to conceal from callers the fact that they're alone at home. It tells about "warm lines"—a telephone number a child can call for advice or simple comfort when he or she is alone. Earlier in the century, advice of this sort was offered to destitute widows or working wives of disabled or unemployed men while the middle class shook its head in sympathy. Now the middle class has "children in self-care" too.

The parents I talked to had younger children, none of whom were in "self-care." The children I visited seemed a fairly jolly and resilient lot. But the parents I spoke to did not feel much supported in their parenthood; like Ann Myerson, many parents in the business world felt obliged to hide concerns that related to children. Female clerical workers were discouraged from making calls home. Many men feared that their doing anything for family reasons—moving to another city, missing the office party, passing up a promotion—would be taken as a sign they lacked ambition or manliness. As for John Livingston's coworkers, the rule was: don't go home until your wife calls.

For all the talk about the importance of children, the cultural climate has become subtly less hospitable to parents who put children first. This is not because parents love children less, but because a job culture has expanded at the expense of a family culture.

As motherhood as a "private enterprise" declines and more mothers rely on the work of lower-paid specialists, the value accorded the work of mothering has declined for women, making it all the harder for men to take it up.

MY WIFE IS DOING IT

Every afternoon Art Winfield knew Adam was waiting for him at day care. Michael Sherman knew that around 6 a.m. one of his twins would call out "Daddy." John Livingston knew that Cary relied on him to get around her mother's discipline. Such men were close enough to their children to know what they were and weren't getting from their mothers.

Uninvolved fathers were not. They *imagined* that their wives did more with the children than they did. For example, one thirty-two-year-old grocery clerk praised his wife for helping their daughter with reading on the weekends—something his wife complained he didn't make time for. But when I interviewed her, I discovered that her weekends were taken up with housework, church, and visiting relatives.

Sometimes I had the feeling that fathers were passing the child-care buck to their wives while the wives passed it to the baby-sitter. Each person passing the role on wanted to feel good about it, and tended to deny the problems. Just as fathers often praised their wives as "wonderful mothers," so mothers often praised their baby-sitters as "wonderful." Even women who complain about day care commonly end up describing the day-care worker as "great." So important to parents was the care of their child that they almost had to believe that "everything at day care was fine." Not only was the role of caretaker transferred from parent to baby-sitter, but sometimes also the illusion that the child was "in good hands."

The reasons men gave for why their wives were wonderful—e.g., that they were patient—were often reasons women gave for why the baby-sitters were wonderful. Just as uninvolved fathers often said that they wouldn't want to trade places with their wives, so wives often said they wouldn't want to trade places with their day-care worker.

As one businesswoman and mother of a three-year-old boy commented: "Our baby-sitter is just fantastic. She's with the kids from seven o'clock in the morning until six o'clock at night. And some kids stay later. I don't know how she does it. *I* couldn't." Another working mother commented: "I couldn't be as patient as Elizabeth [the day-care worker] is. I love my child, but I'm not a baby person."

The day-care worker herself was often in a difficult spot. She depended economically on the parents, so she didn't want to say anything so offensive it might lead them to withdraw the child from her care. And parents didn't have time to listen. As Katharine Wilson, a day-care worker for fifteen years, remarked:

> One out of five parents just drop their children off and run. Another three will come in and briefly talk with you. Then the last person will come in and talk to you quite a bit. Not too many call during the day. They trust we know what we're doing.

Some day-care centers even established a policy of check-in sheets that required parents to come inside the day-care center and sign their child in each morning, thus preventing the hurried few who might otherwise leave their children off at the sidewalk.

Pickup time was often hectic, and not a good time to talk. As one day-care worker observed:

> It's a hell of a life the parents lead. Every time I see them they're in a rush. It's rush in the morning and rush in the

evening. They barely ask me what Danny had for lunch or how he seemed. I think they might feel bad when they see him around four o'clock in the afternoon. He gets kind of restless then. He's waiting. He sees the parents of the other children come and each time the doorbell rings he hopes it's his parents. But, see, they come in the last—six-thirty.

Sometimes a day-care worker becomes worried about a child. As Alicia Fernandez confided:

I've had Emily for a year and a half now. She's never been real open with me and I don't think she is with her mother either. I think, in a way, Emily was hurt that her former sitter had to give her up. It was a hard adjustment coming in to me and in fact I don't think she has adjusted. One day she took the money out of my wallet—the money her mother had given me—and tore it up. I was so shocked. It was my pay. I slapped her across the knees. She didn't cry. I felt bad I'd done that, but even worse that she didn't cry. I thought, hey, something's wrong.

Had she mentioned this to Emily's mother and father? I asked. She replied quickly and quietly: "Oh no. It's hard to talk about that. We just don't get around to it. In a way, I feel badly about it but on the other hand if I told her mother, she might take Emily away."

The day-care worker, who could best judge how Emily's day had gone, felt afraid to confide her concerns to Emily's parents, who badly needed to hear them. Other day-care workers also kept their opinions to themselves. As one noted: "You can feel sorry for them. I have Tim for nine hours. I have Jessica for ten and a half—now Jessie's mother is a single mother. Like I say, at the end of the day they cry." "Do you talk to their parents about the crying?" I asked.

They don't ask, and I don't bring it up. Don't get me wrong. These children are adaptable. They're pliant. As long as there's a sense of love here and as long as you feed them, they know I'm the one who satisfies their needs. That's all I am to them. The children love me and some little children, like Nelson, don't want to go home. He's three now but I've had him since he was seven months old; Stephanie's three and I've had her since she was six weeks. But I do feel sorry for the children, I do. Because I know there are days when they probably don't feel like coming here, especially Mondays.

When day-care workers feel sorry for the children they care for something is wrong. This woman, a thirty-year-old black mother of three, was gentle and kindly, a lovely person to care for children. What seemed wrong to me was the overly long hours, the blocked channels of communication, and the fathers who imagined their wives were "handling it all."

A FATHER'S INFLUENCE

In a time of stalled revolution—when women have gone to work, but the workplace, the culture, and the men have not adjusted themselves to this new reality—children can be the victims. Most working mothers are already doing all they can. It is men who can do more.

Fathers can make a difference that shows in the child. I didn't administer tests to the children in the homes I visited nor gather systematic information on child development. I did ask the baby-sitters and day-care workers for their general impressions of differences between the children of single parents, two-job families in which the father was uninvolved, and two-job families in which the father was actively involved. All of them said that the children of fathers who were actively involved seemed to them "more secure" and "less anxious." Their lives were less rushed. On Monday, they had more to report about Sunday's events: "Guess what I did with my dad. . . ."

But curiously little attention has been paid to the effect of fathers on children. Current research focuses almost exclusively on the influence of *mothers*. A panel of distinguished social scientists chosen by the National Academy of Sciences to review the previous research on children of working mothers concluded in 1982 that a mother's employment has no consistent ill effects on a child's school achievement, IQ, or social and emotional development.[6] Other summary reviews offer similar but more complex findings. For example, in charting fifty years of research on children of working mothers, Lois Hoffman, a social psychologist at the University of Michigan, concluded that most girls of all social classes and boys from working-class families, whose mothers worked, were more self-confident and earned better grades than children whose mothers were housewives. But she also found that compared to the sons of housewives, middle-class boys raised by working mothers were less confident and did less well in school. But what about the influence of the fathers? Research documents a fact one might intuitively suspect: the more involved the father, the better off the child. Professor Norma Radin and her coresearchers at the University of Michigan conducted a number of studies that show that, all else being equal, the children of highly involved fathers are better adjusted socially and emotionally than children of noninvolved fathers and score higher on academic tests. In Dr. Radin's research, "highly involved" fathers are those who score in the top third on an index composed of questions concerning responsibility for physical care (e.g., feeding the children), responsibility for socializing the child (e.g., setting limits), power in decision making regarding the child, availability to the child, and an overall estimate of his involvement in raising his preschooler. In one study of fifty-nine middle-class families with children between the ages of three and six, Dr. Radin found that highly involved fathers had sons who were better adjusted and more socially competent, more likely to perceive themselves as masters of their fate, and had a higher mental age on verbal intelligence tests.[7] A 1985 study by Abraham Sagi found Israeli children of highly involved fathers showed more empathy than other children.

A 1985 study by Carolyn and Phil Cowan, two psychologists at the University of California, Berkeley, found that three-and-a-half-year-old children of involved fathers achieved higher scores on certain playroom tasks (classifying objects, putting things in a series, role-taking tasks) than other children. When fathers worked longer hours outside the home, the Cowans found in their observation sessions, the three-and-a-half-year-olds showed more anxiety. The daughters of long-hours men were, in addition, less warm and less task oriented at playroom tasks, although they had fewer behavior problems. When fathers worked long hours, mothers tended to compensate by establishing warm relations with their sons. But when mothers worked long hours, husbands did not "compensate" with their daughters. In spite of this, the girls did well in playroom tasks. When fathers *or* mothers worked more outside the home, the parent established a closer bond with the *boy*.[8]

The results of active fatherhood also seem to last. In one study, two psychologists asked male undergraduates at the University of Massachusetts, Amherst, to respond to such statements as "My father understood my problems and worries and helped with them, hugged or kissed me goodnight when I was small, was able to make me feel better when I was upset, gave me a lot of care and attention." They were also asked to describe his availability ("away from home for days at a time, . . . out in the evening at least two nights a week, . . . home afternoons when children came home from school," and so on). Young men who ranked their fathers as highly—or even moderately—nurturant and available were far more likely to describe themselves as "trusting, friendly, loyal, and dependable, industrious and honest."[9]

The effects of a man's care for his children are likely to show up again and again through time—in the child as a child, in the child as an adult, and probably also in the child's own approach to fatherhood, and in generations of fathers to come. An exceptionally warmhearted man, like the stepfather of Art Winfield, could light a future way. In the last forty years, many women have made a historic shift into the economy. Now it is time for a generation of men to make a second shift—into work at home.

The Working Wife
as Urbanizing Peasant

❋

WOMEN's move into the economy is the basic social revolution of our time. It embraces the lifetimes of Nancy Holt, Nina Tanagawa, Anita Judson, their mothers and grandmothers. Nancy Holt is a social worker and mother of Joey. Her mother was a Nebraska housewife and mother of four, and her grandmother raised five children on a wheat farm. Nina Tanagawa is an executive and mother of two. Her mother ran the house, raised three children, and helped keep the books in her father's hardware store. Her grandmother raised chickens and cows on a farm. Anita Judson is a billing clerk and mother of two. Her mother worked two jobs as a domestic and raised four children. Her grandmother worked a farm in Louisiana. Working from the present generation back, there is often this pattern: working mother now, urban housewife thirty years ago, farm woman fifty years ago. Sometimes two generations of urban housewives follow the farm woman, sometimes none. All these women worked. What's new is that, in taking paid work outside the home, masses of women live a life divided between two competing urgency systems, two clashing rhythms of living, that of family and workplace. What's new, in scale at least, is child care for pay, the massive spread of the double day, and the struggle within marriage to equalize the load at home. What's new is the pervasive *effect* of the struggle on apparently unrelated events— as in "Joey's Problem."

This recent change is an extension of an earlier one. Before the industrial revolution in America, most men and women lived out their lives on the private family farm—where crops were grown and craft work done mainly for domestic consumption. With industrialization, more crops and goods were produced and distributed to wider markets for money. But industrialization affected men and women at different times and in different ways. In a sense, there is a "his" and a "hers" to its history in America.

Painting the picture in broad strokes, the growth of factories and trades in early American cities first began to draw substantial numbers of men and women away from farm life around the 1830s. Many single girls worked in the early New England textile mills for four and five years until they married, but mill girls represented a tiny fraction of all women and less than 10 percent of all those who worked for wages.[1] In 1860, most industrial workers were men. Only 15 percent of women worked for pay, most of them as domestic servants. As men entered factory work, they gradually changed their basic way of life; they moved from open spaces to closed-in rooms, from loose seasonal time to fixed industrial time, from life among a tight circle of kinfolk and neighbors to a life among more different kinds of people. At first, we might say, men did something like trying to "have it all." In the early New England rural factories, for example, men would work in these factories during the day and go home in the evenings to work in the fields. Or they moved in and out of factory work depending on the season and the crop ready for harvest. But over time, the farmer became an urban worker.

On the whole, the early effects of industrial employment probably altered the lives of men in a more dramatic and immediate way than it altered the lives of women, most of whom maintained a primary identity at home. To be sure, life changed for women, too. Earlier in the century, a young mother might churn butter and raise chickens and hogs. Later in the century, a young mother might live in the city, buy her butter and eggs at the grocery store, take in boarders, be active in church, and subscribe to what the historian Barbara Welter has called a "cult of true womanhood" based on the special moral sensibility ascribed to women. Through this period, most women who married and raised children based their role and identity at home. "Home" changed. But, as the historian Nancy Cott argues in *Bonds of Womanhood*, throughout the nineteenth century, compared to men, women maintained an orientation toward life closer to what had been. If we compare the overall change in the lives of women to those in the lives of men, we might conclude that during this period men changed more.

Today, it is women whose lives are changing faster. The expansion of service jobs has opened opportunities for women. Given that women have fewer children now (in 1800 they gave birth to about eight and raised five or six to adulthood; in 2010 they average two) and given that their wage has been increasingly needed at home, it has become "the woman's turn" to move into the industrial economy. It is now women who are wrenched out of a former domestic way of life.

In the early nineteenth century, it was men who began to replace an older basis of power—land—with a new one—money. It was men who began to identify their "manhood" with having money in a way they had not done before. Through the great value on a man's purchasing power, the modern worship of goods—or what Karl Marx criticized as a "commodity fetishism"—became associated with "being a man."

Today, it is women who are establishing a new basis of power and identity. If women previously based their power on attractiveness to men or influence over children and kin, now they base it more on wages or authority on the job. As Anita Judson, the billing clerk married to the forklift driver, observed, "After I started earning money, my husband showed me more respect." Given the wage gap, and the greater effect of divorce on women, the modern woman may not have a great deal more power than before, but what power she has is *based* differently.

Paid work has come to seem exciting, life at home dull. Although the most acceptable motive for a woman to work is still "because I have to," most of the working mothers I talked to didn't work just for the money. In this way they have begun to participate in a value system once exclusively male and have developed motivations more like those of men. Many women volunteered to me that they would be "bored" or "go bananas just staying home all day," that they were not, on any permanent basis, the "domestic type." This feeling held true even among women in low-level clerical jobs. A nationwide Harris poll taken in 1980 asked women: "If you had enough money to live as comfortably as you'd like, would you prefer to work full time, part time, do volunteer-type work, or work at home caring for the family?" Among working women, 28 percent wanted to stay home. Of all the women in the study, including housewives, only 39 percent wanted to stay home—even if they had enough money to live as comfortably as they liked. When asked if each of the following is an important reason for working or not, 87 percent of working women responded "yes" to "providing you with a sense of accomplishment and personal satisfaction," 84 percent to "helping ends meet," and 81 percent to "improving your family's standard of living."[2] Women want paying jobs, part-time jobs, interesting jobs—but they want jobs, I believe, for roughly the same complex set of reasons peasants in modernizing economies move to cities.*

In many ways, the twentieth-century influx of married women into an industrial economy differs from the earlier influx of men. For one thing, through the latter half of the nineteenth century up until the present, women's tasks at home have been reduced. Store-bought goods gradually replaced homespun cloth, home-made soap and candles, home-cured meats, and home-baked bread. More recently, women have been able to buy an array of preprepared meals, or buy "carry-out," or, if they can afford it, to eat out. Some send out clothes to a "wash and fold" laundry, and

---

*In the United States we speak of farmers, not "peasants." The term "farmer" connotes free ownership of land, and a certain pride, while the term "peasant" suggests the humility of a feudal serf. I draw the analogy between modern American women and the modernizing peasantry because women's inferior social, legal, educational, and economic position had until recently been like that of peasants.

pay for mending and alterations. Day care for children, retirement homes for the elderly, homes for delinquent children, mental hospitals, and psychotherapy are, in a way, commercial substitutes for jobs a mother once did at home.

Products and services in the market often excel over mama's best efforts at home. A woman's skills at home are then valued less. One mother remarked: "Sometimes when I get upset and want to make a point, I refuse to cook. But it doesn't work. My husband just goes and picks up some Colonel Sanders fried chicken; the kids love it." Another mother said, "When I told my husband I wanted him to share the laundry, he just said, 'Let's take it to a laundry.'" The modern industrial versions of many goods and services come to be preferred over the old-fashioned domestic ones, even as colonial cultures came to prevail over old-fashioned "native ways." Just as the First World has raised its culture over the Third World's indigenous culture, so too the store-bought goods and services have marginalized the "local crafts" of the housewife.

THE TWO CULTURES

Not only are many of the products and services of the home available and cheap elsewhere, the status of the full-time housewife has sunk. Wives who "just" stay home have developed the defensiveness of the downwardly mobile. Facing the prospect of becoming a housewife after quitting her job, Ann Myerson said, "If you want to know what shunning feels like, go to a cocktail party. People will ask you what you *do*. Say 'I'm a housewife.'" One illustration in the November 1970 issue of *True* magazine sums up the housewife's predicament: a commuter train is filled with businessmen reading morning newspapers and office memos. A bewildered middle-aged housewife in bathrobe and furry slippers, hair in curlers, searches the aisles for her husband, his forgotten briefcase in hand. Her husband is hiding behind his seat, embarrassed that his wife looks so ridiculous, so out of place. In their suits, with their memo pads and newspapers, going somewhere, the men of the commuter car determine what is ridiculous. They represent the ways of the city; she is a lost peasant in their midst.

Working mothers often feel poised between the cultures of the housewife and the working man. On one hand, many middle-class women feel severely criticized by relatives or neighbors who stay home. Feeling increasingly threatened and militant about their own declining position, they pose the question, "Do you *have* to work?" Nina Tanagawa felt the critical eye of the stay-at-home moms of her daughter's friends. Jessica Stein felt it from affluent neighbors. Nancy Holt and Adrienne Sherman felt scrutinized by their mothers-in-law. Some of these watchful relatives and neighbors cross over the big divide themselves. When Ann Myerson's mother was a housewife, she criticized Ann for her overzealous careerism, but when her mother got a job herself, she questioned Ann's decision to quit.

Many working mothers seemed to feel both superior to housewives they knew and envious of them. Having struggled hard for her accounting degree, Carol Alston didn't want to be confused with "ordinary" women who weren't productive. But seeing housewives slowly pushing their carts down the aisle at the Safeway at midday, she also came to question her own hectic life.

Women who've remained back in the "village" as housewives have often been burdened with extra tasks—collecting delivered parcels, letting in repairmen, or keeping afternoon company with the children of neighborhood mothers who work. One complained that housewives were the only ones who volunteered at Cub Scout meetings. Their working neighbors seldom have time to stop and chat or, sometimes, return favors.

Their traditional source of honor, like the peasant's, has been threatened. Unpaid work, like that of housewives, came to seem like not "real" work. The housewife became "just a housewife," her work became "just housework." In their book *For Her Own Good*, Barbara Ehrenreich and Deirdre English describe how at the turn of the century, the Home Economics Movement struggled against the social decline of the housewife by trying to systematize and upgrade the role into a profession. Women, its leaders claimed, could be dignified "professionals" in their own homes. Ironically, the leaders of the Home Economics Movement thought housework was honorable—not because it was *intrinsically* valuable—but because it was just as real as *paid* work, a concession revealing how much moral ground had already been lost.

CLASS DIFFERENCES

If working wives are the modern-day urbanizing peasant, then there are important differences between some "peasants" and others. In addition to the split between housewives and working women, this social revolution also widens a split between women who do jobs that pay enough to pay a baby-sitter and women who baby-sit or tend to other home needs. Carmen Delacorte, who sat for the children of two other families I talked to; Consuela Sanchez, the Salvadorian woman who baby-sat for the Livingstons' daughter and whose mother was raising Consuela's child back in El Salvador; the Myersons' Filipino baby-sitter, who had an eight-year-old daughter in the Philippines; the Steins' housekeeper and assistant housekeeper: all these women are part of a growing number of workers forming an ever-broadening lower tier of women doing bits and pieces of the housewife's role for pay.

Most likely, three generations back, the grandmothers of all these women—professional women, baby-sitters, housekeepers—were housewives. Since class has a remarkable sticking power, it may be that the granddaughters of working-class housewives moved into the economy mainly as maids, day-care workers, laundry and other service workers—doing low-paid "female" work—while the granddaughters of upper-middle-class and upper-class housewives moved in as lawyers, doctors, professors, and executives. The granddaughters of the middle class may have tended to move into the expanding world of clerical jobs "in between." Both Carmen Delacorte and Ann Myerson form part of the new "peasantry," but as in the industrial revolution of the nineteenth century, some newcomers to the city found it much tougher going than others, and were more tempted to go home.

PRESERVING A DOMESTIC TRADITION?

But women of every social class and in every kind of job face a common problem: how shall I preserve the domestic culture of my mother and grandmother in the age of the nine-to-five or eight-to-six job? In some ways, the experience of Chicana women condenses the experience of all working women. Many Chicanas have experienced the strains of three movements—that from rural to urban life, from Mexican to American life, and from domestic to paid employment. In her research on Chicana working women, the sociologist Beatrice Pesquera discovered that many conceived it to be their job as women to keep alive *la cultura*, to teach their children Spanish songs, stories, religious rituals; to teach their daughters to cook tortillas and chile verde. This was, she argued, eroded by television and ignored by schools in America. So the Chicana was a cultural bridge between past and present, posing yet another task in her second shift. When they don't have time to be the bridge themselves, Chicana working mothers often seek a "tortilla grandma" to baby-sit and provide *la cultura*. Many white working mothers have fought a similar—and often losing—battle to carry forward a domestic culture—a culture of homemade apple pie, home-sewn Halloween costumes, hand-ironed shirts. If she didn't do it on weekdays, she got to it on Saturday.

Many traditional women feel they should carry on *all* of the domestic tradition and that *only women* can carry it on. Having secured a base in the industrial economy, men have relied on women to connect them back to a life outside it. In *The Remembered Gate*, Barbara Berg argues that as Americans moved off the land, the values of farm life moved into the home. The woman at home became the urban agrarian, the one who preserved the values of a bygone rural way of life while living in the city. By "staying back" in this sense, she eased the difficult transition for the men who moved ahead.

Who is easing the transition for women now? Although traditional women want to preserve a "domestic heritage," most working mothers I talked to felt ambivalent about it. "Do I really *need* to cook an elaborate meal every night?" one woman asked. Another mused, "I'm not the type that has to see my face in the kitchen floor. That part of my mother's cleaning routine I let go of, no problem. But I don't give my child as much as my mother gave me. That's why I want my husband involved—to make up for that."

Some men have responded to the declining domestic culture, much as colonizers responded to the marginalization of traditional peasant life. Secure in their modern world, the colonizers could collect peasant rugs, jewelry, or songs, or cultivate a taste for the indigenous cuisine. Today, some successful professional men, secure in their own modern careers, embrace a few tokens of the traditional female culture. They bake bread or pies on Saturdays, or fix a gourmet meal once a month. But very few men go completely "native"; that would take an extra month a year.

UNEQUAL WAGES AND FRAGILE MARRIAGES—
THE COUNTERTENDENCY

Women's move into the economy, as a new urban peasantry, is the basic social revolution of our time, and, on the whole, it has increased the power of women. But other realities also lower it. If women's work outside the home increases their need for male help inside it, two facts—that women earn less and that marriages have become less stable—inhibit many women from pressing men to help more.

Today, while women average eighty cents to the dollar, their wages are more important than ever before to family life, and as half of all workers, they are more important than ever to the national economy. But overall it remains true that, given how things are, women have a greater economic need for marriage than men, and are more likely to fall into poverty outside it.

Meanwhile, what has changed is the extent to which a woman can depend on marriage. The divorce rate has risen steadily through the century and between 1970 and 1980, it doubled. Experts estimate that today 43 percent of all first marriages, 60 percent of all second marriages, and 73 of third ones eventually end in divorce. Whatever causes divorce, as the sociologist Terry Arendell points out in *Divorce: Women and Children Last*, the effect of it is much harder on women. Divorce usually pushes women down the class ladder—sometimes way down. Most divorced men provide surprisingly little financial support for their children. According to the Bureau of the Census in 1985, 81 percent of divorced fathers and 66 percent of separated fathers have court orders to pay child support. Twenty percent of these fathers fully comply; 15 percent pay irregularly. How much child support a father pays is also not related to his capacity to pay.[3]

After divorce, fathers have distressingly little emotional contact with their children as well. According to the National Children's Survey conducted in 1976 and 1981 and analyzed by sociologist Frank Furstenberg, 23 percent of all divorced fathers had no contact with their children during the past five years. Another 20 percent had no contact with their children in the past one year. Only 26 percent had seen their children for a total of three weeks in the last year. Two-thirds of fathers divorced for over ten years had not had any contact with their children in more than a year. In line with this finding, in her study of divorced women, sociologist Terry Arendell found that over half of the children of divorced women had not received a visit or a call from their father in the last year; 35 percent of these children had not seen their fathers in the last five years. Whatever job they took, these women would also have to be the most important person in their children's lives.

The frightening truth is that once pushed down the class ladder, many divorced women and their children get stuck there. This is because they have difficulty finding jobs with adequate pay and because most of them have primary responsibility for the children. Also, fewer divorced women than men remarry, especially older women with children.

In the nineteenth century, before a woman could own property in her own name, get a higher education, enter a profession, or vote, she might have been trapped in a marriage to an overbearing husband and have nowhere else to go. Now we call that woman "oppressed." Today, a woman can legally own property, vote, get an education, work at a job, and leave an oppressive marriage to walk into an apparently "free" form of inequality.

Divorce is an undoing of an economic arrangement between men and women. Reduced to its economic bare bones, traditional marriage has been what the economist Heidi Hartmann calls a "mechanism of redistribution." Through it men supported women to rear their children and tend their homes. In the late nineteenth and early twentieth centuries, unions won a higher "family wage" for male workers, on the grounds that men needed the money more than women to support wives and children. At that time it seemed reasonable that men should get first crack at better-paying jobs, and even earn more than women for the same work because "women didn't support a family." Since this arrangement put men and women in vastly unequal financial positions, the way most women got a living wage was to marry. In the job market, the relation between men and women was as the upper to the lower class. Marriage was the equalizer.

But as marriage—this "mechanism of redistribution"—has grown more fragile, divorced men still earn a "family wage" but no longer "redistribute" it to their children or the ex-wife who cares for them. The media stresses how sexes both have the freedom to divorce, and surely this choice is an important advance. At the same time, the more men and women live outside marriage, the more they divide into separate classes. Three factors—the belief that child care is female work, the failure of ex-husbands to support their children, and higher male wages—have taken the economic rug from under that half of married women who divorce.

Patriarchy has not disappeared, it's changed form. In the old form, women were forced to obey an overbearing husband in the privacy of an unjust marriage. In the new form, women are free with an overall unequal setup. In the old form, women were limited to the home but economically maintained there. In the new form, women earn the bacon and cook it too.

The modern oppression of women outside marriage reduces the power of women *inside* marriage as well. Married women become cautious, like Nina Tanagawa or Nancy Holt who look at their divorcing friends and say, "The extra month a year or a divorce? I'll work the extra month."

In conversation, both men and women expressed sympathy for the emotional pain of divorcing friends. But women told stories with more anxious interest, and more empathy for the plight of the woman. One evening at the dinner table, a mother of two who worked at word processing had this exchange with her husband, a store manager, and her former boss:

A good friend of mine worked as a secretary for six years, putting her husband through dental school. She worked like a dog, did all the housework, and they had a child too. She didn't really worry about getting ahead at the job because she figured they would rely on his work and she would stop working as soon as he set up practice. Well, he went and fell in love with another woman and divorced his wife. Now she's still working as a secretary and raising their little boy. Now he's got two other children by the other woman.

Her husband commented: "That's true, but she was hard to get along with, and she had a drinking problem. She complained a lot. I'm not saying it wasn't hard for her, but there's another side to the story."

Surprised, the wife answered. "Yeah, but she was *had*! Don't you think?"

Her husband said, "Oh, I don't know. They both have a case."

Earlier in our century, the most important cautionary tale for women was of a woman who "fell" from chastity before marriage and came to a bad end because no man would have her. Among working mothers of small children, and especially the more traditional of them, the modern version of the "fallen woman" became the divorcée. Needless to say, not all women fear divorce. But when life is made to seem so cold "out there," women such as Nancy Holt and Nina Tanagawa may try to get warm inside unequal marriages.

THE HAVES AND HAVE-NOTS OF BACKSTAGE SUPPORT FOR WORK

A cycle is set in motion. Because men put more of their "male" identity in work, their work time is worth more than female work time—to the man and to the family. The greater worth of male work time makes his leisure more valuable, because it is his leisure that enables him to refuel his energy, strengthen his ambition, and move ahead at work. By doing less at home, he can work longer hours, prove his loyalty to his company, and get promoted faster. His aspirations expand. His pay rises. He earns exemption from the second shift.

The female side of the cycle runs parallel. The woman's identity is less in her job. Since her work comes second, she carries more of the second shift, thus providing backstage support for her husband's work. Because she supports her husband's efforts at work more than he supports hers, her personal ambitions contract and her earnings, already lower, rise more slowly. Her extra month a year contributes not only to her husband's success but to the expanding wage gap between them, and so the cycle spins on.

The inequality in backstage support is hidden from view. One cannot tell from sheer workplace appearance who goes home to be served dinner and who goes home to cook, any more than we can tell rich from poor these days just by how people dress. Both male and female workers come to work looking the same. Yet one is "poorer" in backstage support than the other. One irons a spouse's uniform, fixes a lunch, washes clothes, types a résumé, edits an office memo, takes phone calls, or entertains clients. The other has a uniform ironed, a lunch fixed, clothes washed, a résumé typed, an office memo edited, phone calls taken, and clients entertained.

There is a curious hierarchy of backstage "wealth." The richest is the high-level executive with an unemployed wife who entertains his clients and runs his household; and a secretary who handles his appointments, arranges his travel, and orders anniversary flowers for his wife. The poorest in backstage support is the single mother who works full time and rears her children with no help from anyone. Between these two extremes lie the two-job couples.

In a study I did of the family life of workers in a large corporation, I discovered that the higher up the corporate ladder, the more home support a worker had. Top executives were likely to be married to housewives. Middle managers were likely to be married to a working spouse who does some or most of the housework and child care. And the clerical worker, if she is a woman, is likely to be single or a single mother and does the work at home herself.[4] At each of these three levels, men and women fared differently. Among the female top executives, 95 percent were married to men who also worked and 5 percent were single or single parents. Among male top executives, 64 percent were married to housewives, 23 percent were married to working wives, and 5 percent were single or single parents. So compared to men, female top executives had less backstage support. As one female manager remarked: "It's all men at my level and most of them are married to housewives. But even the ones whose wives work seem to have more time at the office than I do." As women executives so often quipped, "What I really need is a wife."

In the middle ranks, a quarter of the men were married to housewives, nearly half were married to working wives, and about a third were single. Among women in the middle ranks, half were part of two-job couples and carried most of the second shift. The other half were single or single parents. Among lower-level clerical workers, most were single or single mothers.

Being "rich" or "poor" in backstage support probably influences what traits people develop. Men who have risen to the top with great support come to be seen and to actually be "hard driving," ambitious, and "committed" to their careers. Women with less support are vulnerable to the charge of being "uncommitted." Sometimes, they do become less committed. But women such as Nina Tanagawa did not lack ambition or suffer from what the psychologist Matina Horner calls a "fear of success." Rather, their "backstage poverty" raised the emotional price of success impossibly high.

In an earlier economic era, when men entered industrial life, their wives preserved—through the home—a link to a life they had known before. By "staying back," such wives eased a difficult transition for the men who were moving into the industrial age. In a sense the Nancy Holts of America are like peasants new to factory life but no one is easing the transition for them.

Stepping into Old Biographies or Making History Happen?

✳

THE woman with the flying hair offers a picture of what it should be like to work and raise a family: busy, active, fun. But the female mannequin in the apron, wide-eyed and still, arms folded, peering outside my neighbor's bay window, a picture of the falsely present mother is often a more real picture of life at home when two-job couples "cut back" at home and diminish their idea about what a child, a marriage, a home really needs. She is my neighbor's joke but she also symbolizes a certain emotional reality when men don't share the second shift.

As women have been catapulted into the economy, their pocketbooks, their self-respect, their notion of womanhood, and their daily lives have been transformed. The "motor" of this revolution is the changing economy—the decline in the purchasing power of the male wage, the decline in "male" blue-collar jobs, and the rise in "female" jobs in the growing service sector. New ideas about manhood and womanhood have become a powerful prod, as well, by creating a new code of honor and identity for men and women that fits the evolving circumstances.

But the revolution has influenced women faster than it has men. The unevenness of this revolution has driven a wedge between such husbands and wives as Evan and Nancy Holt, Nina and Peter Tanagawa, Ray and Anita Judson. Home is far from a "haven in a heartless world," as Christopher Lasch has noted; home has become a shock absorber of pressures far outside it.

The gender revolution is primarily *caused* by changes in the economy, but people *feel* it in marriage. In a parallel way, economic shifts have been the "motor" of changing relations between blacks and whites. As the number of unskilled jobs declines, as capital moves out of the central cities to suburbs or to cheap labor in Third World countries, blacks and whites are left to compete for the remaining jobs. It is in the back rooms of investment banks, personnel offices, and union halls that the strain between the races might be said to *originate.* But it is in the school yard, in the prison, on the street that racial tension is actually *felt.* Just as American blacks have "absorbed" a higher unemployment rate "for whites," in the same sense, the growing number of working women have absorbed the contradictory demands of family and work "for men," by working the extra month a year. But unlike most blacks and whites, men and women *live* together; the female absorption of a male problem becomes part of marriage, and strains it.

Although most working mothers I talked with did most of the work of the home, they felt more permission to complain about it than working women fifty or a hundred years ago. A hundred years ago, American women lacked much permission to ask for a man's help in "women's work." As Gwendolyn Hughes pointed out in 1925, in her book *Mothers in Industry,* earlier in the century supermoming wasn't a "strategy," it was a normal way of life. Today women feel entitled to ask for help at home. But most still have to ask.

At the time of my first interviews, more than half of the women I talked to were not trying to change their division of labor. They complained, they joked, they sighed fatalistically; they collected a certain moral credit for doing "so much," but they didn't press for change. Some of these women didn't want their husbands to share because they didn't believe it was right or because they were making up for having surpassed a certain "power mark." Other women in the study wanted their husbands to share but didn't press for it.

Some women who didn't urge their husbands to share at home also didn't "make room" for his hand at home; they played expert with the baby, the dinner, the social schedule. Something in their tone of voice said, "This is my domain." They edged their husbands out, then collected credit for "doing it all."

About a third of the women I talked to were in the course of pressing their husbands to do more. But another *third* of the women I talked to *had* at some point already pushed their husbands to share, didn't get far, and wearied of trying. Some, like Adrienne Sherman and Nancy Holt, tried active renegotiation—holding long discussions, making lists and schedules, saying they can't go on like this. Or they tried passive renegotiation—they played dumb or got sick.

For their part, 20 percent of the men felt they should share the responsibility and work at home and 80 percent did not. Men whose wives pressed them to do more often resisted by reducing their ideas about needs. They claimed they didn't need the bed made, didn't need a cooked meal, or didn't need a vacation planned. Indeed, some men seemed to covertly compete with their wives over who could care the least about how the house looked, how the meal tasted, what the guests would think. Other men denied the fact they didn't share by not acknowledging the extra kinds of work their wives did. Some men made alternative offerings to the home. Peter Tanagawa offered his wife great emotional support for her career instead of more help at home. Seth Stein offered his wife the money and status of his career instead of help at home. Others made furniture, or built additions on the house their wives could have done without.

Some men covertly referred their wives to "all the sacrifices" to their manhood they had already suffered—compared to other men, present and past. They made their wives feel "luckier than other women." Unconsciously, they made a gift out of not being as patriarchal as they *could* be.

If there is one truth that emerges from all the others, it is that the most important injury to women who work the double day is not the fact they work too long or get too tired. That is only the obvious and tangible cost. The deeper problem such women face is that they cannot afford the luxury of unambivalent love for their husbands. Like Nancy Holt, many women carry into their marriage the distasteful and unwieldy burden of resenting their husbands. Like some hazardous waste produced by a harmful system, this powerful resentment became hard to dispose of.

When women repress their resentment, many, like Nancy Holt, pay a certain cost in self-knowledge. The mental tricks that kept Nancy Holt from blowing up at Evan or sinking into depression were also the mental tricks that prevented her from admitting her real feelings and understanding the ultimate causes for them. Her psychological "maintenance program"—a program that kept her comparing herself to other women and not to Evan, readjusting connections she made between love and respect, respect and actions, and reminding herself that she was "lucky" and "equal anyway"—all these habits of thought smoothed the way for a grand rationalization. They softened both sides of a strong contradiction—between her ardent desire for an equal marriage and all that prevented her from having it. They blinded her to what she really felt about her life.

Some women didn't want their husbands to share the second shift and didn't resent their not sharing. But they seemed to pay another price—a devaluation of themselves or their daughters as females. Ann Myerson managed the home because she wanted to protect her husband's time so he could make his "greater contribution" at work. Hers was the "less important" work. Despite herself, she also regretted having daughters, because they too would grow up managing the house in order to protect the greater contributions of their husbands. However driven, however brilliant, Ann felt, girls could never enjoy the privilege of smooth, unambivalent, highly rewarded devotion to work. Instead of seeing a problem in the system of rewards or the arrangement between the sexes, Ann felt it was too bad she didn't have boys who could "cash in" on it. In this, Ann articulated a contradiction I believe every woman faces: women end up doing the second shift when the second shift is secondary. The more important cost to women is not that they work the extra month a year; it is that society devalues the work of the home and sees women as inferior because they do devalued work.

Devalued as the work of rearing children is, it is probably one of the most humanly rewarding. In appreciating the toll of living in a stalled revolution, then, we should count as part of that cost the missing connections between Seth Stein, Evan Holt, and their children. Resentful of Seth's long absences, his older son sullenly withdrew and at bedtime the younger one dashed around frantically. Drawing the one out and calming the other down became one more hassle at the end of Seth's long day. He is missing the feelings his children would feel toward him if they didn't resent his absence. He is missing the tangles and the arguments that ultimately remind a parent that they matter to a child. He is also missing the cuddles, the talks about what holds the clouds up and why people get sad.

Although fathers pay most of this particular emotional cost, in a different way many mothers do too. As the main managers of the second shift, women become the "heavies," the "time and motion" persons of the family-and-work speed-up. They hurry children through their daily rounds—"Hurry up and eat. . . ." "Hurry and get into your pajamas. . . ."—and thus often become the targets of children's aggression.

FUTURE NANCY HOLTS?

As I drive from my office at the University of California, Berkeley, across the Oakland Bay Bridge to my home in San Francisco, I often compare the couples I have been studying to the students I teach. Who will step into the biography of Nancy Holt? Who will be the new Nina Tanagawa? The Jessica Stein? The Adrienne Sherman? The Ann Myerson? And which of the men will be like Art Winfield? Like John Livingston? Like Ray Judson? Will my students eventually rear children like Joey Holt, Alexandra Tanagawa, Victor and Walter Stein, Adam Winfield? Will it be easier for the younger generation in two-job families? Has the turmoil of the 1970s and early 1980s been a temporary phase in preparation for a new kind of marriage in the future? Or will my students also live in a revolution that is stalled?

I wonder about all this as I talk with students in my office at 464 Barrows Hall on the Berkeley campus. Nearly all of my women students badly want lifelong careers. In this they are typical of students more generally. An American Council of Education survey of 200,000 freshmen at more than 400 campuses in March 1988 asked students to name their probable career. Less than 1 percent of women answered "full-time homemaker."[1] In my office, only a handful confide that "all they want" is to be a homemaker, offering long, hesitant explanations for why they would conceivably want to stay home, as if these days this choice for a college woman called for a social version of a medical excuse.

In a 1985–86 survey of University of California, Berkeley, seniors, Anne Machung found that over 80 percent of senior women thought it was "very important" to have a career. At the same time, 80 percent definitely planned to marry or be in a committed partnership, and another 17 percent hoped to be in one. They planned to have two or three children at most, and to have them later in life than their mothers did. Most planned to interrupt their careers from one to five years to have the children but they didn't think this would disadvantage them at work.[2] The students I teach fit this description too. When I show my students a picture of the woman with the flying hair, briefcase in one hand, child in the other, they say she is unreal, but they want to be just like her.

Even for the most exceptional women, the contradictions between work and family are very real. And my students know it. Many know it from their mothers' struggles, and sometimes from their divorces. But, faced with a contradiction and a cultural cover-up, they feel afraid. They applaud the new opportunities at work. They are scandalized by the inequities that remain. But when it comes to matters at home, a distant, vague, distracted look comes into their eyes, and suddenly they become hesitant and inconclusive. They plan to put marriage off. They plan to go slow. If they have a steady boyfriend, they don't talk about how they will share the work at home in the future. That's "too far ahead." It isn't just one or two young women who avoid it; there seems to be a collective decision not to look. For all the media attention given the working mother, young women are not asking what major changes we need to make the two-job family work well.

If Nancy Holt and many women in this book reacted against their mothers' frustrations at the life of an unfulfilled housewife, many of my women students, eighteen to twenty-two, are reacting against their mothers' frustration at being *oppressed working mothers*. To many young women, the working mother is the new ideal. But she is also the new cautionary tale.

Many young men and women grew up inside busy, strained two-job families. When I ask them about the advantages of having grown up in a two-job family, they mention the education, the family vacations, the financial needs their parents' wages met. And they generally agree with the student who said: "It's made me self-reliant. I can cook by myself, do my homework without prodding. I wouldn't be so independent if my mom had been home all the time." When I ask them about the disadvantages, they sometimes recall a bad memory, like this one: "When I was ten, I had to come home and empty the ashtrays and make the salad for dinner and start my homework in the house alone. I survived, but I hated it." Or another: "My mother was always on the go, and my dad worked long hours. I don't feel like I really got to know either of them until I got to college." When asked to put the advantages and disadvantages together, both men and women felt the advantages won. They want to have two-job families, too, but not in the same way.

Bracing for the plunge into adulthood, most of these young students are turning away from Carmen Delacorte's model of womanhood, but not reaching out with confidence to Adrienne Sherman's. Most of my women students—at the University of California, the heartland of student revolt in the 1960s—are wistful for a 50-50 marriage, but don't think they'll get it. Raised as babies in families who struggled over the second shift, they are weary of marital wars. They accept the goals of the revolution but approach them pragmatically, timidly, fatalistically, in the spirit of the "stall." They are poised to step into the biography of Nancy Holt.

Next to the experience of their own working mothers, what most affects their views on marriage is their exposure to divorce. It makes some young women more traditional. As one described: "In her first marriage, my mother really pushed to be equal with my dad. That led to horrible arguments. In her second marriage, she's staying home. She just says, 'Yes, dear . . . yes, dear' and things are calmer. I don't know what I'm going to do. I know I don't want a marriage like her first but I can't see myself in a marriage like her second." Most daughters of divorce don't want to "get caught" unprepared. As one nineteen-year-old student explained to me: "My mother worked as a freelance graphic designer and it was she who took care of my brother and me. She didn't earn much for her work, so after the divorce, her income plummeted and she got really depressed. Meanwhile my dad got remarried. When I called my dad to tell him how depressed she was, he just said she should get a job." If a woman lets go of her place at work to care for a family, she can "get caught." So some women may creep cautiously into the biography of Anita Judson, the billing clerk and mother of two who kept on working to be prepared "just in case."

The problems middle-class women face are doubled in the working class. Blue-collar women are likely to marry blue-collar men, who are the most vulnerable to the vacillations of the near economy. Less-educated women are more likely to defer to their husbands' jobs; one 1986 national study found that 53 percent of women with no high school education, in contrast to 25 percent of women college graduates, believe "that it is more important for a wife to support her husband's career than to have a career herself."[3] Unlike upper-middle-class women, they will still have to work, and won't enjoy the services of a maid.

And how about young men? Are they planning to share the work at home with working wives? In a 1986 study of Berkeley seniors, 54 percent of the women and 13 percent of the men expected to be the one who would miss an important meeting at work for a sick child. Sixty-nine percent of the women and 38 percent of men expected to share the laundry work equally. Fifty percent of women and 31 percent of the men expected to share cooking.[4] A survey by Catalyst found that *half* of the women plan to put the husband's job first, but *two-thirds* of the men said they planned to put their own job first.

In a 1985 in-depth study of Berkeley seniors, Anne Machung asked undergraduate men if they expected to marry a woman who held a job outside the home. "She can work if she wants," most answered. When asked if they would be willing to marry a woman who wanted them to do half the housework and child care, one man answered, "Yes, I could always hire someone." Another answered, "It would depend on how much I liked her and how she asked." A number of men didn't want "lists."

A GENDER STRATEGY FOR THE NATION

Brought to America by the tradition of the European Enlightenment, the belief in human progress easily fit the open American frontier, the expanding national and international economy, and the movements for racial and gender equality. Like most Americans over at least two centuries, most of the men and women I interviewed for this study said they believed "things were getting better." They said they believed men "are doing more at home than before." In small measure, this is true.

But the young do not promise to usher in a new era. Corporations have done little to accommodate the needs of working parents, and the government has done little to prod them. The nuclear family is still the overwhelming choice as a setting in which to rear children. Yet we have not invented the outside supports the nuclear family will need to do this job well. Our revolution is in danger of staying stalled.

Certainly this is what has occurred in the former Soviet Union, the other major industrial society to draw a majority of its childbearing women into paid jobs. Since industrialization, Soviet women had worked outside the home and done the lion's share of the second shift too. "You work?" the Soviet joke went. "You're liberated." A stalled revolution was passed off as the whole revolution. And some argued that there, too, the extra burden on working mothers is behind the rising rate of divorce.[5]

Can we do better than this? The answer depends on how we make history happen. Just as individuals have gender strategies, so do governments, corporations, schools, and factories. How a nation organizes its workforce and day-care centers, how its schools train the young, reflects the work and family roles it envisions for each sex.

While we hear much rhetoric about families, we hear very little talk about government policies that would actually help them. Indeed, comparatively speaking, we are a backward society. In 1993 President Clinton signed the historic Family and Medical Leave Act that gave workers the right to twelve weeks of leave for a new baby or a family medical emergency. But that left out the roughly 50 percent of workers employed in companies with fewer than 50 workers. It didn't apply to part-time workers, most of whom are women, and leave isn't paid.

After giving birth, a German mother receives fourteen weeks of leave at full pay. Italian mothers receive twenty weeks at full pay. In 2002, Canadian mothers won the right to take a full year off from work after childbirth at 60 percent pay. Mothers in Norway can take a year at 80 percent pay. In Japan in 2011 new parents receive $450–500 a month and child care is free. Worldwide, 127 countries—including virtually every industrial nation—mandate some sort of paid family leave. But in the United States, the richest nation in the world, working parents are not guaranteed a penny of paid leave to stay home with a newborn baby.

A profamily policy in the United States would offer paid parental leave to parents—married, single, gay or lesbian—of natural or adoptive children, and paid "care leave" to tend the elderly. Through comparable worth, it would pull up wages in "women's" jobs. It would go beyond half-time work (which makes it sound like a person is only doing "half" of something "whole") by instituting lower-hour, more flexible "family phases" for all regular jobs filled by parents of young children.

The government would give tax credits to developers who build affordable housing near places of work and shopping centers, with nearby meal-preparation facilities, as Dolores Hayden describes in her book *Redesigning the American Dream*. It would create warm and creative day-care centers. If the best day care comes from elderly neighbors, students, grandparents, they could be paid to care for children. Traveling vans for day-care enrichment could roam the neighborhoods as the ice-cream man did in my childhood.

In these ways, the American government could reduce the number of children in "self-care," draw men into children's lives, and make marriages happier. These reforms could even improve the lives of children whose parents divorce, because research has shown that the more involved fathers are with their children *before* divorce, the more involved they are with them *afterward*. If the government encouraged corporations to consider the long-range interests of workers and their families, they would save on long-range costs due to higher absenteeism, turnover, juvenile delinquency, mental illness, and welfare support for single mothers.

These are the real profamily reforms. If they seem utopian today, we should remember that in the past, the eight-hour day, the abolition of child labor, and the vote for women once seemed utopian too. In his book *Megatrends*, John Naisbitt reported that 83 percent of corporate executives believed that more men feel the need to share the responsibilities of parenting; yet only 9 percent of corporations offer paternity leave.

The happiest two-job marriages I saw were between men and women who did not load the former role of the housewife-mother onto the woman, and did not devalue it as one would a bygone "peasant" way of life. They shared that role between them. What couples called "good communication" often meant that they were good at saying thanks for one tiny form or another of taking care of life at home. Making it to the school play, helping a child read, cooking dinner in good spirit, remembering the grocery list, taking responsibility for the "upstairs." These were the silver and gold of the marital exchange. Up until now, the woman married to the "new man" has been one of the lucky few. But as the government and society shape a new gender strategy, as the young learn from example, many more women and men will be able to enjoy the leisurely bodily rhythms and freer laughter that arise when family life is family life and not a second shift.

Postscript

Since the publication of *The Second Shift*, Greg Alston no longer plays scary jokes on his son, Daryl, to toughen him up. But the Livingstons have separated and the Judsons have divorced. Cary Livingston lives mainly with her mother, though her father wants desperately to remain involved. Ray Judson sees Erik and the baby every two weeks, and Ruby if she's around. As the twins grew older, the Shermans plunged back into their careers from which they've now retired—Michael to become an ardent activist in human rights.

Afterword

The movement of millions of women into paid jobs constituted the major revolution in the twentieth-century American family. But the stories I heard told of "stalls" in that revolution. An old-fashioned view of fatherhood—that was one stall. No family-friendly policies at work—that was another stall. Too little value on the importance of the small acts of paying attention that constitute care or appreciation for others—yet another stall. I began to realize I was talking to couples trapped within the stalled gender revolution of the 1980s.

But are working parents in America today better off? A 2010 online post by Katrina Alcorn on the *Huffington Post* Web site, both hilarious and serious, gives one woman's answer and points to a misguided search for answers.[1] Alcorn describes how she balanced a demanding job, a daily commute, and care for her young children. Then just before the first birthday of her youngest child, she collapsed with insomnia and panic attacks. For these problems, she goes to a psychiatrist who prescribes an antidepressant. The antidepressant caused her to undergo night sweats, headaches, cotton mouth, and further sleeplessness, for which the psychiatrist then prescribes sleeping pills. Alcorn still can't sleep and now suffers an eye twitch.

For her sleeplessness, she is now sent to a "sleep lab," where specialists diagnose her with apnea and outfit her with the latest artificial breathing machine. This she describes as "the size of a lunchbox . . . with a corrugated hose that looped over my head and three slim black straps that held rubber nose plugs snug to my face. . . . Oxygen flowed up the vacuum cleaner hose on top of my head and through the nose plugs. When I opened my mouth, air came whooshing out like I was some kind of human leaf blower." After two weeks, Alcorn finds herself with a fierce headache, unable to breathe through her nose, and on the verge of a cold. Finally a sensible pulmonary specialist points out that long-term use of sleeping pills can hinder breathing, antidepressants can cause insomnia, and artificial breathing machines can dry out nasal passages and so induce colds.

In the end, Katrina Alcorn quits her pills, gives up her Darth Vader breathing machine, feels better, and wisely concludes: "It is crazy to put working parents in impossible situations where they are bound to go crazy, and then act like there's something wrong with them for going crazy." Many working parents look fine on the outside, smiling, well-groomed, bright-eyed, she argues, but I feel close to an inner, emotional edge doing what Tina Fey describes as "a tap-dance recital in a minefield."[2] Indeed, just as many Americans live with great financial debt—unpaid school loans, heavily mortgaged homes, a drive-now-pay-later car—so many may be overloaded with emotional debt. In these times of a stalled revolution, the cultural ideal of the breezily confident woman with the flying hair may be leading many to live beyond their emotional means. So it is to the ultimate causes—the larger "stall"—that we must look.

And how far *have* we come since 1989? To begin with, more American couples are doing the Tina Fey tap dance. In 1975, for example, half of mothers with kids under age eighteen were working. But by 2009, that had risen to nearly three-quarters. In 1975, a third of moms with children under age three were in the labor force; in 2009 it was nearly two-thirds—of whom 73 percent worked full time.[3] And for many, the workday also stretches longer.[4]

So if more mothers are working outside the home, are more men picking up the workload at home? Compared to the 1980s, more American men believe in sharing the second shift and fewer men hold to traditional roles. In the 1970s, 70 percent of men born before the baby boom agreed: "It's better for everyone if the man works and the woman cares for home and family." But by the 1990s, half of those same men agreed and among post–baby boom men, a quarter did.[5] Fewer men also disapproved of high-earning wives.

Still, many couples also feel that however much a dad helped at home, his job came before his wife's. Then came the Great Recession of 2008. The higher-paying jobs of welders, machinists, auto assembly-line workers—all jobs usually filled by men—proved more vulnerable to cost-cutting automation and offshoring than the lower-paid but steadier jobs women held as health aides, administrators, or day-care workers. So while over the past twenty-five years more men have come to believe in sharing the second shift, economic trends caused them to keep an anxious eye on their potentially runaway jobs.

So do the husbands of working moms actually share the second shift more than the men of the 1980s I describe in this book? Since the publication of *The Second Shift* in 1989, a startling two hundred studies published in the decade between 1989 and 1999 provide some answers.[6] The most recent, careful, and detailed study by Melissa Milkie, Sara Raley, and Suzanne Bianchi—based on two nationwide surveys—reported the present-day story of married two-job parents of preschool children, just like those in this book.[7] In one survey conducted in 2003–5, 3,500 mothers and 3,000 fathers agreed to receive periodic telephone calls during a twenty-four-hour day. During each call parents were asked what they were doing, how long it took, where they were, and who they were with. A second survey, conducted in 2000, simply asked parents how they used their time, including such activities as taking naps.

Compared to working dads, researchers found, full-time working moms with preschool kids put in an extra five hours a week (in the first study) and seven hours a week at home (in the second). This created a weekly leisure gap of five to seven hours, or an extra *two weeks* a year of twenty-four-hour days.[8] In my 1980s study, I'd found that compared to their husbands, working moms put in an *extra four weeks a year.* So twenty-five years didn't rid women of an extra shift. But it did cut the length of it in half.

In 1989, I had found that working moms felt more rushed than working dads. And that's what the new research found to be still true: half of moms (52 percent) and a third of dads (34 percent) "always felt rushed." I had also found that women did two or three things at once more often. Women still feel that way more than men but don't actually do it more than men. I had found that women slept fewer hours than their husbands and did fewer things for "pure fun" with the kids. Their counterparts today sleep as long as their husbands and do fun things with their kids as often too. But husbands watch 2.7 more hours of television a week and get 7.5 more hours a week of adults-only leisure.

So are couples happier as a result of these changes? This matters, of course, for if couples aren't enjoying life at home, we haven't *really* unstalled this stalled revolution. The Milkie et al. findings on this issue are unsettling. The researchers compared mothers with full-time jobs (thirty-five hours or more) with those who worked part time or stayed home. Moms with full-time jobs reported laughing with their children less often than anyone else in the study—part-time moms, unemployed moms, and all of the fathers. Surprisingly, fathers married to full-time workers— fathers whose help was most needed—read to, laughed with, and praised their children *less* often than fathers married to part-time or stay-at-home moms. And mothers in full-time jobs (25 percent) were less likely to say they were "completely satisfied with how well their children are doing in life" than were part-time (35 percent) or nonworking (58 percent) moms. About a third of dads were "satisfied," a proportion that did not vary with the hours their wives worked. Overall, most parents—59 percent of mothers, 66 percent of fathers—were not "completely satisfied with how their children were doing."

So why would that be? Could such worried parents be responding to a more widespread reality of American life? One clue lies in a 2007 UNESCO report comparing American children with those in twenty other advanced nations. The report focuses on the health, schooling, social relationships, and self-reported happiness of children ages eleven to fifteen, and it offers sobering news:[9] out of twenty-one countries, the United States ranked twentieth. It was at or near the bottom, researchers found, in rankings on children's health, poverty, family and peer relations, chances of risky behavior (drinking alcohol, drugs, fighting, for example), and personal relationships.[10]

Children were also given a picture and told, "Here is a picture of a ladder. The top of the ladder, 10, is the best possible life for you and the bottom is the worse possible life for you. In general where on the ladder do you feel you stand at the moment? Tick the box next to the number that best describes where you stand." In terms of the proportion of children marking a box above the middle rung, the United States—the world's richest country—ranked eighteen out of twenty-one countries.[11]

So why, in the welfare of its children, does the United States rank so far lower than most other advanced nations? Could it be that so many American mothers work? It is, after all, common for guilty American parents to worry that a mother's job itself makes for unhappy children. But if so, we couldn't understand Norway, which boasts *both* the world's highest rates of maternal employment *and* one of the world's highest rates of child well-being. Seventy-five percent of all working-age Norwegian women work for pay while Norway also ranks seventh out of twenty-one nations in the overall welfare of its children. In short, Norway has undergone a gender revolution, but avoided a *stalled* revolution. Norwegian parents of new or newly adopted babies enjoy an eleven-month paid leave, and new fathers are offered a month's paid leave, exclusive to them, to be forfeited if they decline.[12] Parents receive cash benefits for children ages one to three who lack a full-time place at a public day-care center. Should an elderly parent fall ill, a person with a job can sign up at the local municipality for a "care salary," and take leave from work to care for the parent. And to top it off, a full-time workweek in Norway is thirty-five hours.

Americans shake their heads in disbelief at Norway's wonder-land of limited hours and family-friendly benefits. The country is so small, detractors point out. And its economy is thriving, blessed as it is with the well-spent revenue from North Sea oil. But larger surrounding countries—Sweden, Denmark, and Finland—have no such oil, yet enjoy both thriving economies and family-friendly state policies. France, Germany, the Netherlands, Belgium, and other European nations are not far behind. In short, women can both work and raise thriving children in societies determined to re-move the "stall" from a stalled revolution.

For the United States to catch up with its more successful neighbors, we'd need to reconsider some of our beliefs about com-munity and government. Many Americans resist the idea of gov-ernment help in the abstract: they want to fix the stalled revolution *privately*. But when you get down to specifics, a light appears in their eyes. Paid family and medical leave for new parents or those coping with family illness? Good idea. Affordable subsidized child care? Good idea. A neighborhood toy exchange, or a skill bank that allows neighbors to exchange unpaid services—computer help for mowing a lawn, math tutoring for fresh lasagna? Good idea. Gov-ernment incentives for companies offering flexible hours and job shares? Sure. But no one of us can accomplish all these reforms alone.

In celebration of National Telework Week, Joan Blades, the founder of the Internet-driven organization MomsRising, recently renewed the call for flexi-place—work from home or neighbor-hood workstations.[13] Compared to office-based workers, research shows, home-based workers get more done and save companies money. Working from home, we also unclog freeways, save gas, and green our nation while saving precious time for giggling children at home.

But at the very root of a successful gender revolution is, I believe, a deep value on care—making loving meals, doing projects with kids, emotionally engaging family and friends. Most women in America are no longer homemakers. But the choice arises—do we devalue that role, or do we value its emotional core and share that now with men? And here we must address a strange imbalance between two values associated with the early women's movement. As that movement rolled forward—during the days I first jotted notes envisioning this book—it put forward two big ideas. One was female *empowerment*—the idea that women should express their talents, be all they can be, and stand equal to men. The second big idea was valuing—and sharing—the duties of caring for others.

Without our noticing, American capitalism over time embraced empowerment and sidetracked care. So in the absence of a countermovement, care has often become a hand-me-down job. Men hand it to women. High-income women hand it to low-income women. Migrant workers who care for American children and elderly, hand the care of their own children and elderly to paid caregivers as well as grandmothers and aunts back in the Philippines, Sri Lanka, Mexico, and other countries of the global South. And those Filipina, Sri Lankan, or Mexican paid caregivers at the end of this care chain pass child-care duties to oldest daughters. The big challenge in the years ahead—and the challenge at the heart of this book—is to value and share the duties of caring for loved ones. Facing it, we could—and why not in our lifetimes?—finally celebrate a world beyond this unstalled revolution.

Appendix

Research on Who Does the Housework and Child Care

❋

When I read Gwendolyn Salisbury Hughes's description of women factory workers in Philadelphia after World War I doing laundry and washing their front steps on Saturday mornings, I was reminded of the stories I was hearing from women over sixty years later. But in 1918, when Gwendolyn Hughes was collecting her information, no one would have thought to do a survey comparing men's work at home with women's. Outside of a small social circle, in 1918 this comparison was hard to imagine.

In contrast, through the mid-1960s, 1970s, and 1980s there has been an explosion of research that compares working women to men in their relative contributions to the home. One of the largest time-use studies was conducted by John Robinson at the University of Michigan's Survey Research Center. In his 1965 survey, published in 1977, Robinson gave the 1,244 men and women the so-called yesterday interview in which respondents were asked to remember on one day what they did the previous day. The study overrepresented urban, educated people. The same interview was conducted by Alexander Szalai in 1965–66 in twelve other countries in Western and Eastern Europe, including West Germany, Belgium, France, East Germany, Hungary, Bulgaria, Czechoslovakia, Poland, Yugoslavia, and the former USSR.

A second major study, by Kathryn Walker and Margaret Woods, sampled 1,296 men and women (all married couples) living in Syracuse, New York, in 1967 (the report was published in 1976). Their methods differed from those of Robinson, but both found a large leisure gap between working men and women. Both found that husbands of working wives do little more at home than husbands of housewives. Both found that husbands of working wives actually put in altogether *fewer* hours of work (paid work combined with work at home) than did husbands of housewives—because husbands of working wives could now afford to cut back on their paid work. These husbands did *proportionally* more than husbands of housewives (25 percent versus 15 percent of home work) but that's because *both* spouses did less at home when the wife went out to work.

Are men doing more now? Studies done in the late 1970s and 1980s come up with mixed findings. Some studies find no increase. The 1977 nationwide "Quality of Employment" survey done by the University of Michigan combined the hours of paid and unpaid work men and women each do and found a daily leisure gap of 2.2 hours, about the same gap researchers found in the 1960s. Another study—this one in 1985—by Bradley Googins of Boston University's School of Social Work, took as its subjects the 651 employees of a Boston-based corporation. Of these employees, the married mother averaged 85 hours a week on job, homemaking, and child care. The married father averaged 66 hours—a nineteen-hour-per-week leisure gap. In 1983, Grace Baruch and Rosalind Barnett's study of 160 middle-class Boston families found no difference in the help around the house between men whose wives worked and men whose wives didn't. In her 1983 study of 1,500 white working couples, Shelley Coverman found that women did a total of 87 hours of paid and unpaid work while men did 76—leaving a leisure gap of 11 hours a week. In her 1981 study of professional women with children, Sara Yogev found a leisure gap of 30 hours.

In her 1977 study, Harriet Presser asked how much husbands increased their work at home after their wives took outside jobs. She found 44 percent of the husbands did more work at home, 45 percent did the same amount, and 11 percent actually did less. One study by Greg Duncan and James Morgan (1978) presents some stark statistics on the extra hours of work marriage costs women and saves men. They reported hours of housework per year as follows: 1,473 for married women, and 886 for single women, 301 for married men, and 468 for single men. All of this evidence points to "no change."

But other recent studies find a decrease in the leisure gap. One study—a replication of the earlier University of Michigan study by Robinson—found that women worked only a tiny bit longer than men each day. Between 1965 and 1975 Robinson and his coworkers found the leisure gap between men and women had virtually disappeared. *Men* weren't doing *more* housework and childcare. *Women* were doing *less,* and putting in four to five hours less on the job as well. Rather than renegotiating roles with their husbands, these wives pursued a strategy of cutting back at home and at work.

If this study is representative of women and men in the general population, then "cutting back"—not male sharing—is the new response to the strains of being a supermom. But I don't believe this study is representative of the general population, and the researchers themselves were puzzled. During 1965 through 1975, when this study was done, hours of women's paid labor did not shrink and the proportion of women parttimers did not increase in the United States. According to the Bureau of Labor Statistics (Table 677), the proportion of women working part time was 19 percent in 1965, 22 percent in 1970, 21 percent in 1975, 21 percent in 1980, and 20 percent in 1982. In short, most women continued to work full time. The proportion who worked part time didn't change between 1965 to 1982.

But the hours at work of women in this *study* did decline, and the decline was probably an artifact of the researchers' method. In hopes of improving the accuracy of their study, the researchers periodically reinterviewed the same respondents at different times of day. So detailed and repeated were the questions in this study that about a quarter of the people dropped out of it—among them, presumably, the busiest. Ironically, the women most burdened by the very crunch the researchers were investigating probably didn't have time to fill out such a lengthy questionnaire.

Observing the findings of this study, Joseph Pleck cautiously hailed the day when the problem of the leisure gap would pass. But the fact is, for most women that day has not come. Even if all women could iron out the leisure gap by working part time, is part-time work a solution *if it's just for women*? Given the increasing danger of marginalizing family life, I believe it's important to offer and legitimate well-paid part-time jobs (see Chapter 17), but for men as well. I think it would be a mistake to settle for part-time work "just for women." This division of labor would lead to economic and career inequities between men and women, which would make women economically vulnerable in an age in which half of marriages don't last. A better solution might be to share the part-time option or alternate part-time phases of each spouse's work life.

MY STUDY: A NATURALISTIC APPROACH

Anne Machung and I interviewed 145 people altogether, two-thirds of them several times over. We interviewed 100 husbands and wives (50 two-job couples) and 45 other people, including baby-sitters, day-care workers, schoolteachers, traditional couples with small children, and divorcées who had been in two-job couples. I did the in-depth observations of 12 families, and these families were selected from among the 50 couples in our study as good examples of common patterns we found. We supplemented the in-depth study with a quantitative analysis of all 50 families.

Characteristics of the Couples

Of the men we interviewed, the mean age was thirty-three, of the women, thirty-one. Forty-seven percent had one child, 38 percent had two, and 15 percent had three; no couple had more than three. As a whole, those we interviewed were disproportionately middle class. Twelve percent were blue-collar workers (craft workers, operatives, service workers), 17 percent clerical and sales, 25 percent managers and administrators, 46 percent professional and technical workers. (According to the Bureau of Labor Statistics, in the United States as a whole in 1982, 44 percent were blue-collar workers, 25 percent were clerical or sales, 12 percent were managers and administrators, 17 percent were professional and technical workers, and 3 percent farmers. These add up to 101 percent due to rounding error.)

As for education, 6 percent of the people we interviewed had a high school education or less, 31 percent had some college, 19 percent had a B.A. or B.S., 12 percent had some graduate education, and 32 percent had graduate degrees. As for home ownership, only 2 percent already owned a home, 55 percent were in the process of buying one, and the rest rented. In this study, 8 percent of families had regular outside help, 13 percent had occasional help, and 79 percent had no help at all. (Nationwide, 85 percent of all the families have no form of outside help.)

Working couples who are poorer—and especially the women in those couples—have it harder. In her 1986 dissertation on lower- and working-class Chicanas, Denise Segura reported that when she asked wives whether their husbands helped at home, they responded with "half smiles, painful silences, tensing of facial muscles and at times, outright laughter." The problems of the second shift are probably nowhere resolved any better than in the couples we've studied here.

Seventy percent of our couples were white, 24 percent were black, 3 percent Chicano or Latino, and 3 percent Asian. Although I found more conservative attitudes among Chicanos, I found no difference between whites and Chicano men in their help at home. Nor did I find a difference between whites and blacks. (One of Joseph Pleck's studies, 1982, showed a smaller weekly leisure gap among black husbands and wives—11 hours—than among whites—17 hours—but I didn't find this.)

Ways of Seeing

Initially we contacted couples by distributing a short questionnaire on work and family life to every thirteenth name drawn from the personnel list of a large corporation. Fifty-three percent returned the questionnaire. At the end of this short questionnaire we explained what we were interested in and asked if respondents would be willing to volunteer for an in-depth interview. To supplement our list, we later asked the people we interviewed for the names of neighbors and friends who were also two-job couples with children under six.

We asked men and women, "Can you tell me about your typical day?" We found that wives were much more likely to spontaneously mention something to do with the house; 3 percent of wives but 46 percent of husbands didn't mention the house at all in their spontaneous description of a "typical day." Three percent of the women and 31 percent of the men made no spontaneous mention of doing something for a child—like brushing hair or fixing a meal.

Working mothers also more often mentioned caring for people within the larger family circle: their own parents, their husbands' parents, relatives, neighbors, friends, baby-sitters. One woman made sandwiches every Saturday for the neglected children of a neighboring working couple. Another helped her baby-sitter through a marital crisis. Another phoned daily to a relative bedridden with a back injury. Another made Christmas cookies for neighbors. Similarly, when gifts or phone calls came, they often came from busy working mothers. Men, especially working-class men, were often generous about giving time to move furniture, repair cars, or build additions on houses. But in most of these families, the communal circle of informal help seemed to be based more solidly on the informal work of women.

We also noticed that men spoke about chores in a different way—more in terms of chores they "liked and disliked," would do or wouldn't do. Women more often talked about what needed doing.

Men and women also tell somewhat different stories about how much each contributes. For example, 25 percent of husbands and 53 percent of wives answer that the wife "always" anticipates household needs. Some researchers have tried to avoid this sort of "subjective wart" on otherwise objective findings—by taking one or the other person's word for what each partner does. To avoid this source of bias, our solution was to acknowledge and *use* the problem of subjective bias by *averaging* the husband's and wife's estimates of the amount of time each contributed to the set of chores about which I asked them. The tasks fell into three categories: housework, parenting, and management of domestic life. Under housework we included such things as putting out the garbage, picking up, vacuuming, making beds, cleaning bathrooms, doing laundry, routine meal preparation, cleanup, grocery shopping, sewing, car repairs, lawn, household repairs, care for houseplants, care for pets, dealing with the bank. Under child care we included both physical care of the child (tending a child while sick, feeding, bathing the child, taking the child to day care or to doctors) and educating the child (for example, daily discipline, reading). Under management of domestic life we included remembering, planning, and scheduling domestic chores and events, which included such tasks as making up the grocery list, paying bills, sending birthday and holiday cards, arranging baby-sitting, and preparing birthday parties for the child.

We found that 18 percent of men shared the second shift in the sense of doing half of the tasks in all three categories. These 18 percent of men didn't necessarily do half of the *same* tasks as their wives did; they did half of the tasks in each category overall (these 18 percent did 45 to 55 percent; none did more); 21 percent did a moderate amount (between 30 and 45 percent); and 61 percent did little (between 30 percent and none).

The Relation Between Ideology and Male Help at Home

I divided the fifty husbands I studied into three groups: those who shared the housework and child care (i.e., did 45 to 55 percent), those who did a moderate amount (30 to 45 percent), and those who did little (30 percent or less). Of all the *traditional* men, 22 percent shared, 44 percent did a moderate amount, and 33 percent did little. (These add up to 99 percent instead of 100 percent because percentages were rounded off.) Of all the *transitional* men, 3 percent shared, 10 percent did a moderate amount, and 87 percent did little. Of the *egalitarian* men, 70 percent shared and 30 percent did a moderate amount. The numbers are small but suggestive.

The Relation Between the Wage Gap and the Leisure Gap

A debate still rages in social science research between two camps. One, represented by Gary Becker in his *Economic Approach to Human Behavior*, claims that wives do more housework because couples reason that "it's good for everybody" if husbands focus on work, since they generally earn more. Women's greater work at home is thus part of a family strategy to maximize economic utility. Implicitly, he argues that this collective strategy involves little struggle and, indeed, has nothing to do with ideology or male privilege. The second camp, best represented by Joan Huber and Glenna Spitze in *Sex Stratification*, argues that such arrangements are as much cultural as they are economic. And according to their own massive study, it is the size of the wife's paycheck and not the wage gap between spouses that influences the amount of work a husband does at home.

In search of an invisible "economic hand" that might explain why some couples do and some don't share the work at home in my own study, I set about dividing our fifty couples into three groups—high-wage gap (in which the husbands earned much more than the wives), middle-wage gap, and low-wage gap. I found no statistically significant relation between the wage gap between husband and wife and the leisure gap.

To cross-check this finding, I reanalyzed a subsample of another sixty-five couples (both of whom worked full time and cared for children under age fifteen) drawn from a larger national study done by the Survey Research Center at the University of Michigan in 1981. (This was the same 1977 sample that showed the disappearing leisure gap.) I divided the couples into four groups: the husband earned 75 percent or more of the total family income, between 55 and 75 percent, between 45 and 55 percent, and the wife earned more. I found that the less the wife earned (relative to her husband) the more housework she did. Women in group one contributed 72 percent of all the housework; in the second group, they contributed 66 percent; in the third, 55 percent; and in the fourth, 49 percent. Although women who earned more than their husbands did less housework, they did not have more leisure. The reason for this was that the *low*-earning women who did more housework worked shorter hours, so they could do the housework and have more leisure. Still puzzled, I looked again at my own fifty couples, teased apart the low-wage-gap group, and discovered that—in contrast to the couples in the University of Michigan study—the women who outearned their husbands often did so because their husbands weren't doing so well at work. (This may not have been the case for high-earning wives in the Michigan study.) Looking more closely, I discovered the principle of "balancing"—wives "making up" for doing "too well" at work by doing more at home.

Taking off from Huber and Spitze, then, I conclude that the leisure gap between wives and husbands reflects something more than these couples' pragmatic adaptation to the higher wages of American men—an interplay of gender strategy.

Notes

Chapter I

1. For the 1975 and 2009 figures on mothers' participation in paid employment, see Tables 5 and 7 in U.S. Department of Labor & U.S. Bureau of Labor Statistics (December 2010) "Women in the Labor Force: A Databook" (Report 1026; http://www.bls.gov/cps/wlf-databook-2010.pdf). For 2009 figures for mothers with children under age 1, see Bureau of Labor Statistics (May 2010) Table 6 "Employment Status of Mothers with Own Children Under 3 Years Old by Single Year of Age of Youngest Child and Marital Status, 2008-09 Annual Averages" (http://bls.gov/news.release/famee.t06.htm). For figures on part-time work in 1975 and 2009 see table 20 in "Women in the Labor Force" report, cited above. For data on part-time work of women with infants in 2009, see Table 6 (cited above).

2. Alexander Szalai, ed., *The Use of Time: Daily Activities of Urban and Suburban Populations in Twelve Countries* (The Hague: Mouton, 1972), p. 668, Table B. Another study found that men spent a longer time than women eating meals (Shelley Coverman, "Gender, Domestic Labor Time and Wage Inequality," *American Sociological Review* 48 [1983]: 626). With regard to sleep, the pattern differs for men and women. The higher the social class of a man, the more sleep he's likely to get. The higher the class of a woman, the less sleep she's likely to get. (Upper-white-collar men average 7.6 hours sleep a night. Lower-white-collar, skilled and unskilled men all averaged 7.3 hours. Upper-white-collar women average 7.1 hours of sleep; lower-white-collar workers average 7.4; skilled workers 7.0 and unskilled workers 8.1.) Working wives seem to meet the demands of high-pressure careers by reducing sleep, whereas working husbands don't.

For more details on the hours working men and women devote to housework and child care, see the Appendix of this book.

3. Grace K. Baruch and Rosalind Barnett, "Correlates of Fathers' Participation in Family Work: A Technical Report," Working Paper no. 106 (Wellesley, Mass.: Wellesley College Center for Research on Women, 1983), pp. 80–81. Also see Kathryn E. Walker and Margaret E. Woods, *Time Use: A Measure of Household Production of Goods and Services* (Washington. D.C.: American Home Economics Association, 1976).

4. Peplau, L. A., and K. P. Beals. "The Family Lives of Lesbians and Gay Men." In A. Vangelisti, ed., *Handbook of Family Communication*, 2004.

Chapter 2

1. In a 1978 national survey, Joan Huber and Glenna Spitze found that 78 percent of husbands think that if husband and wife both work full time, they should share housework equally (*Sex Stratification: Children, Housework and Jobs.* New York: Academic Press, 1983). In fact, the husbands of working wives at most average a third of the work at home.

2. The concept of "gender strategy" is an adaptation of Ann Swidler's notion of "strategies of action." In "Culture in Action—Symbols and Strategies," *American Sociological Review* 51 (1986): 273–86, Swidler focuses on how the individual uses aspects of culture (symbols, rituals, stories) as "tools" for constructing a line of action. Here, I focus on aspects of culture that bear on our ideas of manhood and womanhood, and I focus on our emotional preparation for and the emotional consequences of our strategies.

3. For the term "family myth" I am indebted to Antonio J. Ferreira, "Psychosis and Family Myth," *American Journal of Psychotherapy* 21 (1967): 186–225.

4. F. T. Juster, 1986.

Chapter 3

1. Lee Rainwater and W. L. Yancey, *The Moynihan Report and the Politics of Controversy* (Cambridge, Mass.: M.I.T. Press, 1967), p. 32.

2. In her book *Redesigning the American Dream* (New York: W. W. Norton, 1984), p. 91, Dolores Hayden describes how, in 1935, General Electric and *Architectural Forum* jointly sponsored a competition for who could design the best house for "Mr. and Mrs. Bliss"—the model couple of the period (Mr. Bliss was an engineer, Mrs. Bliss was a housewife with a college degree in home economics. They had one boy, one girl). The winner proposed a home using 322 electrical appliances. Electricity, the contest organizers proposed, was Mrs. Bliss's "servant."

3. Helen Gurley Brown, *Having It All* (New York; Simon and Schuster, 1982), p. 67.

4. Shaevitz, Marjorie H., *The Superwoman Syndrome* (New York: Warner, 1984), p. xvii.

5. Ibid., p. 112. All quotes within this paragraph are from ibid.

6. Ibid., pp. 205–6.

7. Ibid., pp. 100–101.

8. Hilary Cosell, *Woman on a Seesaw: The Ups and Downs of Making It* (New York: G. P. Putnam's Sons, 1985), p. 30.

9. Bob Greene, "Trying to Keep Up with Amanda," *San Francisco Chronicle,* June 16, 1984, "People" section.

Chapter 9

1. The combination of high work demands with low control over the pace of these demands creates more strain in women's jobs. This may account for the higher observed rates of mental strain among women workers—rates often implicitly attributed to "female frailty" or "excitability." See Cranor et al. (1981).

Similarly, in their study "Women, Work and Coronary Heart Disease," *American Journal of Public Health* 70 (1980): 133–41, Suzanne G. Haynes and Manning Feinleib suggest that women service workers (especially those married to blue-collar husbands, with three or more children) actually suffer more coronary disease than top-level male executives. These female workers combine the "low-autonomy" atmosphere of clerical work with the low-autonomy situation of the family-work speed-up. For research on the effect of marriage and work on mental stress, see Walter R. Gove, "The Relationship Between Sex Roles, Mental Health, and Marital Status," *Social Forces* 51 (1972): 34–44; Walter Gove and Michael

Geerken, "The Effect of Children and Employment on the Mental Health of Married Men and Women," *Social Forces* 56 (1977): 66–76; and Peggy Thoits, "Multiple Identities: Examining Gender and Marital Status Differences in Distress," *American Sociological Review* 51 (1986): 259–72.

2. One study found that male workers enjoy longer coffee breaks and longer lunches than female workers. According to Frank Stafford and Greg Duncan, men average over an hour and forty minutes more rest *at work* than women do each week. See Frank Stafford and Greg Duncan, "Market Hours, Real Hours and Labor Productivity," *Economic Outlook USA,* Autumn 1978, pp. 103–19.

3. Wiseman, Paul. "Young, Single, Childless Women Out-earn Male Counterparts," *USA Today*, September 2, 2010. Figures are based on U.S. Census Bureau information analyzed by the New York research firm Reach Advisors.

4. Blades, Joan, and Kristin Rowe-Finkbeiner, *The Motherhood Manifesto*, New York: Nation Books, 2006, p. 7.

Chapter 10

1. See Nancy Chodorow, *The Reproduction of Mothering* (Berkeley: University of California Press, 1980).

Chapter 13

1. Of the 100 men and women in the 50 "mainstream" couples I studied, 18 percent of the husbands were traditional, 62 percent transitional, and 20 percent egalitarian. Among the wives, 12 percent were traditional, 40 percent were transitional, and 48 percent were egalitarian. (Berkeley couples were omitted because they probably reflect an untypically liberal subculture.) Below, I've shown how husbands' gender ideologies match those of their wives.

The Marital Mix of Gender Ideology*

*Husband's Gender Ideology
with Regard to Marital Roles*

Wife's Gender Ideology	Traditional	Transitional	Egalitarian	Total Wife's
Traditional	10% (5)	2% (1)	—	(6)
Transitional	6% (3)	32% (16)	2% (1)	(20)
Egalitarian	2% (1)	28% (14)	18% (9)	(24)
Total	(9)	(31)	(10)	(50)

*Percentages are of all the 50 *marriages* studied.

Thus, of all the marriages I studied, 60 percent were between husbands and wives who shared similar ideologies, and 40 percent were between husbands and wives who disagreed. The most common type of disagreement was between an egalitarian woman and a transitional man.

Chapter 14

1. See William J. Goode, "Family Disorganization," Chapter 11 in *Contemporary Social Problems*, 4th ed., Robert K. Merton and Robert Nisbet (eds.) (New York: Harcourt Brace Jovanovich, 1976). Also see Louis Roussel, *Le Divorce et les Français*, Vol. II, "L'Expérience des Divorcés," Travautet Documents, Cahier No. 72 (Presses Universitaires de France, 1975), pp. 26–29. In many ways, the fact that wives work both benefits and stabilizes marriage. In virtually all the research on women's work, working women report themselves as happier, higher in self-esteem, and in better mental and physical health than do housewives. See Lois Hoffman and F. I. Nye, *Working Mothers* (San Francisco: Jossey Bass, 1974), p. 209. A woman's work also adds money to a marriage through the so-called dowry effect. By making a family richer, a woman's wages may protect the family from the strains of poverty associated with marital disruption. See Valerie Kincade Oppenheimer, "The Sociology of Women's Economic Role in the Family," *American Sociological Review* 42

(1977): 387–405; D. T. Hall and F. E. Gordon, "Career Choices of Married Women," *Journal of Applied Psychology* 58 (1973): 42–48.

2. Ronald C. Kessler and James McRae, *Institute for Social Research Newsletter*, University of Michigan, 1978. See also S. S. Feidman, S. C. Nash, and B. G. Aschenbrenner, "Antecedents of Fathering," *Child Development* 54 (1983): 1628–36; M. W. Yogman, "Competence and Performance of Fathers and Infants," in A. Macfarlane, ed., *Progress in Child Health* (London: Churchill Livingston, 1983).

3. Joan Huber and Glenna Spitze, *Sex Stratification: Children, Housework and Jobs* (New York: Academic Press, 1983).

4. According to George Levinger's study, men voiced fewer complaints. But the top four were mental cruelty (30 percent), neglect of home or children (26 percent), sexual incompatibility (20 percent), and infidelity (20 percent). For women, the top four were mental cruelty (40 percent), neglect of home or children (39 percent), financial problems (37 percent), and physical abuse (37 percent). ("Sources of Marital Dissatisfaction Among Applicants for Divorce," *American Journal of Orthopsychiatry* 36 [1966]: 803–7.)

Chapter 15

1. Other studies find that a man's upbringing bears only a slight relationship to the amount of work at home he does as an adult. See Lois Hoffman, "Parental Power Relations and the Division of Household Tasks," in F. I. Nye and L. W. Hoffman, eds., *The Employed Mother in America* (Chicago: Rand McNally, 1963), pp. 215-30; M. Bowling, "Sex Role Attitudes and the Division of Household Labor," paper presented at the American Sociological Association, Chicago, 1975; Rebecca Stafford, Elaine Backman, and Pamela DiBona, "The Division of Labor among Cohabiting and Married Couples," *Journal of Marriage and the Family* 39 (1977): 43–57; C. Perucci, H. Potter, and D. Rhoads, "Determinants of Male Family Role Performance," *Psychology of Women Quarterly* 3 (1978): 53–66; M. Roberts and L. Wortzel, "Husbands Who Prepare Dinner: A Test of Competing Theories of Marital Role Allocations," unpublished paper, Boston University, 1979; S. Hesselbart, "Does Charity Begin at Home? Attitudes Toward Women, Household Tasks, and Household Decision-Making," paper presented to the American Sociological Association, 1976; and Gayle Kimball, *50–50 Marriage* (Boston: Beacon Press, 1983).

2. Surprisingly, most researchers find little or no relationship between the amount of time a man spends at paid work and the proportion of housework he does. See Robert Clark, Ivan Nye, and Viktor Gecas, "Husbands' Work Involvement and Marital Role Performance," *Journal of Marriage and the Family* 40 (1978): 9–21; Stafford, Backman, and DiBona (1977); Perucci, Potter, and Rhoads (1978). But also see John Robinson, *How Americans Use Time* (New York: Praeger, 1977), and Walker and Woods (1976). For a thorough review of the evidence, see Joseph H. Pleck, *Working Wives, Working Husbands* (Beverly Hills: Sage Publications, 1985), p. 55.

3. I found a slight—but not statistically significant—difference. Despite a good deal of research on the possible link between the wage gap between husband and wife and the leisure gap between them, I'm aware of only one researcher, the economist Gary Becker (*A Treatise on the Family* [Cambridge, MA: Harvard University Press, 1981]), who found such a link. For more on research about this link, see the Appendix.

4. Pleck (1985), p. 151.

5. See Bob Kuttner, "The Declining Middle" *Atlantic Monthly*, July 1983; Paul Blumberg, *Inequality in an Age of Decline* (New York: Oxford University Press, 1980); Michael Harrington and Mark Levinson, "The Perils of a Dual Economy," *Dissent* 32 (1985): 417–26; and Andrew Hacker, "Women Versus Men in the Work Force," *New York Times Magazine*, December 9, 1984. For the argument that the labor market is *not* dividing into two parts, see Neal H. Rosenthal, "The Shrinking Middle Class: Myth or Reality?" *Monthly Labor Review* 108 (1985): 3–10.

6. Sheila B. Kamerman and Cheryl D. Hayes, eds., *Children of Working Parents: Experience and Outcomes* (Washington, D.C.: National Academy Press, 1983), p. 238.

7. See Norma Radin, "Primary Caregiving and Role Sharing Fathers of Preschoolers," in M. E. Lamb, ed., *Nontraditional Families: Parenting and Child Development* (Hillsdale, N.J.: Erlbaum, 1982), and her "The Role of the Father in Cognitive/Academic Intellectual Development," in M. E. Lamb, ed., *The Role of the Father in Child Development*, 2nd ed. (New York: Wiley, 1981); Norma Radin and Graeme Russell, "Increased Father Participation and Child Development Outcomes," in Lamb, *Nontraditional Families*, pp. 191–218; H. B. Biller, "The Father and Personality Development: Paternal Deprivation and Sex-Role Development," in M. E. Lamb, *The Role of the Father in Child Development* (New York: Wiley, 1976); A. Sagi, "Antecedents and Consequences of Various Degrees of Pa-

ternal Involvement in Child-Rearing: The Israeli Project," in Lamb, *Nontraditional Families*, pp. 205–32; and Michael E. Lamb, ed., *The Father's Role: Applied Perspectives* (New York: Wiley-Interscience, 1986). In Robert Blanchard and Henry Biller's study of forty-four white third-grade boys, they compared boys whose fathers were absent before they were five, absent after five, present for less than six hours a week, and present for more than two hours a day. The boys were similar in their age, I.Q., social class, and the presence of male siblings. The boys who saw their fathers the most did much better on the Stanford Achievement Tests (which measure comprehension of verbal, scientific, and mathematical concepts) than did boys whose fathers were involved less than six hours a week, and did much better than boys whose fathers were totally absent ("Father Availability and Academic Performance Among Third-Grade Boys," *Developmental Psychology* 4 [1971]: 301–15).

8. Carolyn and Philip Cowan found that a father's involvement increased his daughter's sense of being master of her fate and improved her scores in math ("Men's Involvement in Parenthood: Identifying the Antecedents and Understanding the Barriers," in P. Berman and F. A. Pedersen, eds., *Fathers' Transitions to Parenthood* [Hillsdale, NJ.: Erlbaum, 1986]).

9. See Mark W. Router and Henry B. Biller, "Perceived Personality Adjustment Among College Males," *Journal of Consulting and Clinical Psychology* 40 (3) (1973): 339–42.

Chapter 16

1. Alice Kessler-Harris, *Out to Work* (New York: Oxford University Press, 1982). Also see Julie A. Mattaie Bradby, *An Economic History of Women in America* (New York: Schocken Books, 1982).

2. Louis Harris and Associates, "Families at Work," General Mills American Family Report, 1980–81. Other research also shows that even working-class women who do not have access to rewarding jobs prefer to work. See Myra Ferree, "Sacrifice, Satisfaction and Social Change: Employment and the Family," in Karen Sacks and Dorothy Remy, eds., *My Troubles Are Going to Have Trouble with Me* (New Brunswick, NJ.: Rutgers University Press, 1984), pp. 61–79. Women's paid work leads to their personal satisfaction (Charles Weaver and Sandra Holmes, "A Comparative Study of the Work Satisfaction of Females with Full-Time Employment and Full-Time Housekeeping," *Journal of Applied Psychology* 60 [1975]:

117–28) and—if a woman has the freedom to choose to work or not—it leads to marital happiness. See Susan Orden and N. Bradburn, "Working Wives and Marriage Happiness," *American Journal of Sociology* 74 (1969): 107–23.

3. See U.S. Bureau of the Census, *Current Population Reports: Households, Families, Marital Status and Living Arrangements*, series P-20, no. 382 (Washington, D.C.: U.S. Government Printing Office, 1985). Also see *Statistical Abstracts of the U.S. National Data Book, Guide to Sources* (Washington, D.C.: U.S. Government Printing Office, 1985). Spousal support is awarded in less than 14 percent of all divorces, and in less than 7 percent of cases do women actually receive it. See Lenore Weitzman, *The Divorce Revolution* (New York: Free Press; London: Collier Macmillan, 1985).

4. These findings are based on questionnaires I passed out to every thirteenth name on the personnel roster of a large manufacturing company. Of those contacted, 53 percent replied. The results show that the typical form of a worker's family life differs at different levels of the corporate hierarchy. The traditional family prevails at the top. Dual-work families prevail in the middle, and single-parent families and singles prevail at the bottom, as the chart below shows:

Family Type

Level in Company	Traditional Family	Dual Work	Single/ Single Parent	Total
Top executive	54%	39%	8%	101%*
Middle manager	13%	50%	37%	100%
Clerical worker	—	50%	50%	100%

*This adds up to 101 due to rounding error.

Chapter 17

1. "What Do Cal Freshmen Feel, Believe, Think?" *Cal Report* 5 (March 1988): 4. In her study of Barnard senior women, Mirra Komarovsky found only 5 percent wanted to become housewives (*Women in Colleges: Shaping New Feminine Identities* [New York: Basic Books, 1985]).

2. See Anne Machung, "Talking Career, Thinking Job, Gender Differences in Career and Family Expectations of Berkeley Seniors," *Feminist Studies* 15 (1), Spring 1989.

3. *Public Opinion*, December–January 1986.

4. Machung (1989).

5. For more on the role of Soviet men in housework and child care, see Michael Paul Sacks, "Unchanging Times: A Comparison of the Everyday Life of Soviet Working Men and Women Between 1923 and 1966," *Journal of Marriage and the Family*, November 1977, pp. 793–805; and Gail Lapidus, ed., *Women, Work and Family in the Soviet Union* (New York: M. E. Sharpe, 1982).

Afterword

1. Katrina Alcorn, *Huffington Post* Internet Post, April 8, 2010, "Peaceful Revolution: If You Give a Mouse a Prozac . . ."

2. Tina Fey, "Confessions of a Juggler," *The New Yorker*, February 14, 2011, p. 64.

3. Compared with the 1980s, fewer mothers are married, have preschool kids, and work full time. If we follow the statistics, it seems more have quit, cut back hours, or divorced. Still, whether married, cohabiting, or divorced, most mothers of preschool children—six out of ten mothers of children under three—are in the labor force. And of those, only a quarter (27 percent) work part time. Bureau of Labor Statistics, Current Population Survey, Table 6, "Employment Status of Mothers with Own Children Under 3 Years old by Single Year of Age of Youngest Child, and Marital Status, 2007–2009 Annual Averages."

4. The combined weekly work hours of married couples has risen by 20 percent—from fifty-six hours a week in 1969 to sixty-seven hours in 2000. Based on a Bureau of Labor Statistics study, the figures apply to couples ages twenty-five to fifty-four. "Working in the 21st Century" (http://www.bls.gov/opub/working/page17b.htm). According to a 2009 Time Use survey, employed men work now, as in the past, about an hour more than employed women, and even among full-time workers (men average 8.3 hours and women 7.5). "American Time Use Survey" 2009 (http://www.bls.gov/news.release/status.nr0.htm). On hours of work for employed women and men, 1980 to 2009, see the Bureau of Labor Statis-

tics, Department of Labor, "Women in the Labor Force, 2010," Table 21 (http://www.bls.gov/cps/wlf-table21-2010.pdf).

5. Teresa Ciabattari, *Gender and Society*, August 2001, 15(4): 574–91, Table 3. Another study based on the nationwide General Social Survey showed a similar rise in the acceptance of the equality of the sexes between 1974 and 2004. But it also revealed a pause in 1994 and subsequent flattening of the upward trend through 2004. This pause did not signal, the authors surmise, a return to 1950s domesticity, but rather a shift that Maria Charles and David Grusky call "egalitarian essentialism." This view mixes the new (women should have equality of choice) with old (women are better with children and should choose to stay home when they can). Women can be equal, this view holds, and stay home with the children because they've freely chosen to do so. These choices are often premised, of course, on the assumption that we can't reshape jobs, get more government support, and alter the prevailing notion of manhood.

6. Scott Coltrane, "Research on Household Labor: Modeling and Measuring the Social Embeddedness of Routine Family Work," *Journal of Marriage and Family* 2000, 62(4): 1208–33. Studies tracking the years between 1969 and 1999 reported men doing some more housework (an annual 262 hours more) and women doing quite a lot less (783 hours less). The housework gap between the sexes shrank in those decades from thirty-three hours a week to less than thirteen. See "Time Use: Diary and Direct Reports" by F. Thomas Juster, Hiromi Ono, and Frank. P. Stafford (Institute for Social Research, University of Michigan, unpublished report, Tables 9 and 10, pp. 39–49).

7. See Melissa A. Milkie, Sara B. Raley, Suzanne M. Bianchi, "Taking on the Second Shift: Time Allocations and Time Pressures of U.S. Parents with Preschoolers," December 2009, *Social Forces*, 88(2): 487–518.

8. Ibid, p. 502. If the researchers added in what they call "secondary activities"—tasks one did while also doing other things—they found women working an extra 9.3 hours per week, or extra 20 days a year. Ibid., Table 2, p. 517.

9. "Child Poverty in Perspective: An Overview of Child Well-being in Rich Countries," UNICEF, *Innocenti Report Card* 7, Florence, Italy, 2007 (http://www.unicef-irc.org/publications/pdf/rc7_eng.pdf).

10. Ibid, p. 2, for overall rankings. The United States, along with the United Kingdom ranked in the bottom third in five out of the six dimensions reviewed. The Netherlands won highest marks. There was no rela-

tionship between how rich a country was and the welfare of its children. The Czech Republic outranked the United States, for example.

11. Ibid, p. 37.

12. International Labour Office, Bureau for Gender Equality, *Gender Equality and Decent Work: Good Practices at the Workplace*, 2005.

13. Joan Blades and Nanette Fondas, *The Custom-Fit Workplace*, 2010: San Francisco: Jossey Bass.

Selected Reading

Abidin, R. *Parent Education and Intervention Handbook.* Springfield, Mass.: Thomas, 1980.

Arendell, Terry. *Mothers and Divorce.* Berkeley: University of California Press, 1986.

Bailyn, Lotte. "Involvement and Accommodation in Technical Careers: An Inquiry into the Relation to Work at Mid-Career." In *Organizational Careers: Some New Perspectives*, edited by J. Van Maanen. London: Wiley International, 1977.

Bain, Mary Jo, Laura Lein, L. O'Donnell, C. A. Stueve, and B. Wells. "Childcare Arrangements of Working Parents." *Monthly Labor Review*, October 1979, pp. 157–62.

Baranskaya, Natalya. "A Week Like Any Other." Translated by Emily Lehrman. Originally appeared in *Novy Mir*, 11 (1969). *The Massachusetts Review*, Autumn 1974, pp. 657–703.

Baruch, Grace K., and Rosalind Barnett. "Correlates of Fathers' Participation in Family Work: A Technical Report." Working paper no. 106. Wellesley College, Center for Research on Women, Wellesley, Mass., 1983.

Becker, Gary. *The Economic Approach to Human Behavior.* Chicago: University of Chicago Press, 1976.

———. *A Treatise on the Family.* Cambridge, Mass.: Harvard University Press, 1981.

Berg, Barbara. *The Remembered Gate: Origins of American Feminism.* New York: Oxford University Press, 1978.

Berk, Richard A., and Sarah Fenstermaker Berk. *Labor and Leisure at Home: Consent and Organization of the Household Day.* Beverly Hills, Calif.: Sage Publications, 1979.

Berk, Sarah Fenstermaker, and A. Shih. "Contributions to Household Labor: Comparing Wives' and Husbands' Reports." In *Women and Household Labor,* edited by S. F. Berk. Beverly Hills, Calif.: Sage Publications, 1980, pp. 191–228.

Bernard, Jessie. *The Future of Marriage.* New York: World, 1972.

Bernardo, H. D., L. C. Shehan, and R. G. Leslie. "A Residue of Tradition: Jobs, Careers and Spouse's Time in Housework." *Journal of Marriage and the Family* 49 (1987): 381–90.

Best, Fred. *Flexible Life Scheduling: Breaking the Education-Work-Retirement Lockstep.* New York: Praeger, 1980.

Biller, H. B. "The Father and Personality Development: Paternal Deprivation and Sex-Role Development." In *The Role of the Father in Child Development,* edited by M. E. Lamb. New York: John Wiley, 1976.

Blades, Joan, and Kristin Rowe-Finkbeiner. *The Motherhood Manifesto,* New York: Nation Books, 2006, p. 7.

Blanchard, R. W., and H. B. Biller. "Father Availability and Academic Performance Among Third-Grade Boys." *Developmental Psychology* 4 (1971): 301–15.

Blumberg, Paul. *Inequality in an Age of Decline.* New York: Oxford University Press, 1980.

Bohen, H., and A. Viveros-Long. *Balancing Jobs and Family Life: Do Flexible Work Schedules Help?* Philadelphia: Temple University Press, 1981.

Bowling, M. "Sex Role Attitudes and the Division of Household Labor." Paper presented at the American Sociological Association, Chicago, 1975.

Bradburn, Susan R., and Norman M. Orden. "Working Wives and Marriage Happiness." *American Journal of Sociology* 74 (1969): 392–407.

Bradby, Barbara. "The Destruction of Natural Economy." In *The Articulation of Modes of Production*, edited by Harold Wolpe. London, Boston, and Henley: Routledge and Kegan Paul, 1980, pp. 93–127.

Brown, Helen Gurley. *Having It All*. New York: Simon and Schuster, 1982.

Campbell, A., P. Converse, and W. Rodgers. *The Quality of American Life*. New York: Russell Sage, 1976.

Chodorow, Nancy. *The Reproduction of Mothering*. Berkeley: University of California Press, 1980.

Clark, Robert, Ivan Nye, and Viktor Gecas. "Husbands' Work Involvement and Marital Role Performance." *Journal of Marriage and the Family* 40 (1978): 9–21.

Cooler, Cary L. *Stress Research: Issues for the Eighties*. Chichester, England, and New York: John Wiley, 1983.

Cosell, Hilary. *Woman on a Seesaw: The Ups and Downs of Making It*. New York: G.P. Putnam's Sons, 1985.

Cott, Nancy F. *The Bonds of Womanhood*. New Haven: Yale University Press, 1977.

Courtney, Alice, and Thomas Whipple. *Canadian Perspectives on Sex Stereotyping in Advertising*. Ottawa: Advisory Council on the Status of Women, 1978.

Coverman, Shelley. "Gender, Domestic Labor Time and Wage Inequality." *American Sociological Review* 48 (1983): 623–36.

Cowan, Carolyn, and Philip A. Cowan. "Parents' Work Patterns, Marital and Parent-Child Relationships and Early Child Development." Paper presented at Meetings of the Society for Research in Child Development, Toronto, Canada, April 1985.

———. "Men's Involvement in Parenthood: Identifying the Antecedents and Understanding the Barriers." In *Fathers' Transitions to Parent-*

hood, edited by P. Berman and F. A. Pedersen. Hillsdale, NJ.: Erlbaum, 1986.

Cowan, Paul, and Rachel Cowan. *Mixed Blessings: Marriage Between Jews and Christians.* New York: Doubleday, 1987.

Cranor, Linda A., Robert Karasek, Jr., and Christopher C. Carlin. "Job Characteristics and Office Work: Findings and Health Implications," Columbia University, Department of Sociology and Industrial Engineering and Operations Research, Mimeo: Paper presented at the National Institute for Occupational Health Issues Affecting Clerical/Secretarial Personnel, July 22–24, 1981. Cincinnati, Ohio.

Dale, Barbara, and Jim Dale. *The Working Woman Book.* Kansas City and New York: Andrews, McMeel and Parker, 1985.

Duncan, Greg J., and James N. Morgan (eds.). *Five Thousand American Families—Patterns of Economic Progress.* Vol. 6, Ann Arbor: Survey Research Center, University of Michigan, 1978.

Edder, Janet. "New Programs Offer Assistance for Latchkey Children." *The New York Times*, September 5, 1985.

Ehrenreich, Barbara, *The Hearts of Men.* Garden City, N.Y.: Anchor Books, 1983.

Ehrenreich, Barbara, and Deirdre English. *For Her Own Good: Fifty Years of the Experts' Advice to Women.* Garden City, NY: Anchor Press, 1978.

Ehrensaft, Diane. *Parenting Together: Men and Women Sharing the Care of Their Children.* New York: Free Press, 1987.

Epstein, Cynthia Fuchs. *Women in Law.* New York: Basic Books, 1981.

Estes, Carol, and Anne Machung. "Berkeley Work-Family Project." The Women's Center for Continuing Education, University of California, Berkeley, 1986.

Farkas, G. "Education, Wage Rates, and the Division of Labor Between Husband and Wife." *Journal of Marriage and the Family* 38 (1976): 473–84.

Feidman, S. S., S. C. Nash, and B. G. Aschenbrenner. "Antecedents of Fathering." *Child Development* 54 (1983): 1628–36.

Feinstein, Karen Wolk. *Working Women and Families.* Beverly Hills and London: Sage Publications, 1979.

Ferree, Myra. "Sacrifice, Satisfaction and Social Change: Employment and the Family." In *My Troubles Are Going to Have Trouble with Me,* edited by Karen Sacks and Dorothy Remy. New Brunswick, NJ.: Rutgers University Press, 1984, pp. 61–79.

Ferreira, Antonio J. "Psychosis and Family Myth." *American Journal of Psychotherapy* 21 (1967): 186–225.

Fuchs, R. Victor. "Sex Differences in Economic Well Being." *Science,* April 1986, pp. 459–64.

Furstenberg, Frank, C. Nord, J. Peterson, N. Zill. "The Life Course of Children of Divorce, Marital Disruption and Parental Contact." *American Sociological Review* 48 (1983): 656–68.

Garey, Anita Ilta, and Karen V. Hansen. *At the Heart of Work and Family: Engaging the Ideas of Arlie Hochschild.* New Brunswick, NJ: Rutgers University Press, 2011.

Gerson, Kathleen. *Hard Choices.* Berkeley and Los Angeles: University of California Press. 1985.

Gilbert, L. A. *Men in Dual Career Families.* Hillsdale, NJ.: Erlbaum, 1985.

Glazer, Barney G., and Anself L. Strauss. *The Discovery of Grounded Theory: Stategies for Qualitative Research.* Chicago: Aldine, 1967.

Goode, William. *After Divorce.* Glencoe, Ill.: Free Press, 1956.

Googins, Bradley, with Dianne Burden. "Balancing Job and Homelife Study: Managing Work and Stress in Corporations," School of Social Work, 1987. Boston University, unpublished manuscript.

Gove, Walter R. "The Relationship Between Sex Roles, Mental Health, and Marital Status." *Social Forces* 51 (1972): 34–44.

Gove, Walter, and Michael Geerken. "The Effect of Children and Employment on the Mental Health of Married Men and Women." *Social Forces* 56 (1977): 66–76.

———. *At Home and at Work: The Family's Allocation of Labor.* Beverly Hills: Sage Publications, 1983.

Greene, Bob. "Trying to Keep Up with Amanda." *San Francisco Chronicle*, June 16, 1984, "People" section.

Hacker, Andrew. "Women Versus Men in the Work Force." *New York Times Magazine*, December 9, 1984.

Hall, D. T., and F. E. Gordon. "Career Choices of Married Women: Effects on Conflict, Role Behavior and Satisfaction." *Journal of Applied Psychology* 58 (1973): 42–48.

Harrington, Michael, and Mark Levinson. "The Perils of a Dual Economy." *Dissent*, Fall 1985, pp. 417–26.

Harris, Louis, and Associates. "Families at Work." The General Mills American Family Report, 1980–81.

Hartmann, Heidi. "The Family as the Locus of Gender, Class and Political Struggle: The Example of Housework." *Signs: Journal of Women in Culture and Society* 6 (1981): 366–94.

Hayden, Dolores. *Redesigning the American Dream.* New York: W.W. Norton, 1984.

Hayes, Cheryl D. (ed.). "Making Policies for Children: A Study of the Federal Process." Washington, D.C.: National Academy Press, 1982.

Hayes, Cheryl D., and Sheila Kamerman (eds.). *Children of Working Parents: Experiences and Outcomes.* Washington, D.C.: National Academy Press, 1983.

Haynes, Suzanne G., and Manning Feinleib. "Women, Work and Coronary Heart Disease: Prospective Findings from the Framingham Heart Study." *American Journal of Public Health* 70 (1980): 133–41.

Hite, Shere. *Women and Love.* New York: Knopf, 1988.

Hochschild, Arlie. "Inside the Clockwork of Male Careers." In *Women and the Power to Change*, edited by Florence Howe. New York: McGraw-Hill, 1971, pp. 47-80.

———. *The Managed Heart: Commercialization of Human Feeling.* Berkeley: University of California Press, 1983.

———. "Why Can't a Man Be More Like a Woman?" *New York Times Book Review*, November 15, 1987.

————. "The Economy of Gratitude." In *The Sociology of Emotions: Original Essays and Research Papers*, edited by David D. Franks and E. Doyle McCarthy. Greenwich, Conn.: JAI Press, in press.

————. "Ideology and Emotion Management: A Perspective and Path for Future Research." In *Research Agendas in the Sociology of Emotions*, edited by Theodore Kemper. Albany, N.Y.: SUNY Press, in press.

Hoffman, Lois. "Parental Power Relations and the Division of Household Tasks." In *The Employed Mother in America*, edited by F. I. Nye and L. W. Hoffman. Chicago: Rand McNally, 1963.

Hoffman, Lois, and F. I. Nye. *Working Mothers*. San Francisco: Jossey Bass, 1974.

Holmstrom, Lynda. *The Two-Career Family*. Cambridge, Mass.: Schenkman, 1972.

Hood, Janet. *Becoming a Two-Job Family*. New York: Praeger, 1983.

Horner, Matina S. "Femininity and Successful Achievement: A Basic Inconsistency." In *Feminine Personality and Conflict*, edited by Judith Bardwick, Elizabeth Douvan, Matina S. Horner, and David Gutmann. Belmont, Calif.: Brooks/Cole, 1970.

Huber, Joan, and Glenna Spitze. *Sex Stratification: Children, Housework and Jobs*. New York: Academic Press, 1983.

Hughes, Gwendolyn Salisbury. *Mothers in Industry: Wage-Earning Mothers in Philadelphia*. New York: New Republic, 1925.

Hunt, Janet G., and Larry L. Hunt. "Dilemmas and Contradictions of Status: The Case of the Dual Career Family." *Social Problems* 24 (1977): 407–16.

Juster, F. T. "A Note on Recent Changes in Time Use." In *Studies in the Measurement of Time Allocation*, edited by F. T. Juster and F. Stafford. Ann Arbor: Institute for Social Research, 1986.

Juster, F. Thomas, and Frank P. Stafford (eds.) *Time, Goods, and Well-Being*. Ann Arbor, Mich.: Survey Research Center, Institute for Social Research, University of Michigan, 1985.

Kamerman, Sheila. *Parenting in an Unresponsive Society*. New York: Free Press, 1980.

————. "Childcare and Family Benefits: Policies of Six Industrialized Countries." *Monthly Labor Review* 103 (1980): 23–28.

Kamerman, Sheila, and Cheryl D. Hayes (eds.). *Children of Working Parents: Experiences and Outcomes.* Washington, D.C.: National Academy Press, 1983.

Kanter, Rosabeth. *Work and Family in the U.S.* New York: Russell Sage, 1977.

Kessler, Ronald C., and James McRae, Jr. "The Effect of Wives' Employment on the Mental Health of Married Men and Women," *Journal of Health and Social Behavior* 47 (April 1982): 216–27.

Kessler-Harris, Alice. *Out to Work.* New York: Oxford University Press, 1982.

Kimball, Gayle. *50–50 Marriage.* Boston: Beacon Press, 1983.

Komarovsky, Mirra. *Women in Colleges: Shaping New Feminine Identities.* New York: Basic Books, 1985.

Kuttner, Bob. "The Declining Middle." *Atlantic Monthly,* July 1983, pp. 60–69.

Lamb, Michael E. (ed.). *Nontraditional Families: Parenting and Child Development.* Hillsdale, N.J.: Erlbaum, 1982.

————. *The Father's Role: Applied Perspectives.* New York: Wiley-Interscience, 1986.

Lapidus, Gail (ed.). *Women, Work and Family in the Soviet Union.* New York: M. E. Sharpe, 1982.

Lazarus, Richard. *Psychological Stress and the Coping Process.* New York: McGraw-Hill, 1966.

Lein, Laura. *Families Without Villains.* Lexington, Mass.: Lexington Books, 1983.

Levering, Robert. *The 100 Best Companies to Work for in America.* Reading, Mass.: Addison-Wesley, 1984.

Levinger, George. "Sources of Marital Dissatisfaction Among Applicants for Divorce." *American Journal of Orthopsychiatry* 36 (1966): 803–7.

Linder, Staffan B. *The Harried Leisure Class*. New York: Columbia University Press, 1970.

Machung, Anne. "Talking Career, Thinking Job: Gender Differences in Career and Family Expectations of Berkeley Seniors." Forthcoming in *Feminist Studies* 15 (1), Spring 1989.

Mainardi, Pat. "The Politics of Housework." In *Sisterhood Is Powerful*, edited by Robin Morgan. New York: Vintage, 1970, pp. 447–54.

Matthaie, Julie A. *An Economic History of Women in America*. New York: Schocken Books, 1982.

Meissner, Martin, Elizabeth Humphrys, Scott Meis, and William Scheu. "No Exit for Wives: Sexual Division of Labor and the Cumulation of Household Demands." *Review of Canadian Sociology and Anthropology* 12 (1975): 424–39.

Model, S. "Housework by Husbands; Determinants and Implications." *Journal of Family Issues* 2 (1981): 225–37.

Morgan, J. "A Potpourri of New Data Gathered from Interviews with Husbands and Wives." In *Five Thousand American Families—Patterns of Economic Progress*, vol. 6, edited by G. Duncan and J. Morgan. Ann Arbor: Institute for Social Research, University of Michigan, 1978, pp. 367–401.

Naisbitt, John. *Megatrends*. New York: Warner Books, 1982.

Nash, John. "Historical and Social Changes in the Perception of the Role of the Father." In *The Role of the Father in Child Development*, edited by M. Lamb. New York: John Wiley, 1976, pp. 65–68.

Nash, J. "The Father in Contemporary Culture and Current Psychological Literature." *Child Development* 36 (1965): 261–97.

Nye, F. Ivan, with Howard M. Bahr et al. (eds.). *Role Structure and Analysis of the Family*. Beverly Hills: Sage Publications, 1976.

Nye, F. Ivan, and Lois Waldis Hoffman (eds.). *The Employed Mother in America*. New York: Rand McNally, 1963.

Oakley, A. *The Sociology of Housework*. New York: Pantheon, 1974.

Olson, D. H., C. S. Russell, and D. H. Sprenkle. "Marital and Family Therapy: A Decade Review." *Journal of Marriage and the Family* 42 (1980): 973–93.

Oppenheimer, Valerie Kincade. "The Sociology of Women's Economic Role in the Family." *American Sociological Review* 42 (1977): 387–405.

Orden, Susan, and N. Bradburn. "Working Wives and Marriage Happiness." *American Journal of Sociology* 74 (1969): 392–407.

Oren, Laura. "The Welfare of Women in Laboring Families: England 1860–1950." *Feminist Studies* 1 (1973): 107–23.

Owen, M., L. Chase-Lansdale, and M. E. Lamb. "Mothers' and Fathers' Attitudes, Maternal Employment, and the Security of Infant-Parent Attachment." Unpublished paper, University of Michigan, 1981.

Peplau, L. A., and K. P. Beals. "The Family Lives of Lesbians and Gay Men." In A. Vangelisti, ed., *Handbook of Family Communication*, 2004.

Perucci, C., H. Potter, and D. Rhoads. "Determinants of Male Family Role Performance." *Psychology of Women Quarterly* 3 (1978): 53–66.

Pesquera, Beatrice. "Work and Family: A Comparative Analysis of Professional, Clerical and Blue Collar Chicana Workers." Ph.D. dissertation, Department of Sociology, University of California, Berkeley, 1986.

Pleck, Joseph H. "Husbands' and Wives' Family Work, Paid Work, and Adjustment." Working Paper No. 95, Wellesley College Center for Research on Women, Wellesley, Mass., 1982.

———. *Working Wives, Working Husbands.* Beverly Hills: Sage Publications, 1985.

Pleck, Joseph H., Graham L. Staines, Linda Lang. "Work and Family Life: First Reports on Work-Family Interference and Workers' Formal Child Care Arrangements, from the Quality of Life Employment Survey." Working Paper No. 11, Wellesley College Center for Research on Women, Wellesley, Mass., 1978.

Potter, K. H., and D. Rhoads. "Determinants of Male Family Role Performance." *Psychology of Women Quarterly* 3 (1978): 53–66.

Presser, Harriet B. "Female Employment and the Division of Labor Within the Home: A Longitudinal Perspective." Paper presented at the Population Association of America, St. Louis, Mo., 1977.

Radin, Norma. "Father-Child Interaction and the Intellectual Functioning of 4-Year-Old-Boys." *Developmental Psychology* 6 (1972): 353–61.

———. "The Role of the Father in Cognitive/Academic Intellectual Development." In *The Role of the Father in Child Development*, 2nd ed., edited by M. E. Lamb. New York: John Wiley, 1981, pp. 379–427.

———. "Primary Caregiving and Role Sharing Fathers of Preschoolers." In *Nontraditional Families: Parenting and Child Development*, edited by M. E. Lamb. Hillsdale, NJ.: Erlbaum, 1982, pp. 173–204.

Radin, Norma, and R. Goldsmith. "Caregiving Fathers of Preschoolers: Four Years Later." *Merrill Palmer Quarterly* 31 (1985): 375–83.

Radin, Norma, and Graeme Russell. "Increased Father Participation and Child Development Outcomes." In *Nontraditional Families: Parenting and Child Development*, edited by M. E. Lamb. Hillsdale, NJ: Erlbaum, 1982, pp. 191–218.

Rainwater, Lee, and W. L. Yancey. *The Moynihan Report and the Politics of Controversy.* Cambridge, Mass.: M.I.T. Press, 1967.

Reuter, Mark W., and Henry B. Miller. "Perceived Personality Adjustment Among College Males." *Journal of Consulting and Clinical Psychology* 40(3) (1973): 339–42.

Roberts, M., and L. Wortzel. "Husbands Who Prepare Dinner: A Test of Competing Theories of Marital Role Allocations." Unpublished paper, Boston University, 1979.

Robinson, John P. *How Americans Use Time.* New York: Praeger, 1977.

———. *Changes in Americans' Use of Time, 1965–75: A Progress Report.* Cleveland, Ohio: Communications Research Center, Cleveland State University, 1977.

Rosenthal, Neal H. "The Shrinking Middle Class: Myth or Reality?" *Monthly Labor Review* 108 (1985): 3–10.

Russell, Graeme. "Maternal Employment Status and Fathers' Involvement in Child Care." *Australian and New Zealand Journal of Sociology* 12 (1982): 28–35.

———. "Shared-Caregiving Families: An Australian Study." In *Nontraditional Families: Parenting and Child Development*, edited by Michael E. Lamb. Hillsdale, NJ.: Erlbaum, 1982, pp. 139–71.

Sacks, Michael Paul. "Unchanging Times: A Comparison of the Everyday Life of Soviet Working Men and Women Between 1923 and 1966." *Journal of Marriage and the Family*, November 1977, pp. 793–805.

Sagi, A. "Antecedents and Consequences of Various Degrees of Paternal Involvement in Child-Rearing: The Israeli Project." In *Nontraditional Families: Parenting and Child Development*, edited by M. E. Lamb. Hillsdale, NJ.: Erlbaum, 1982, pp. 205–32.

Scanzoni, John. *Opportunity and the Family.* New York: Free Press, 1970.

Segura, Denise. "Chicana and Mexicana Women in the Labor Market: A Study of Occupational Mobility and Stratification." Ph.D. dissertation, Sociology Department, University of California, Berkeley, 1986.

Shaevitz, Marjorie H. *The Superwoman Syndrome.* New York: Warner Publications, 1984.

Smith, A. D., and W. Reid. *Role Sharing Marriage.* New York: Columbia University Press, 1986.

Smith, R. (ed.). *The Subtle Revolution: Women at Work.* Washington, D.C.: Urban Institute, 1979.

Stafford, Frank. "Women's Use of Time Converging with Men's." *Monthly Labor Review*, December 1980, pp. 57–58.

Stafford, Frank, and Greg Duncan. "The Use of Time and Technology by Households in the United States." In *Time, Goods, and Well-Being*, edited by F. Thomas Juster and Frank P. Stafford. Ann Arbor, Mich.: Survey Research Center, Institute for Social Research, University of Michigan, 1985, pp. 250–64.

Stafford, Rebecca, Elaine Backman, and Pamela DiBona. "The Division of Labor Among Cohabiting and Married Couples." *Journal of Marriage and the Family* 39 (1977): 43–57.

Statistical Abstracts of the U.S. National Data Book, Guide to Sources. Washington, D.C.: U.S. Government Printing Office, 1985.

Strasser, Susan. *Never Done: A History of American Housework.* New York: Pantheon, 1982.

Strober, Myra, and Charles Weinberg. "Strategies Used by Working and Nonworking Wives to Reduce Time Pressures." *Journal of Consumer Research* 6 (1980): 338–48.

Swidler, Ann. "Culture in Action—Symbols and Strategies." *American Sociological Review* 51 (1986): 273–86.

Szalai, Alexander (ed.). *The Use of Time: Daily Activities of Urban and Suburban Populations in Twelve Countries.* The Hague: Mouton, 1972.

Thoits, Peggy. "Multiple Identities: Examining Gender and Marital Status Differences in Distress." *American Sociological Review* 51 (1986): 259–72.

Two-Career Families: An Annotated Bibliography of Relevant Readings. New York: Catalyst, 1982.

U.S. Bureau of the Census. *Current Population Reports: Households, Families, Marital Status and Living Arrangements.* Series P-20, no. 382. Washington, D.C.: U.S. Government Printing Office, 1985.

U.S. Bureau of Labor Statistics. *Full and Part-Time Status of the Civilian Labor Force: 1965–1982.* "Employment and Earnings," Table 677, "Full and Part-Time Workers, 1965–1982," p. 410. U.S. Department of Labor, Washington, D.C.

U.S. Bureau of Labor Statistics. *Occupation of Employed Workers by Sex and Race: 1960-1982.* Bulletin 2096, Employment and Earnings, No. 693. In *National Data Book and Guide to Sources, Statistical Abstract of the U.S.,* 104th ed. Washington, D.C.: U.S. Department of Commerce, Bureau of the Census, 1984.

U.S. Bureau of Labor Statistics. *Employment and Earnings, Characteristics of Families. First Quarter.* Washington, D.C.: U.S. Department of Labor, 1988.

U.S. Bureau of Labor Statistics. *Employment Characteristics of Families— 2009.* Table 6, "Employment Status of Mothers with Own Children Under 3 Years Old by Single Year of Age of Youngest Child and Marital

Status, 2008–09 Annual Averages." Washington, D.C.: U.S. Department of Labor, 2010.

U.S. Department of Labor and U.S. Bureau of Labor Statistics. *Women in the Labor Force: A Databank*. Report 1026. Washington, D.C.: U.S. Department of Labor, 2010.

Vanek, J. "Time Spent in Housework." *Scientific American*, May 1974, pp. 116–20.

Verbrugge, L. "Women's Social Roles and Health." In *Women: A Developmental Perspective*, edited by P. Berman and E. Ramey. Washington, D.C.: National Institutes of Health, 1982, pp. 49–78.

Walker, Kathryn E., and Margaret E. Woods. *Time Use: A Measure of Household Production of Goods and Services*. Washington, D.C.: American Home Economics Association, 1976.

"Warning: Health Hazards for Office Workers: An Overview of Problems and Solutions in Occupational Health in the Office." Working Women Education Fund, Cleveland, Ohio, 1981.

Weaver, Charles, and Sandra Holmes. "A Comparative Study of the Work Satisfaction of Females with Full-Time Employment and Full-Time Housekeeping." *Journal of Applied Psychology* 60 (1975): 117–28.

Weitzman, Lenore. *The Divorce Revolution*. New York: Free Press, 1985.

Welter, Barbara. "The Cult of True Womanhood." *American Quarterly* 18 (1966): 151–74.

"What Do Cal. Freshmen Feel, Believe, Think? Results of an Annual Survey." *Cal Report* 5 (1988): 4.

"When They Both Work, Who Cleans the Toilets?" *San Francisco Chronicle*, October 11, 1982.

"When You Can't Be Home, Teach Your Child What to Do." *Changing Times*, August 1984.

Wiseman, Paul. "Young, Single, Childless Women Out-earn Male Counterparts." *USA Today*, September 2, 2010.

Yogev, Sara. "Do Professional Women Have Egalitarian Marital Relationships?" *Journal of Marriage and the Family* 43 (1981): 865–71.

Yogev, Sara, and J. M. Brett. "Patterns of Work and Family Involvement Among Single and Dual-Earner Couples." *Journal of Applied Psychology* 70 (1985): 754–68.

———. "Restructuring Work for Family: How Dual-Earner Couples with Children Manage." Unpublished paper, Center for Urban Affairs and Policy Research, Northwestern University, Evanston, Ill., 1987.

Yogman, M. W. "Competence and Performance of Fathers and Infants." In *Progress in Child Health*, edited by A. Macfarlane. London: Churchill Livingston, 1983.

Nonprofit Organizations Engaged in Helping Working Families

MomsRising

Since 2006, this one-million-strong organization has pressed for such causes as fair pay, paid maternity and paternity leave, paid sick days, early care and education, and toxic-free bottles, toys, and home environments.

The Labor Project for Working Families

A national nonprofit founded in 1992, the LPWF partners with labor unions to advocate for family-friendly workplaces and the right of workers to care for themselves and their families.

Take Back Your Time

Since 2002, the organization has worked to raise awareness about "time poverty" in America. Vacations are not, they argue for example, an idle luxury, but crucial to a healthy, civically engaged, environmentally responsible, family-friendly society. They also raise awareness of child "nature-deficit disorder."

Every Child Matters Education Fund

Founded in 2001, this organization works to create a lobby for struggling families that otherwise lack it, to press political candidates to address the urgent need for various child-friendly programs.

National Organization of Women

Funded in l966, N.O.W. remains the largest organization in America pressing for women's rights, including the economic rights of mothers and caregivers, and economic equity.

National Partnership for Women and Families
(formerly the Women's Legal Defense Fund)

The Family and Medical Leave Act was written by a member and the organization fought for nine years to enact it. Since 1971, it fought to end discrimination against pregnant workers, to litigate on-the-job sexual harassment, wage discrimination, and child-support enforcement.

Index